PERSHING COUNTY

100 years

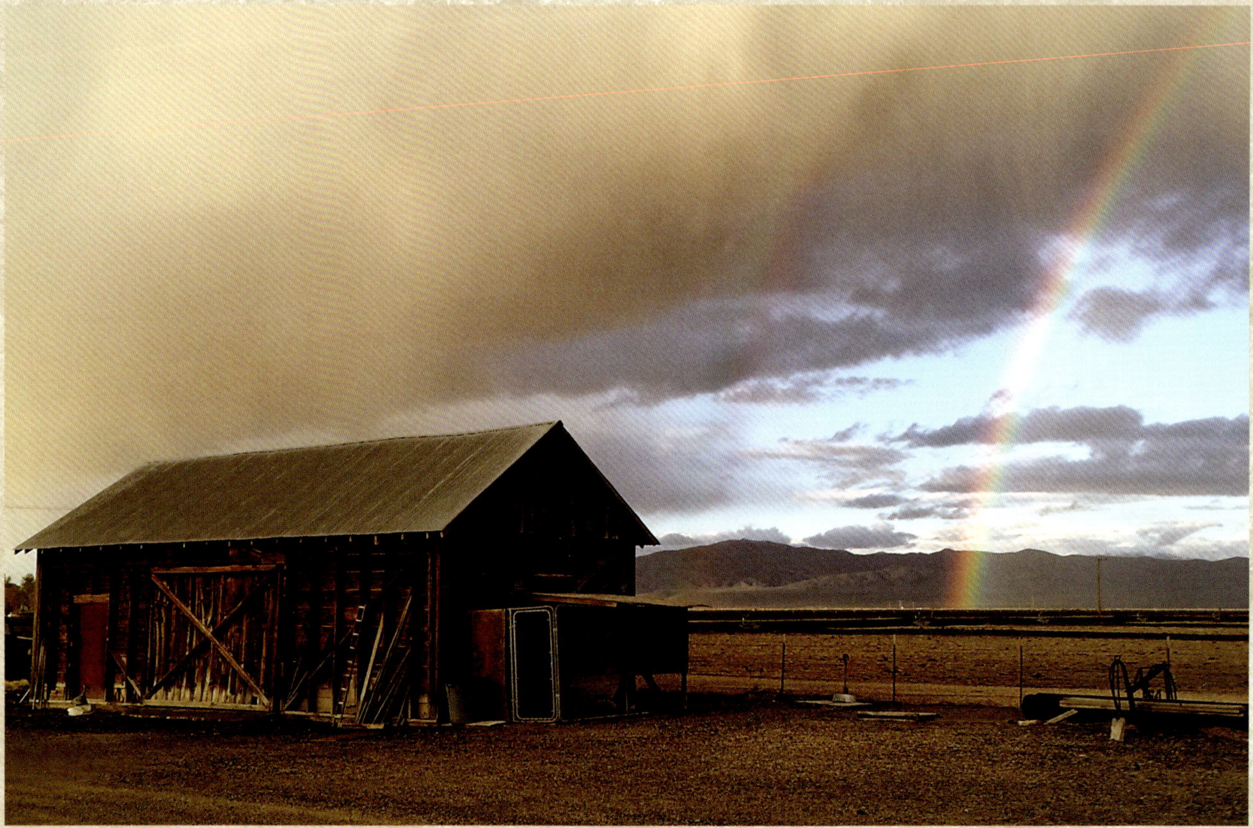

PERSHING COUNTY

100 years

Pat Ferraro Klos
Deanne Davidson
Lynda Quilici
and Jane Fundis Tors

BAOBAB PRESS

Baobab Press, Reno, Nevada 89509 USA

Unless otherwise indicated, all photos in this book are by Deanne Davidson
Printed in China
Design by Kathleen Szawiola

Library of Congress Control Number: 2018936826

ISBN 978-1-936097-16-6

FIRST PRINTING
18 19 20 21 22 23
5 4 3 2 1

Frontispiece: *Double Rainbow above the West Humboldt Range in Lower Valley.*

Contents

Preface

JANE FUNDIS TORS

In 1905, when Humboldt County still encompassed what is today Pershing County, newspaperman and self-described "state-builder" Allen C. Bragg set off by horse and buggy on an ambitious, 1,200-mile tour of the region and its boundless nooks and crannies, including its early communities, ranches, mines, and businesses. He was impressed by the Big Meadows and the "thriving village" of Lovelock, the hub of a large and highly productive section of Humboldt County, which "a generation ago was a barren waste."

"Lovelock is 'on the trail' to be a city of considerable magnitude," he wrote. "I think if I could come back to this dusty ball fifty years hence I should see a city of at least 50,000 souls, for Lovelock valley, if put to its highest uses would support 50,000 or 75,000 busy men and woman and it would be an ideal spot to raise children and start them in life with bright prospects."

Though his population prediction was off, Bragg captured what so many have known and experienced in Pershing County: the lure and promise of mining, the sustaining role of agriculture that resulted from the steadfast persistence of the men and women who carved out and cared for its many farms and ranches, the vital importance of the Humboldt River and the perpetual search to find or harness more water, and an independent and pioneering conviction. Although much of Bragg's account focuses on the land and industry, he was struck by other aspects of the region that reflected a sense of community and caring people. Calling Lovelock a "town of homes," he noted the lawns and shade trees, the early school employing two teachers, the churches, and the myriad businesses, including a drugstore, bakery, hotels, saloons, department store, creamery, flour mill, lumberyard, and more.

Bragg's account and exploration extended beyond the town of Lovelock. He was smitten by the beauty of Unionville, and his first view of the "weirdly fascinating" Black Rock Desert left him drawn to enter the playa: "That desire was almost resistless. I could not keep my mind and hardly my eyes off this wonderful, wonderful sight."

Many who have connected with Pershing County are held by a sense of place that carries meaning, memories, curiosity, and identity. It is a place of wide-open spaces that beckon one to explore and to exhale a bit deeper. While some may see the high desert surrounding the Big Meadows as barren, those who appreciate Pershing County and the Great Basin see an explosion of colors—purples, blues, greens, yellows, and all shades of whites and grays. It is an expansive canvas, yet one that allows a single wildflower to loom large and not go unnoticed.

This book looks at the hundred-year story of Pershing County, which spun off from Humboldt County in 1919 to become the youngest and last of Nevada's sixteen counties. It is a place of contradiction that serves to remind us that diversity energizes lives, places, and histories. The seasons are distinct, and each brings its own beauty. It is a rural setting, yet close enough to urban areas that residents can come to know and understand both. It has been known as a stopping-off point for people, from the nineteenth-century pioneers to modern-day travelers, yet it is also a place marked by the deep roots of those who call it home, often for generations, or in regards to the Native Americans, for millennia.

While a particular history is invariably shaped by long-held plans or visions, much of what happens actually springs from serendipity. My parents, Pete and Gloria Fundis, began dating after she was assigned to a student-teaching stint at Pershing County High School. After marrying, they were contemplating moving on to pursue careers and start their family elsewhere. Then, on November 6, 1959, my grandfather, John Walter Fundis, and Robert Munk, husband of Leona Munk and father of Deanne Davidson, were killed in a car accident. The sudden loss of two respected and thriving local businessmen was a tragedy that rocked the town and set a new course for many, including my parents, who decided to stay in Lovelock to help with the family business, Fundis Company, a trucking company that operated in Lovelock from 1947 to 2004 and continues to operate in Reno under new ownership.

Lovelock would become the place where my sister, brother, and I were born and grew up. Some of my fondest memories of growing up involved our entire family loaded into the pickup truck, often accompanied by other

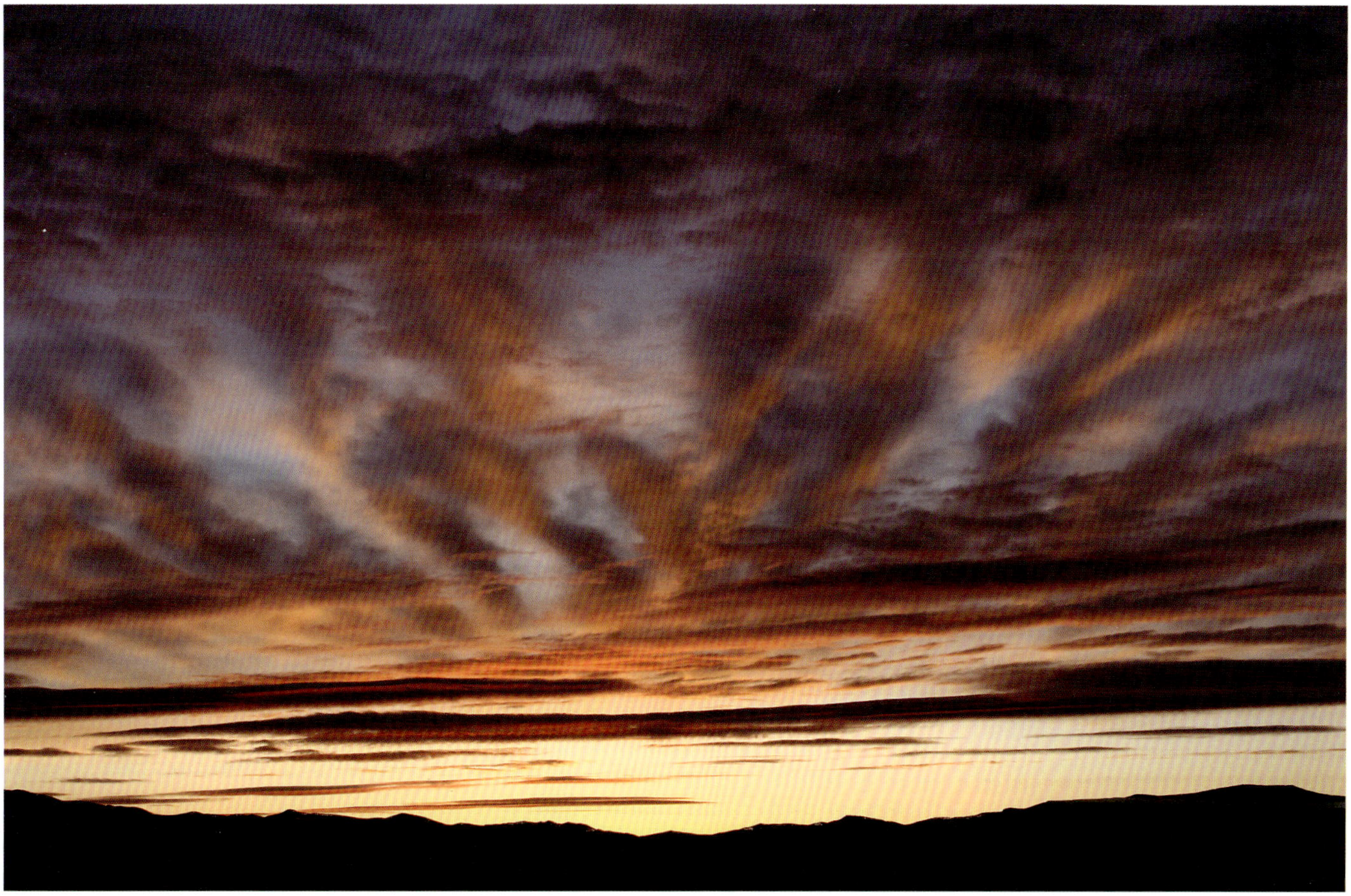

A Pershing County sunset.

friends and families, to explore some remote canyon or hunt for our Christmas tree, or the many summer afternoons spent picnicking or waterskiing at Rye Patch Reservoir, or the hours spent cruising town and laughing with high-school friends. It was a community where people were more apt to "stop by" and visit at someone's house (the back door, in the case of our house) or the coffee counter at a restaurant, than to call on the phone, though that happened often as well. At one point, all four of the women involved with the creation of this book lived within two blocks of one another. It was this two-block area that marked the boundary of how far we were allowed to ride our bikes as children. What a blessing to have had such strong, smart, kind, and giving women and role models in my life!

Outside of the former Fundis Company shop on the southern edge of town, the letters L-O-V-E-L-O-C-K are embedded in a grass knoll. Pete and Gloria had the vision to rescue those letters, which once were set alongside the original train depot, and create the mini-park that continues to welcome visitors today. In 1987 they joined with our cousin Brad Quilici and his wife, Lynda, to create a whimsical, life-size Christmas village in the mini-park. The tradition continued for ten years, and we had such fun setting it up, always on an inevitably cold day that made the steam rise from our cups of hot chocolate. Over the holiday season, practically the entire town would visit the display, often walking through it or taking family pictures. Gloria tells the story of returning home one evening from a trip to Reno. It had been snowing lightly, and the pavement around the display was full of the little footprints of the children who had walked through, undoubtedly to be with and touch the characters and decorations, including Santa and Mrs. Claus. Many cautioned that such a display would attract vandals. It never did. The display in Pete's Park, as we called it, had become a community touch point--a place and tradition that brought people of all ages together.

So many memories of Pershing County are of friendships and experiences that span generations. It's part of the character of the place, where all the Pershing County High School class reunions happen on the same afternoon and then come together that night for one multigenerational celebration. Begun in 1917, the annual Alumni Banquet & Ball is older than the county itself.

Bragg expressed a desire to come back in a hundred years and take his tour again. Now, at the county's centennial and 113 years after his account, this book takes that ride through Pat Ferraro Klos's informative text, Deanne Munk Davidson's photography, and Lynda Killfoil Quilici's original art. In creating this book, we enjoyed rekindling memories and revisiting special places in Pershing County. It is our intent that *Pershing County: 100 Years* conveys our appreciation for the people and the place, as well as our optimism for its future.

Acknowledgments

No book covering a hundred years of anything can come to fruition without lots of help from friends, family, and professionals. This book is no exception. Without the guidance and patience of the staffs at the University of Nevada Press, Special Collections and University Archives of the University of Nevada, Reno, and the Nevada Historical Society, especially Michael Maher and Karalea Clough, this book never would have happened.

Special thanks go to Pershing County resident Devoy Brinkerhoff Munk and former resident Sharon Stiff Calvert, who shared stories, files, and photos. Friends Donna Phillips, Press and Delores Clewe, Kathy Arobio Garcia, and Alicia Arias Dyer either traveled with us, listened to our stories over and over, answered questions, or gave unfailing support. Family members Greg Ferraro, Mike Klos, Gloria Fundis, Ann Kolman, LuRuth Walls, and Brad Quilici supported us in spirit and reality. Bart Campbell and Longhorn Bar manager Crystal Abel told us stories about the bar mural, which led us to Curtis McGowan and Monet Paputsidis, who dug into long-forgotten family archives about their uncle George Perry, the muralist.

We are forever grateful to Pershing County commissioners past and present for factual material we would not otherwise have uncovered: Rob McDougal, Bob Maher, and Paul Davidson, Deanne's husband, who was always available to us and helped us as our driver. Valuable information about ranching, farming, and brands came from Dan Duncan and Carolyn Gottschalk Espil. Dana Bennett, president of the Nevada Mining Association, and Brandon MacDougall, shift supervisor at Coeur Rochester, shared mining statistics and information about current mining trends. Assistant Supervisor Kirsten Gottschalk Hertz made the history of Pershing County Hospital available; the background of the County Library came from County

Librarian Kathie Brinkerhoff; and Extension Agent Steve Foster was a wealth of information on agricultural issues.

Pat Rowe and Elaine Pommerening, descendants of George Lovelock, deserve special recognition for all their help in gathering the George Lovelock clan together for a memorable photo. They, too, answered questions and shared photos that make the book all the richer. As a member of the Lovelock City Council, Pat Rowe's knowledge of events gave us a heads-up several times. Former Pershing County Commissioner Roger Mancebo and his wife, Marilyn, and rancher Tom Moura and his wife, Darlene, have generously shared their family history, which dates back to the beginnings of Pershing County.

We would also like to thank Shaun Griffin for the use of his poem, "Rain Outside Lovelock, Late March," as well as the photographic contributions of the *Lovelock Review-Miner* and Adrian Louis.

A very special thank you to Spencer Jones for the generous use of his Burning Man and Black Rock Desert archives.

And lastly, we give our thanks to the staff at Baobab Press—Christine Kelly, publisher; Danilo Thomas, managing editor; Margaret Dalrymple, editor; and Kathleen Szawiola, designer—for putting our work into readable form and for doing all the heavy lifting for the Burning Man chapter. Will Roger Peterson and Crimson Rose from the Burning Man organization met with this writer and told me how to proceed, but the rest of the work was done by Baobab Press. This book represents a special and rewarding collaboration that Nevadans should enjoy for many years.

A LITTLE HISTORY

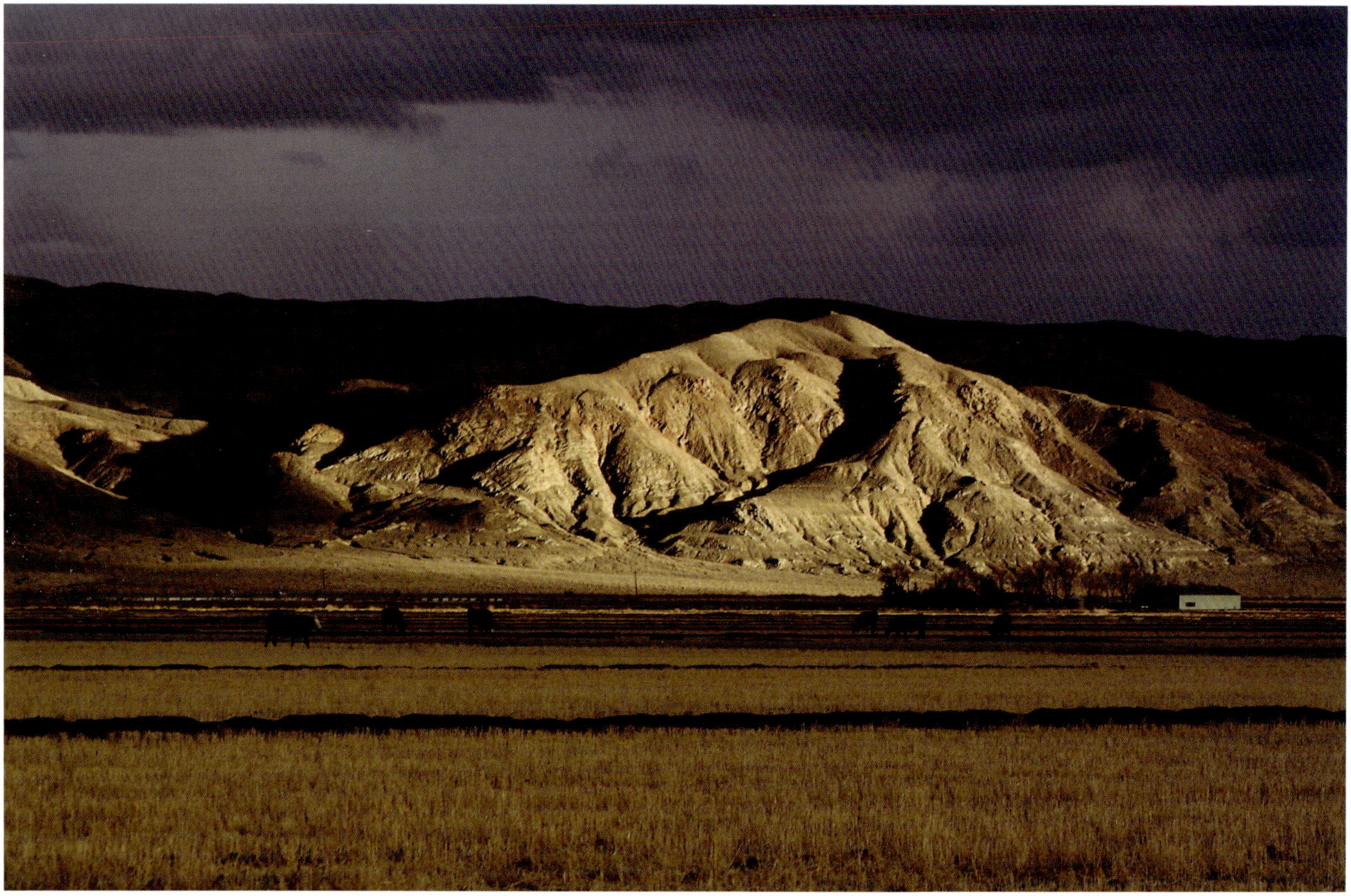

Looking across Lower Valley.

The land of Pershing County was home to indigenous peoples long before the Europeans arrived. Ancient Humboldt Lake covered much of the region, and the earliest native peoples fished and hunted along its shores, leaving fascinating reminders of their culture in places like Lovelock Cave and the Leonard Rockshelter. Although the cave is located in modern Churchill County and the rockshelter in Pershing County, they are part of the same ecosystem and cultural territory that the ancient residents of the region considered their world.

In 1825 the Hudson's Bay Fur Company sent Peter Skene Ogden and his men on a trapping expedition to the still relatively unexplored Great Basin, where they came upon a river as yet unknown to Europeans. They were in the area a second time between 1828 and 1830, following the river to find beaver and other desirable fur-bearing animals. They reached the Humboldt Sink on two occasions but then turned south toward Walker Lake, apparently not finding the local animal life to their liking. Ogden is considered to be the first white man to discover the Humboldt River. Other fur trappers continued to exploit the riches of the Humboldt watershed until the region was overwhelmed by the tide of gold-rush immigration in the 1850s.

Many of the migrant routes across the continent included a stop along the Humboldt River where the river gradually vanished into the Humboldt Sink. Here, among the marshes and sloughs they found a vast, lush meadow. The pioneers rested their livestock while they cut the native grass for hay and stocked up on water before continuing their journey west. Their success was subject to the vagaries of the river, which furnished abundant water and fodder in wet years but only scanty quantities in times of drought.

At a point near today's Imlay, about forty miles northeast of the Big Meadows, the main overland trail split into various routes—the Applegate Trail, the Humboldt Trail, the Truckee Trail, the Oregon Trail, the Emigrant

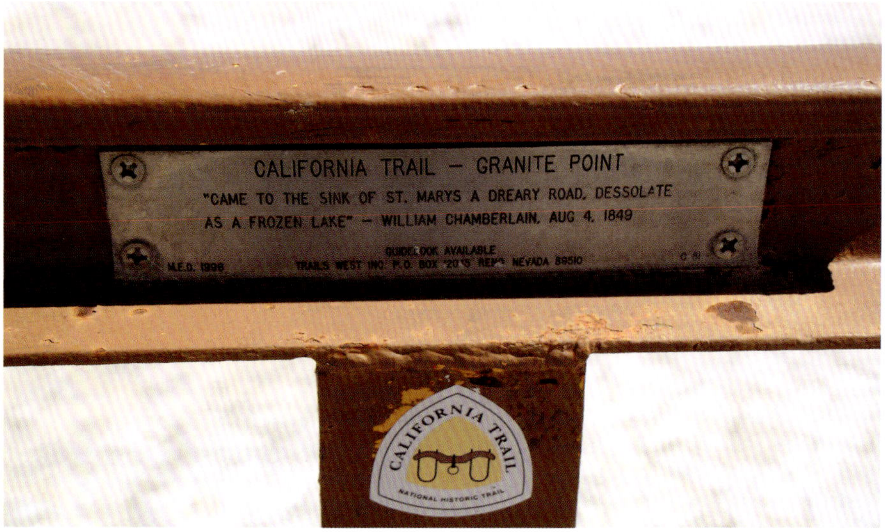

California Trail marker.

Trail, and the California Trail—some leading west over the Sierra Nevada, others into northern California and farther north to Oregon. Despite the challenge of crossing the Sierra Nevada—by 1841 emigrant parties like the Bidwell-Bartleson Party were struggling to find a crossing over this formidable mountain range, and in 1846 the famous Donner Party's trek ended in disaster when they were trapped in the Sierra by an early, heavy snowfall—the slow stream of emigrants continued. After gold was discovered in California in 1848, wagon trains heading for the gold country made the Big Meadows a regular stop before heading into the dreaded Forty-Mile Desert toward the Sierra Nevada. Soon the slow stream of immigrants became a torrent of thousands.

By the 1860s, the first farmers and cattlemen had settled in the meadows north of the Humboldt Sink. According to Nevada historian James Hulse, "hundreds of families raised crops, hay, grain and cattle in the vicinity of what became known as Lovelock."

Not all of these settlers arrived directly from the East. Some, like George Lovelock, after whom the town of Lovelock is named, brought his family west over the Sierra Nevada to California's Honey Lake Valley in 1855. In 1861 he followed a stream of miners who left California to seek their fortune in the mountains and canyons of Nevada. Eventually he landed in the small settlement that became his namesake.

By the 1860s, the hills and mountains of what was later to be known

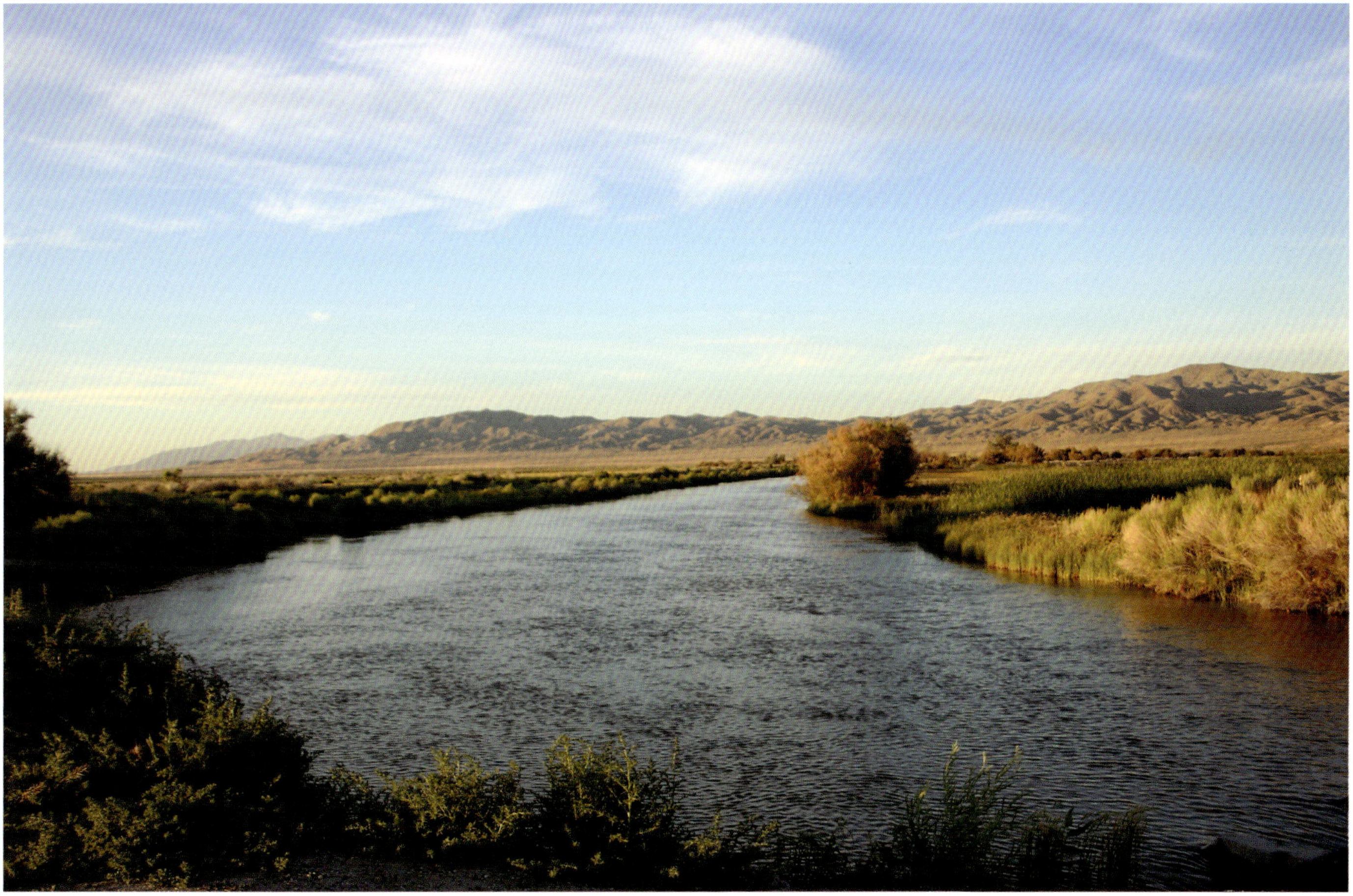

Grasses and willows thrive on the banks of the Humboldt River.

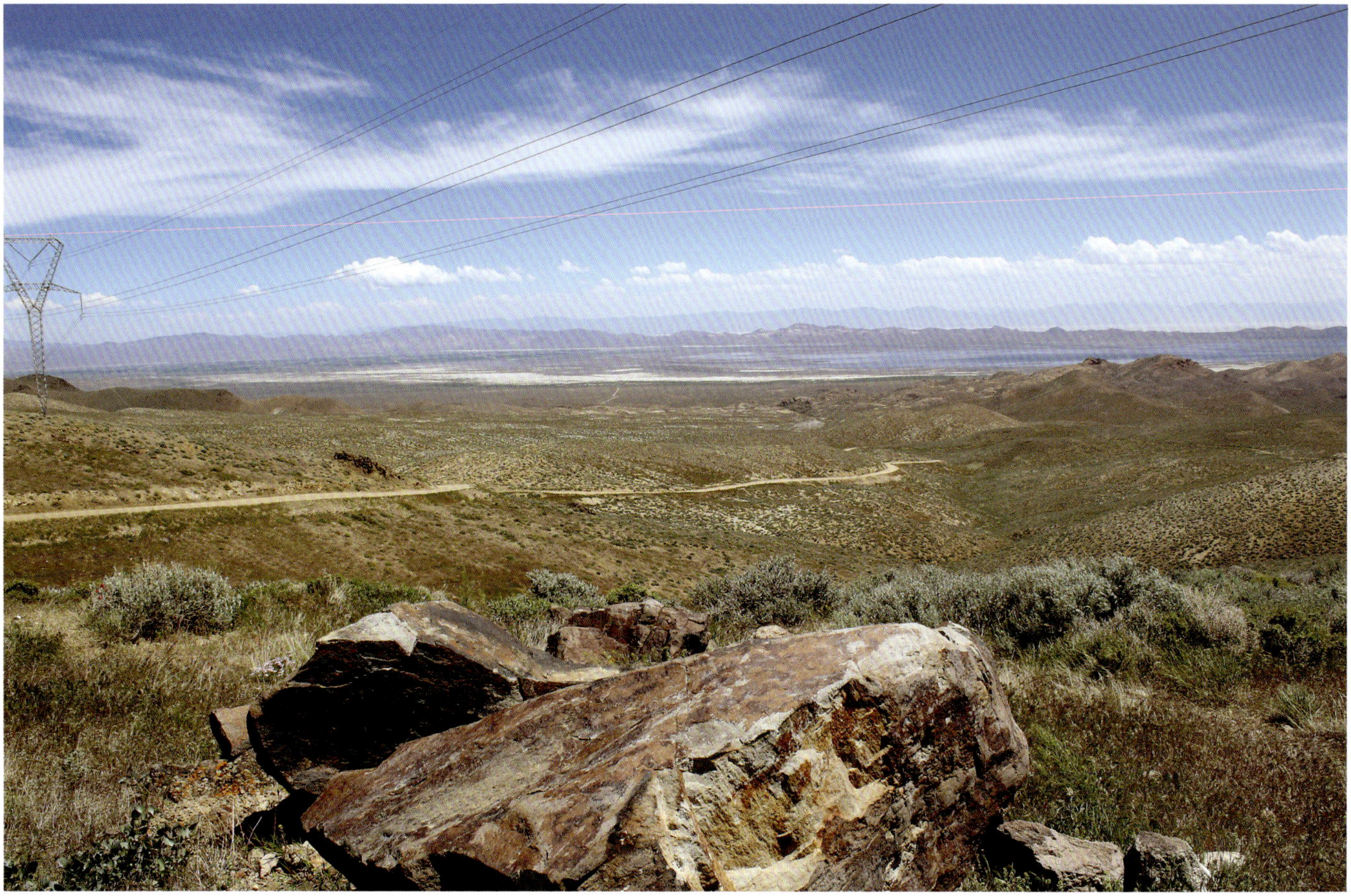

The Lovelock Valley and Humboldt Sink from Ragged Top.

as Pershing County were dotted with tailings from mining camps as the fevered search for gold and silver moved beyond California's gold country into neighboring Nevada. Some of these camps were short-lived, abandoned in a few months when the local lode was exhausted, but others flourished for years. Author Michael Ybarra calls the tailings from the now-abandoned mines "the scat of the gods." This scat beckons modern-day outdoor enthusiasts and historians to search for new forms of wealth. Indeed, photography, rockhounding, artifact hunting, and storytelling await excavation from the forgotten, provocatively named camps of Blue Wing, Ragged Top, Perth, Velvet, Arabia, Limbo, Mazuma, Placeritos, Dun Glen, Bonnie Briar, Kodak, and Seven Troughs. Unionville, the most famous of these camps, survived longer than many. It was immortalized in Mark Twain's *Roughing It*.

On September 20, 1868, the Central Pacific Railroad was completed through this part of Nevada. The Big Meadows and the surrounding area were now connected to the rest of the world. A railroad station was built some ninety miles from Reno at a trading post that was owned by George Lovelock. Small hotels sprang up around the station, eateries proliferated, homes were built, businesses opened, legal and medical services appeared, and local government developed. Lovelock's Station became known as the town of Lovelock.

However, most government was located in Winnemucca, the seat of Humboldt County, which at that time included all of the land that is now

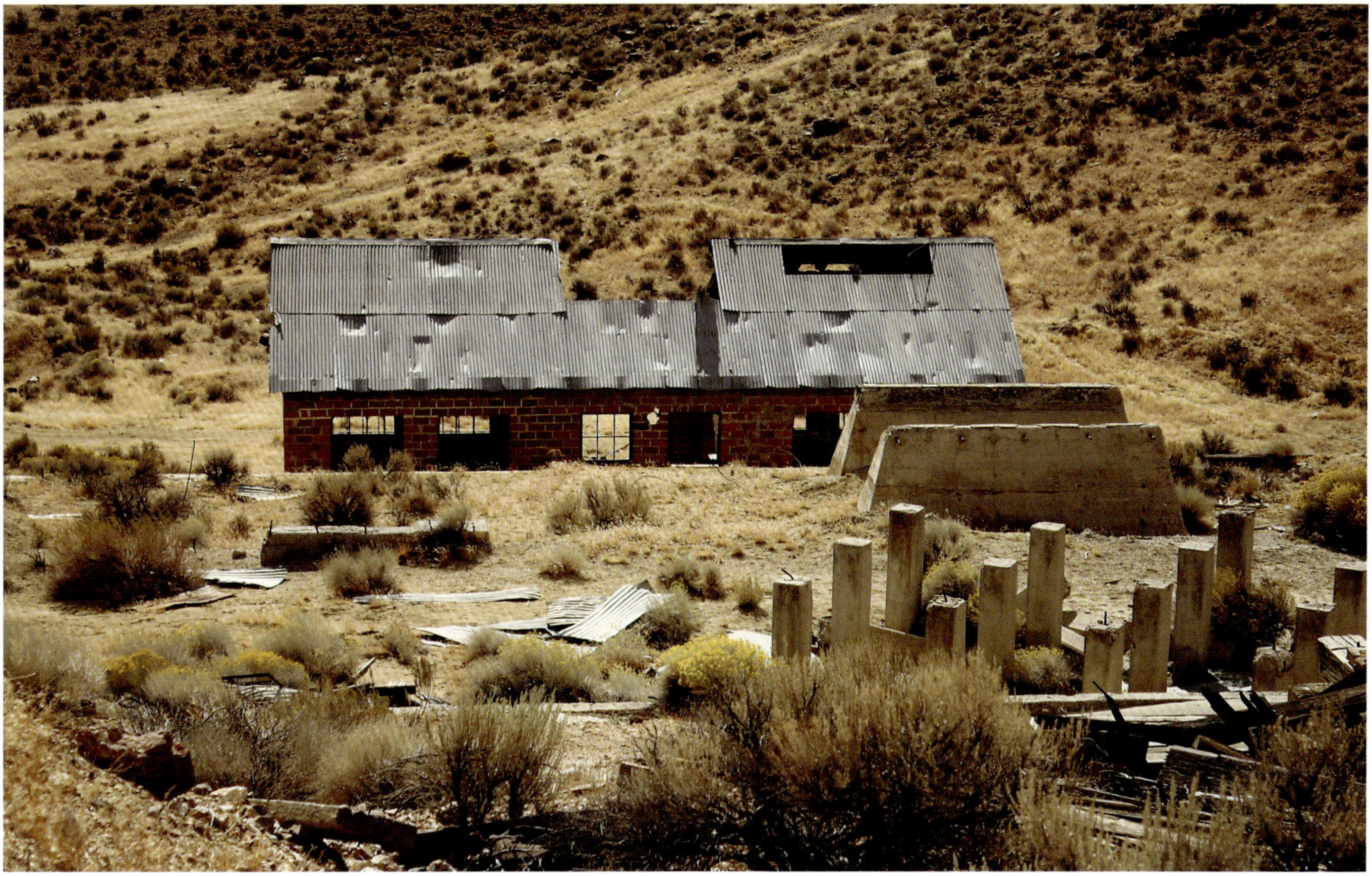

The ruins of Seven Troughs.

Pershing County. By the turn of the century, many people in Lovelock were advocating for more self-governance. On July 20, 1918, a fire in Winnemucca partially destroyed the Humboldt County Courthouse. The matter of building a new courthouse arose, exacerbating the rumblings in Lovelock about more local control of finances and other civic decisions. In February 1919, spokesmen for Lovelock's merchants wrote to Humboldt County officials stating that Lovelock taxpayers favored the division of Humboldt County into two separate jurisdictions. Then a committee of community leaders went to Carson City, the state's capital, to speak for the creation of a new county with Lovelock as its seat. One of these men, William C. Pitt of Lovelock, stated that he loved the "old county" but that the time for "advancement" had come.

On March 12, 1919, the Nevada legislature voted to create Pershing County. Word of the division bill was telegraphed to Lovelock within five minutes of the final vote in Carson City, and James T. Goodin telegraphed the news to General John J. "Black Jack" Pershing that the new county was to be his namesake. Pershing, who had a long and distinguished military career, was named commander of the American Expeditionary Force when the U.S. entered World War I in 1917, and he received the news at his military headquarters in France. Nevada's governor, Emmet D. Boyle, signed the bill creating Pershing County at 3:18 p.m. on March 18, 1919. The new county consisted of 3,859,840 acres of surface area, or 6,031 square miles, 76 percent of which was managed by the federal government.

The creation of the new county was celebrated in many ways. A local poet, Mrs. R. M. Hardy, was inspired to write the following:

Nevada's Baby County

In the enemies' front trenches,
Amidst the taunts and scorn,
In agonizing travail,
Thus the man-child was born.
Three times, we almost gave him up,
And ordered out the hearse,
But with Uniacke for doctor,
And Friedman for head-nurse,
This feisty, husky infant
You see before you now,
One year ago in Carson

Stepped out and made his bow.
Born of battle in the sagebrush,
Descendant of warrior bold,
You can see why he's so sturdy,
And his feet are never cold!
Neither is he ever "yellow",
And his backbone's all in place.
He's a devil of a fellow!
And it's going to be great
To watch this Pershing youngster
Growing up to Man's estate.

Like most parts of Nevada, Pershing County experienced booms and busts in its first one hundred years. When prices for silver, gold, tungsten, and diatomite were high, the miners grew wealthy. When the market for hay, beef, and field crops was strong, the farmers and ranchers prospered, tax revenues were plentiful, and the county coffers were full. However, a single major change can throw a small community like Lovelock into a tail-spin. In the 1960s, when the interstate highway system was constructed,

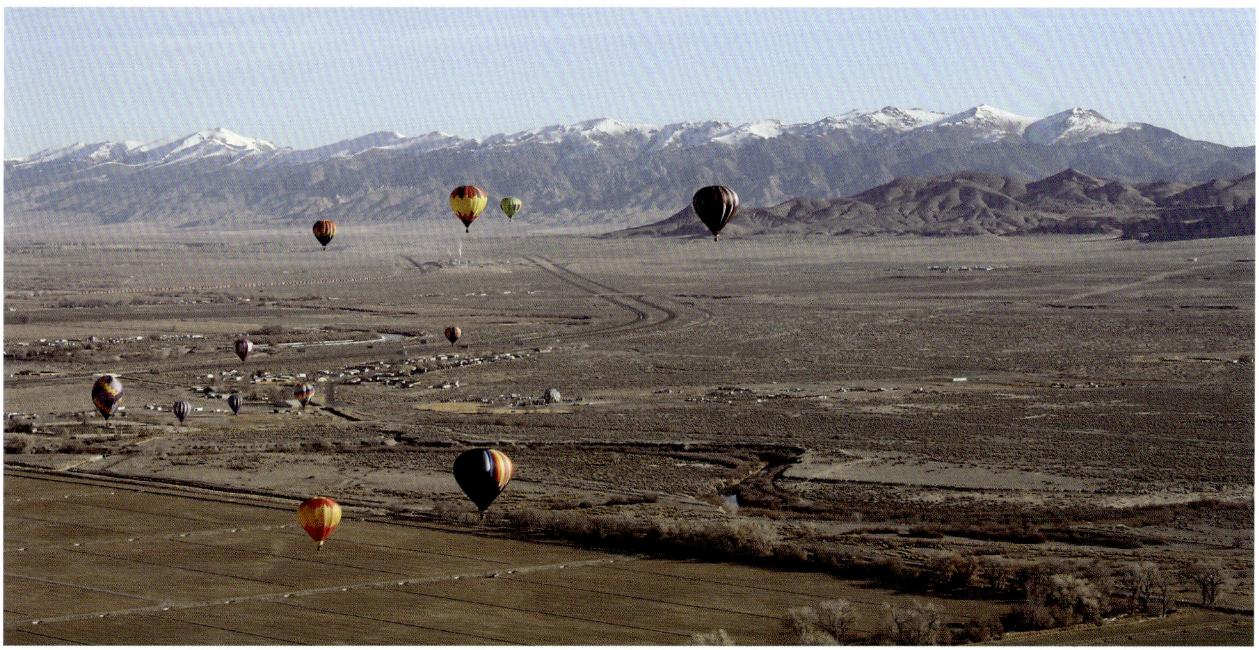

The Humboldt River Valley from the Lovers Aloft Balloon Festival.

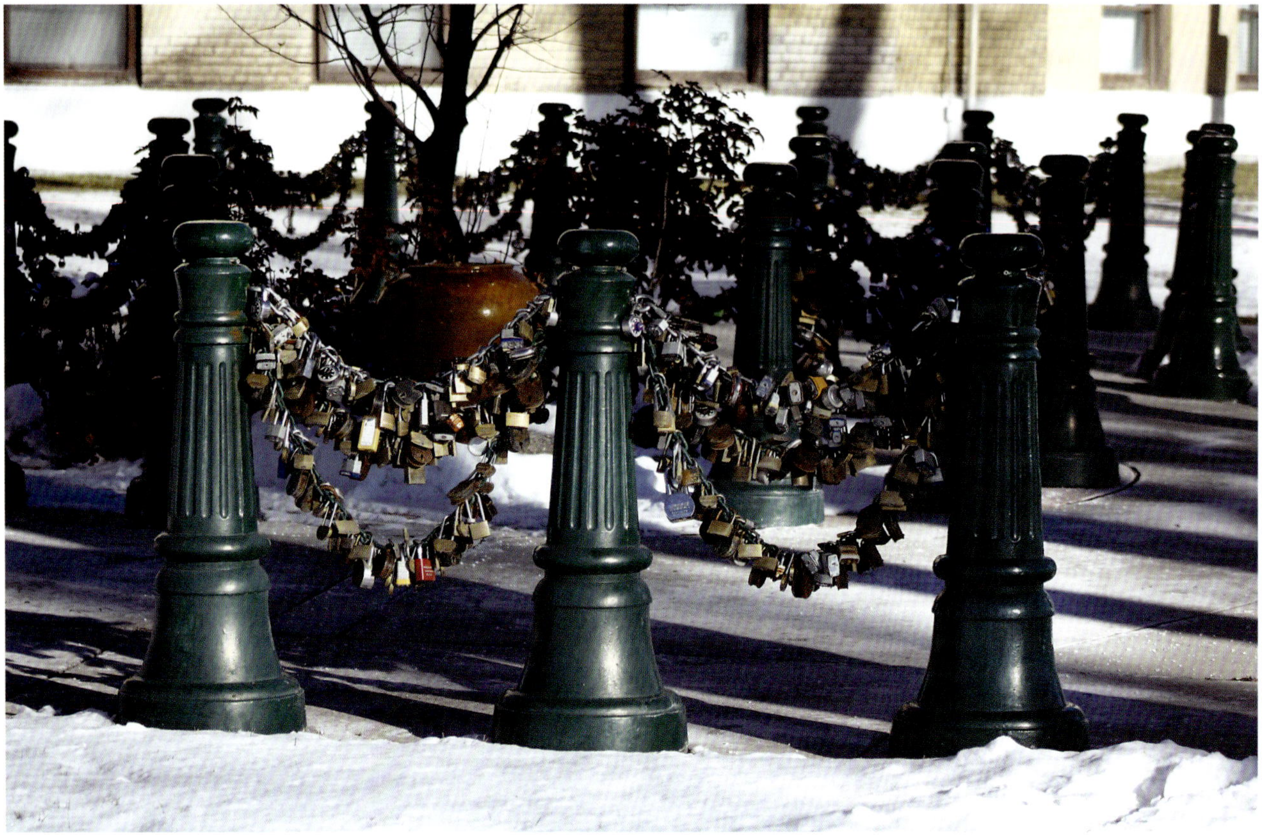

The Lovers Lock Plaza, Lovelock.

Interstate 80 bypassed Lovelock. Transcontinental highway traffic no longer stopped at Lovelock's single traffic light, tourists no longer filled their gas tanks at the Two Stiffs Selling Gas or dropped some coins into the slot machines at Felix's Bank Club.

Today, the residents of Lovelock, the county seat and major community in Pershing County, are working to infuse new life into their charming historic town. Some signs of change can be seen in the efforts of the Chamber of Commerce to promote Lovers Lock Plaza, established on Valentine's Day 2007 in the courthouse park; the Lovers Aloft Balloon Festival over the Humboldt River; a 2016 film festival celebrating the career of silent-film star Edna Purviance, a native of Lovelock; the Lovelock Ranch Rodeo; the popular Portuguese parade and *festa*; and an annual summer event, Frontier Days.

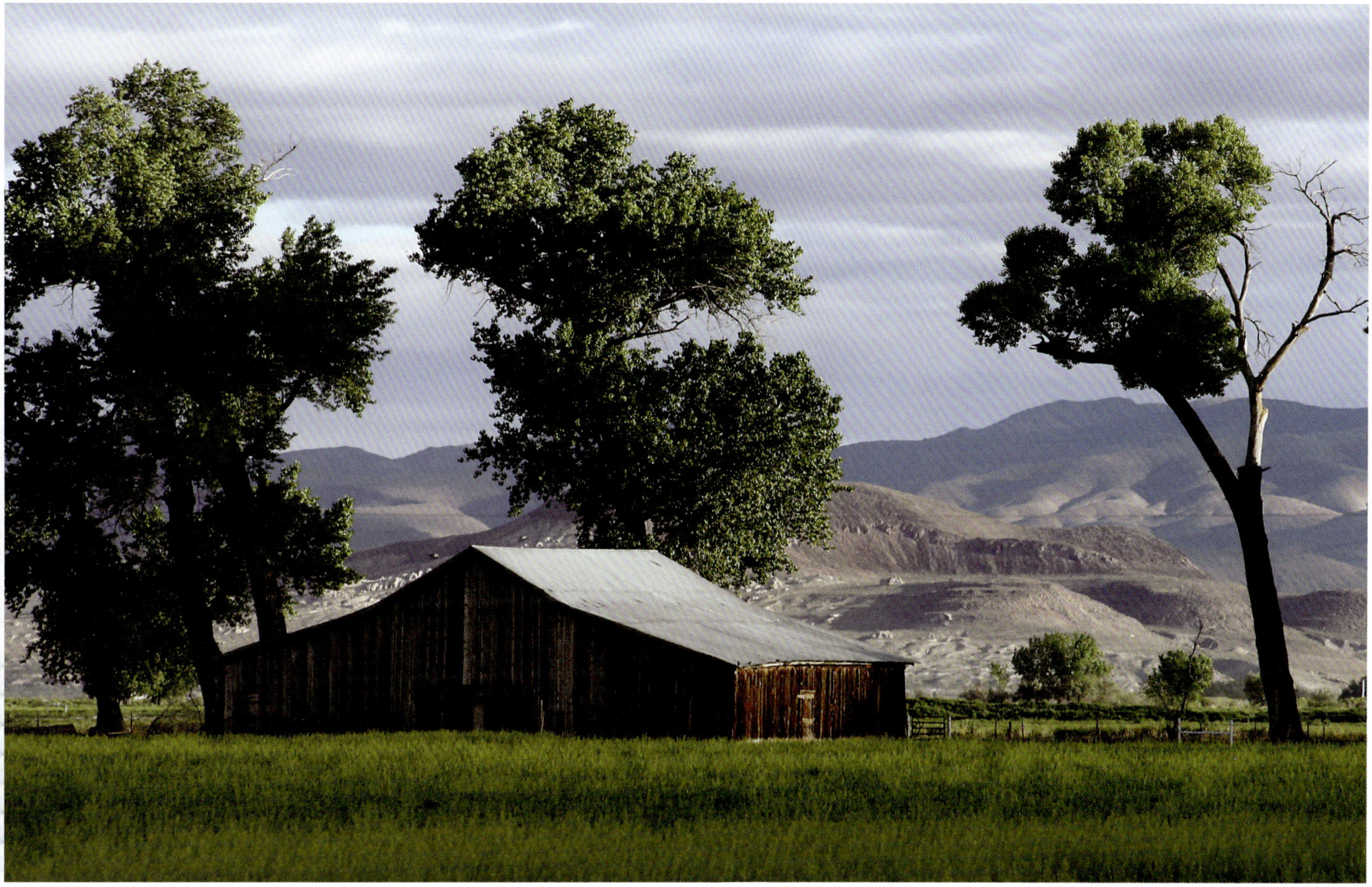

The Anker Ranch, Lower Valley.

Pershing County offers other attractions that draw visitors. Tens of thousands of people attend the annual Burning Man gathering in the northern part of the county; birders follow the seasonal and permanent avian populations in the rich bird habitats created by the Humboldt River; hunters comb the hillsides for deer and game birds; geologists and amateur rock-hunters search the mountains and old mine tailings for their next find; and water-sports enthusiasts use the Rye Patch Reservoir for boating and fishing. The county has much to offer historians, photographers, rockhounds, ghost-towners, outdoors aficionados, and anyone seeking the delightful ambiance of an historic small town. All are welcome in Nevada's "baby county" as it celebrates its hundredth birthday—2019.

THE LAND

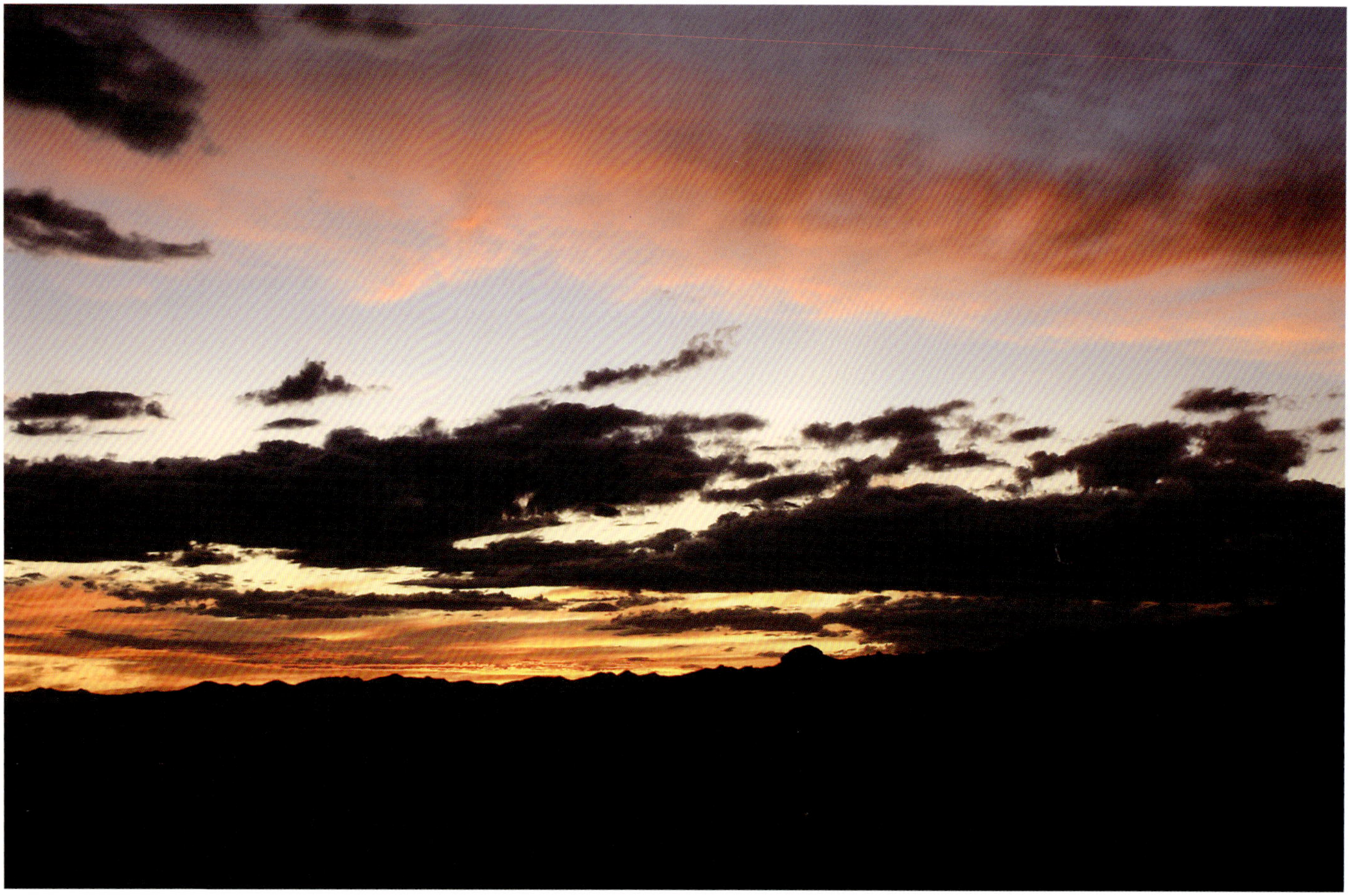

The westerly skies of Pershing County.

The land in north-central Nevada is beautiful, but the air is even more magnificent. Clear and arid, it offers vast vistas of the diverse landscape under an endless sky. The unfiltered light rippling from Pershing County's sunsets tantalizes the eye as it illuminates and shadows mountain, sand, and stream, creating memorable views that tempt the visual artist into trying to capture the unparalleled moment.

Water is the source of Pershing County's success—indeed, of its very existence. Water is what separates meadow from desert. As Mark Twain said, "Whiskey is for drinking and water is for fighting." In Pershing County, water has been both the foundation of life and the reason for any number of heated debates over its use and control. Due to the extremely dry climate and the necessity of water for raising crops and livestock, every drop of water makes a difference here!

Nevada's Nile, the Big Meadows, Lovelock Valley—these are all names that celebrate the fertile land surrounding present-day Lovelock. This rich agricultural area exists because of the Humboldt River, which is sometimes described as "the crookedest river in the world." The Greek tragedian Aeschylus said, "Geography is the mother of all history," and no place in Nevada offers a better example than the tilled, cultivated, irrigated land of lower Pershing County. Without this water, ancient peoples would not have settled here millennia ago nor would later arrivals have produced a recent history of abundant agriculture.

The Humboldt River cuts a trench into the clays that form the bed of ancient Lake Lahontan, and it determines the life of the region. The first European explorers called it the Unknown River, then Mary's River, and finally the Humboldt River. It is a vital water source that regularly flooded and spread out over a vast expanse of land, creating natural meadows of rich grass that are the home to an array of wildlife that sustained ancient man

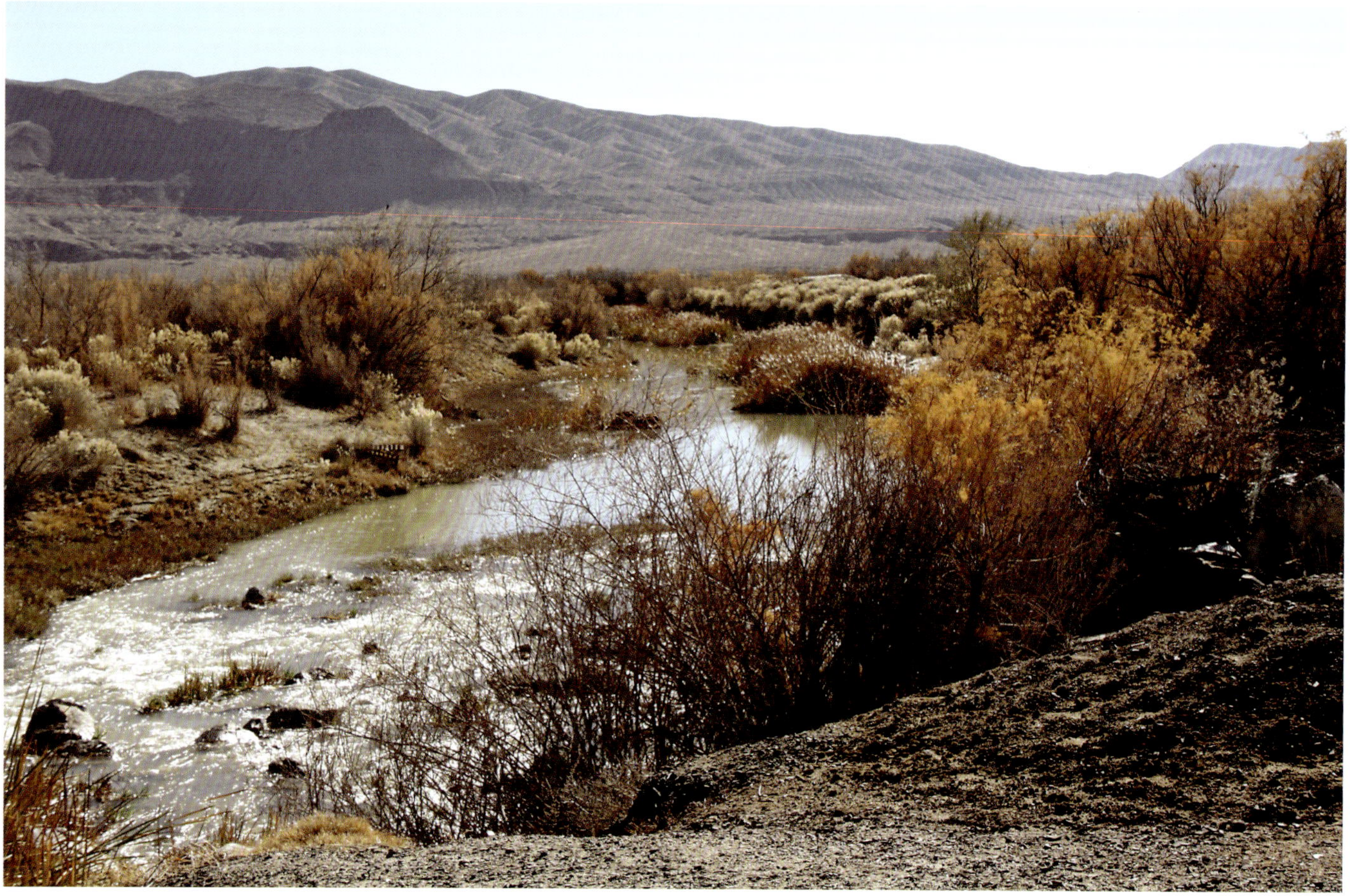

The Humboldt River flowing out of the Big 5 in Lower Valley.

for thousands of years. Today, the river supports the modern life of Pershing County and draws visitors to explore its canyons and valleys, hillsides and mountaintops, as well as the wetlands and irrigated areas that provide excellent bird habitat.

Lovelock's Upper and Lower Valleys are home to more than 150 species of birds, including white-faced ibis, American avocet, black-necked stilts, American white pelicans, sandhill cranes, great blue herons, great egrets, and several species of sandpipers. The isolated canyons provide habitat for a variety of raptors and game birds like chukar, quail, doves, and pheasant.

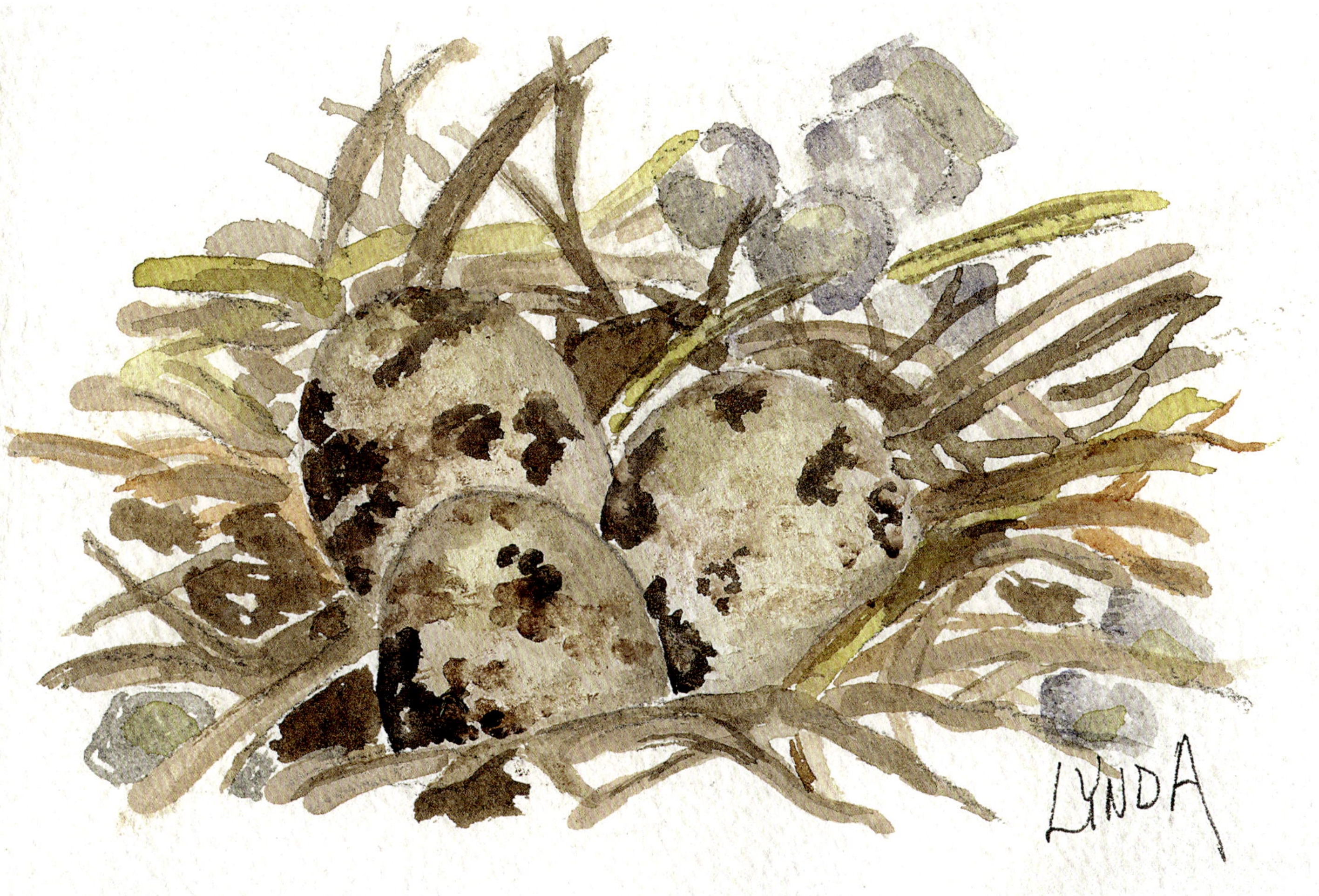

Kildeer are a common bird in Pershing County's wetlands. This clutch of eggs will add another generation to the population. Watercolor by Lynda Quilici.

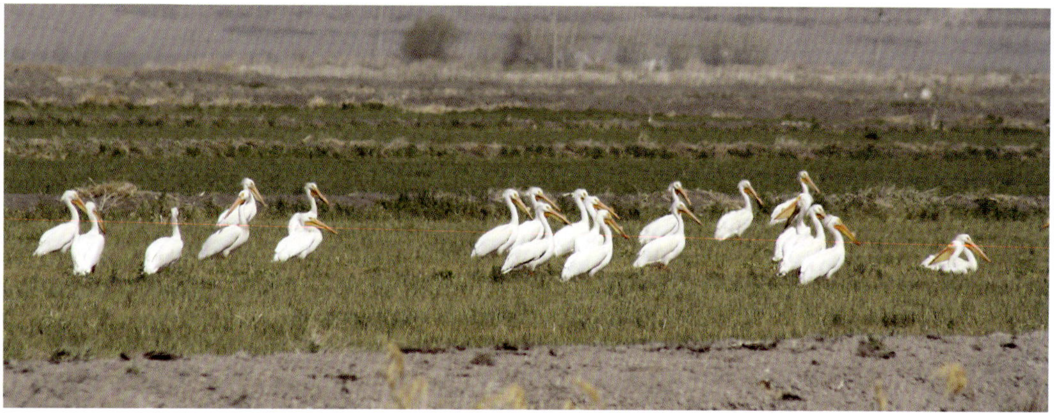

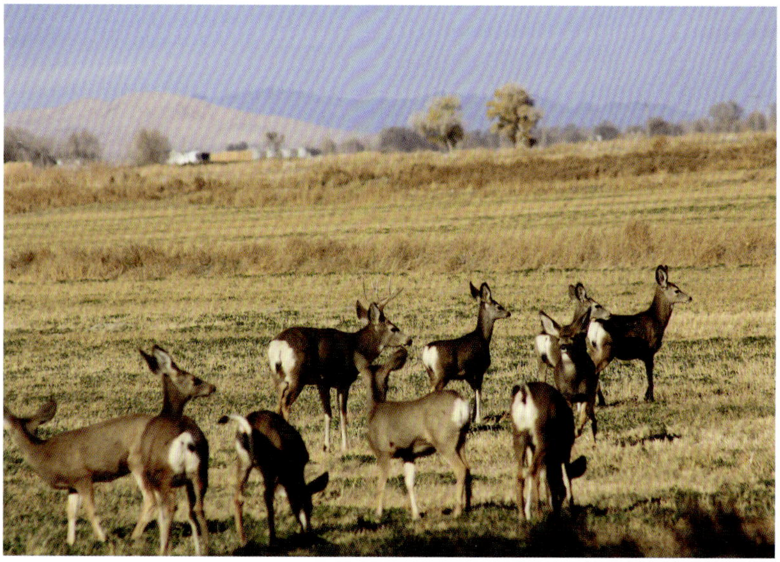

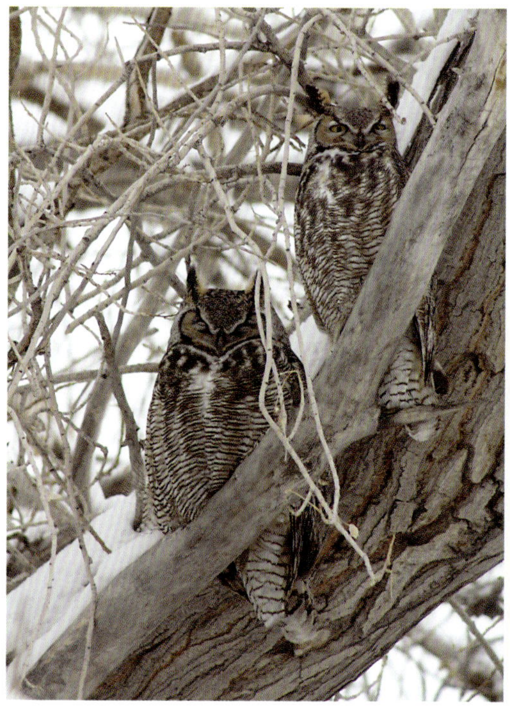

TOP: *Pershing County's wetlands host dozens of bird species. White pelicans are frequent visitors to and residents of Nevada's desert lakes.*

MIDDLE: *Mule deer are abundant in rural Nevada. They often visit agricultural areas and are sometimes found grazing near cattle herds.*

BOTTOM: *Owls are one of the county's common nocturnal birds.*

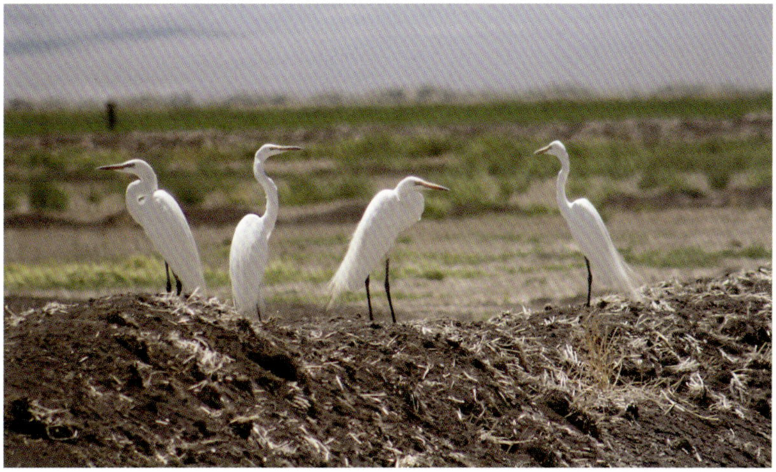

LEFT: *Herons are another water-loving species common in Pershing County's wetlands.*

MIDDLE: *Doves are found all over Pershing County, although they seem to favor farmland.*

BOTTOM: *Wild burros are a domestic species that has flourished for generations in the vast open spaces of the arid West. They, as well as wild horses, are common in Nevada's backcountry.*

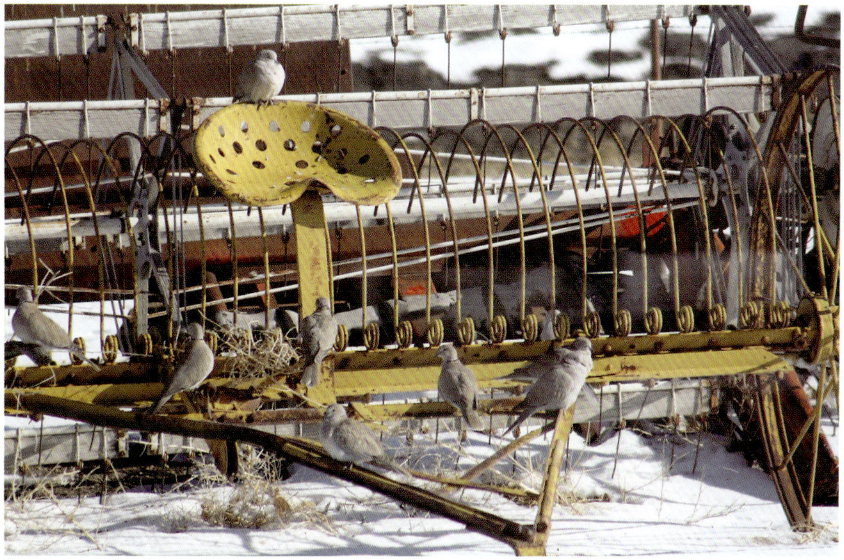

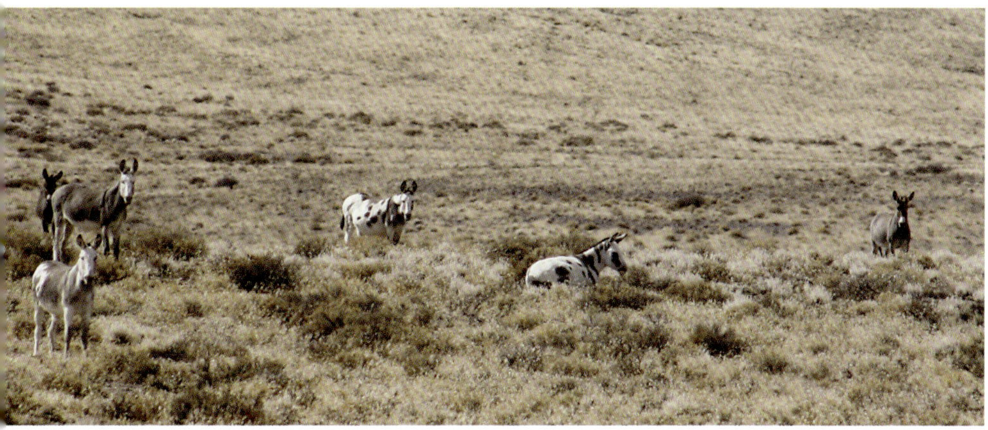

Each season in Pershing County brings its own character and beauty to the land. In spring, the warmth and stored moisture produce carpets of flowers in the desert country. For three short months, from March to May, about forty species of wildflowers bloom in the Lovelock area. Sand verbena, evening primrose, and cheerful orange mallow bloom beside the tall, deep-blue spikes of larkspur and lupine, and pink penstemon (beard-tongue). There are delicate lavender and yellow-throated Phacelia, wild onion and wild garlic, desert daisies, and blue asters. In the early autumn, wild sunflowers and rabbit brush bring swaths of bright yellow blooms to the landscape.

Nevada bouquets:

RIGHT: *lupine and paintbrush*
BELOW: *paintbrush and daisies*

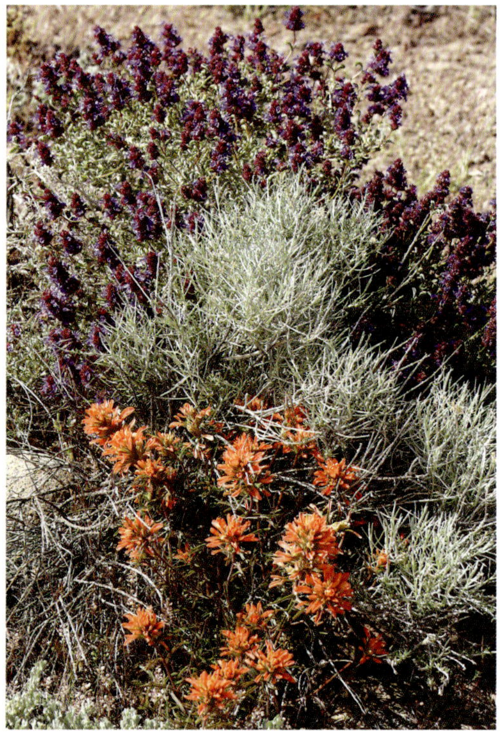

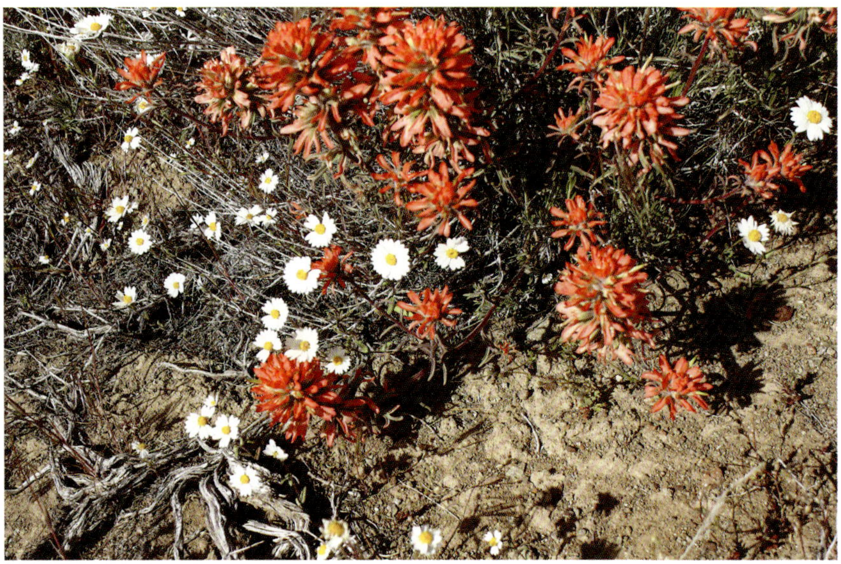

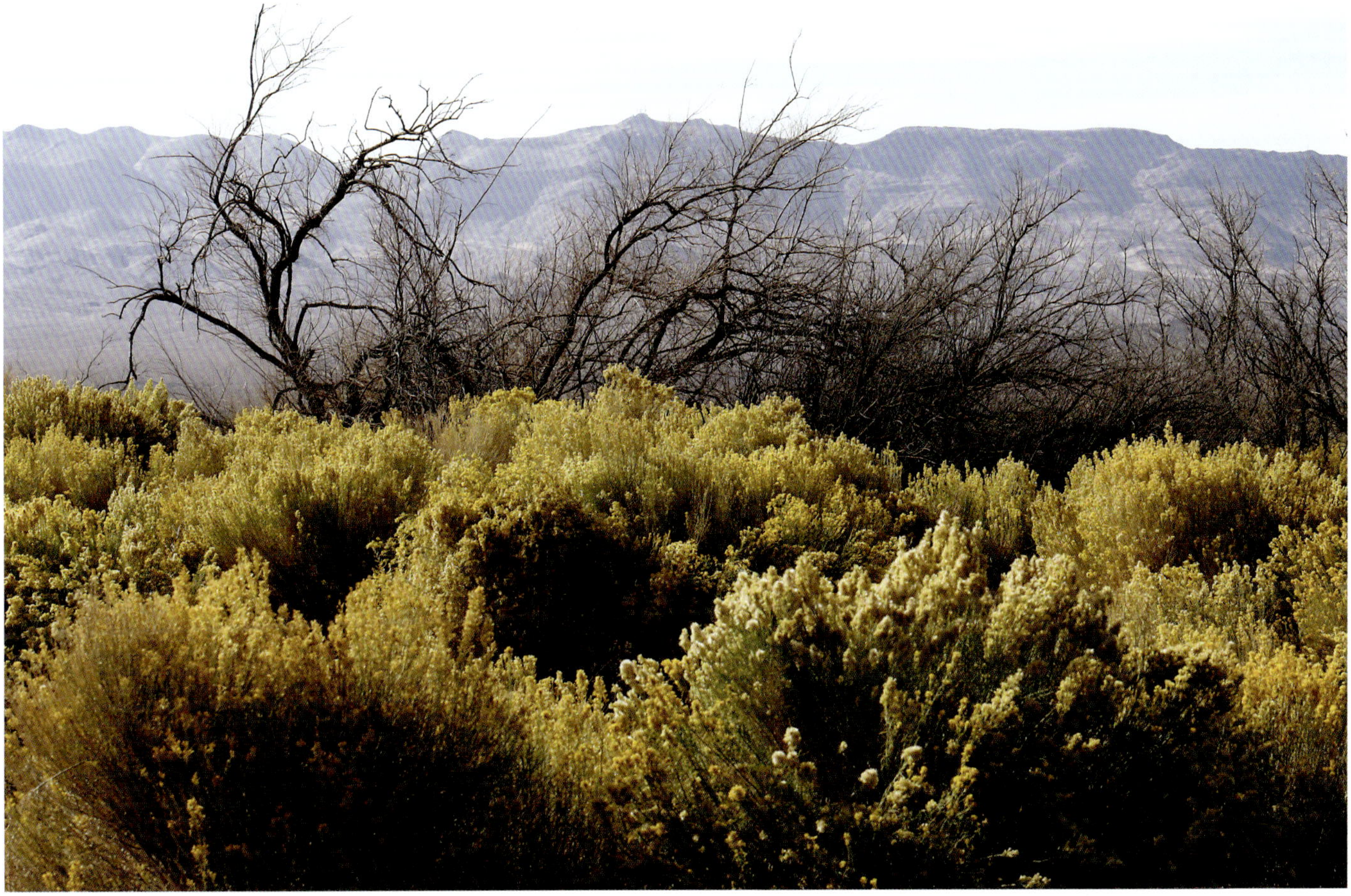

Rabbitbrush is a common species of the high-desert steppe community. It frequently shares habitat with sagebrush. In the late summer, its blooms bring brilliant color to roadsides throughout the county.

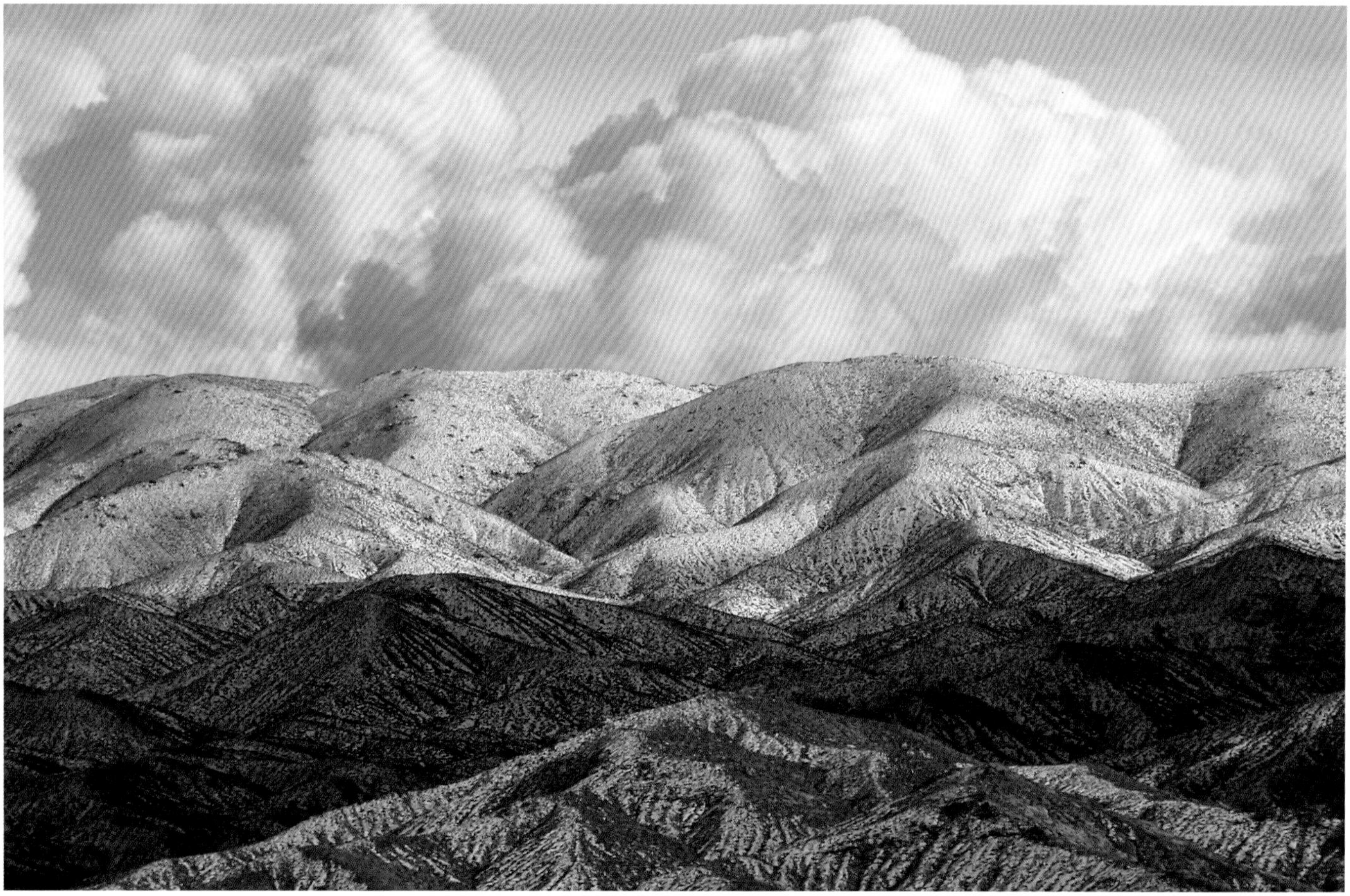

Winter snows bring a new dimension of majesty to Pershing County's mountains.

Winter brings a palette of grays, somber brown-black, and ever-changing whites. The land rests under rain-stippled winter snow. Bitter-cold mornings often bring a freezing fog called *pogonip* (white death) in the local Paiute language. This hoarfrost covers trees, bushes, fence lines, and abandoned buildings, and the dense fog drapes the county's summer gold in wintry ghosts.

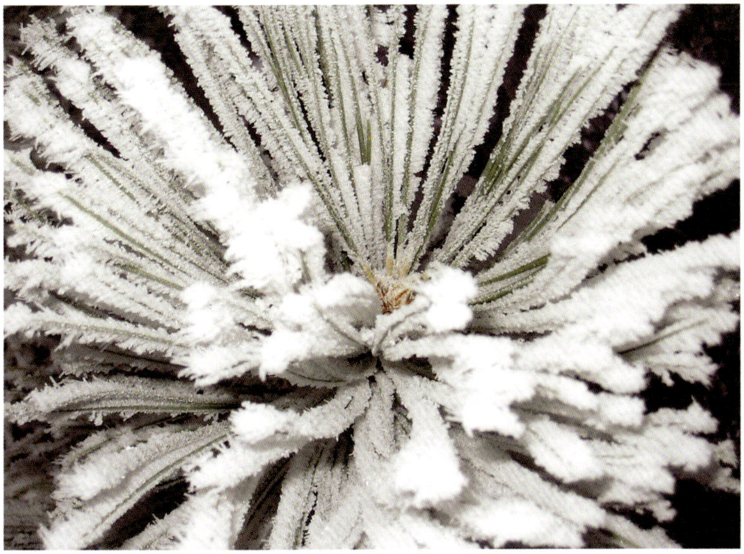

LEFT: *Winter's pogonip covers even ordinary objects with beauty. Here, pogonip bejewels a clump of pine needles.*

BELOW: *Pogonip can turn an entire landscape into an icy ghost of its summertime image.*

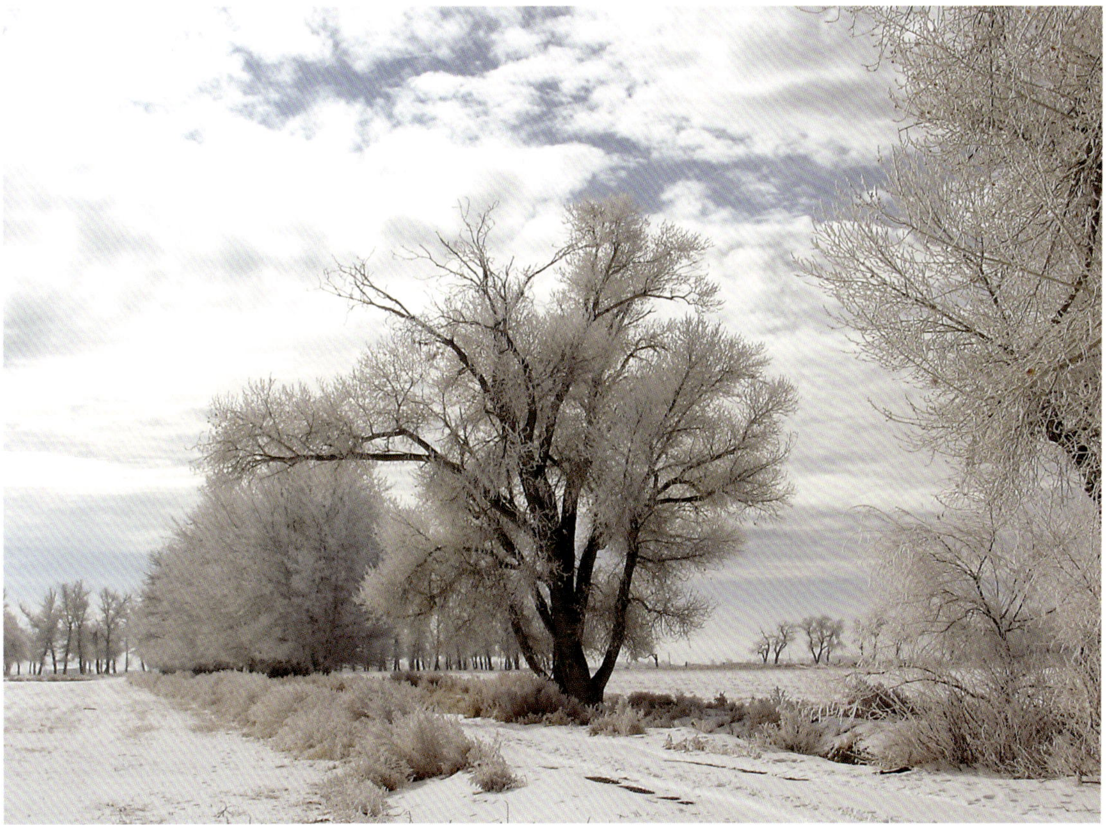

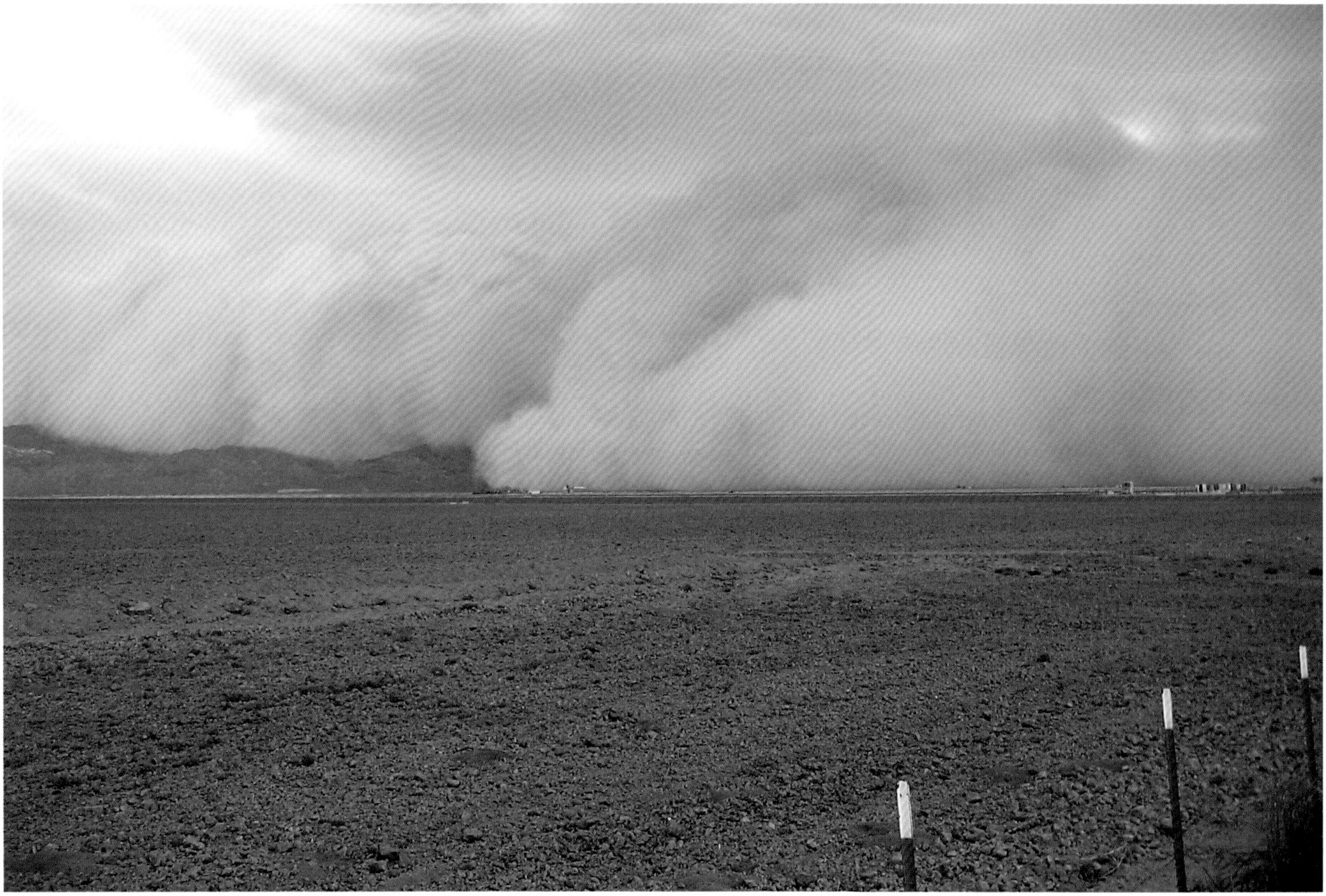

The haboob *is another weather phenomenon common in Pershing County. These brief, intense dust storms seem more typical of the Arabian desert than the rural North American high desert, but they are nonetheless a fact of life here.*

Rain Outside Lovelock, Late March

The first whiskers poke
        from the greasewood.
Clouds sulk the ridge beyond
        an alfalfa farm.
        A roadside cross pretends to grieve
and the few willows reach to
        Rye Patch, a last body
of water before the dry, endless miles.
        This could be the road to Inuvik
        and there is no warrior
at the horizon. The landscape is quarantined:
        a desert peach offers pink rosaries
to the slopes bladed for minerals,
        once white and hard with tranquility,
now dust in the atmosphere.
        This is what the desert surrenders
to the magpie bloated on the centerline,
        to fresh prints at the petroglyphs,
        to the feral galaxy of spring.

—SHAUN GRIFFIN

Summer brings another unusual weather phenomenon, a sudden dust storm propelled by high winds called a *haboob* (an Arabic term). This is a massive low cloud of dust or sand that moves quickly over the land, sweeps over cultivated fields and open rangeland, then just as suddenly disappears.

Besides the miracles that water has wrought in the desert that comprises this region, Pershing County offers a wealth of minerals. Gold and silver deposits attracted tens of thousands of early miners, a few of whom wrested fortunes from the mountains and streams, but the county's earth contains dozens of other minerals as well. Some of these have commercial value, such as copper, tungsten, lead, and sulfur, while others, such as tourmaline, turquoise, garnets, and numerous colorful quartzes, excite gem and mineral collectors.

The landscape is also dotted in places with another fascinating rock, tufa. This soft, friable, and porous sedimentary rock is found in areas once covered by ancient Lake Lahontan. It is formed by the interaction of water and dissolved calcium carbonate, especially at the mouth of a hot spring or on a

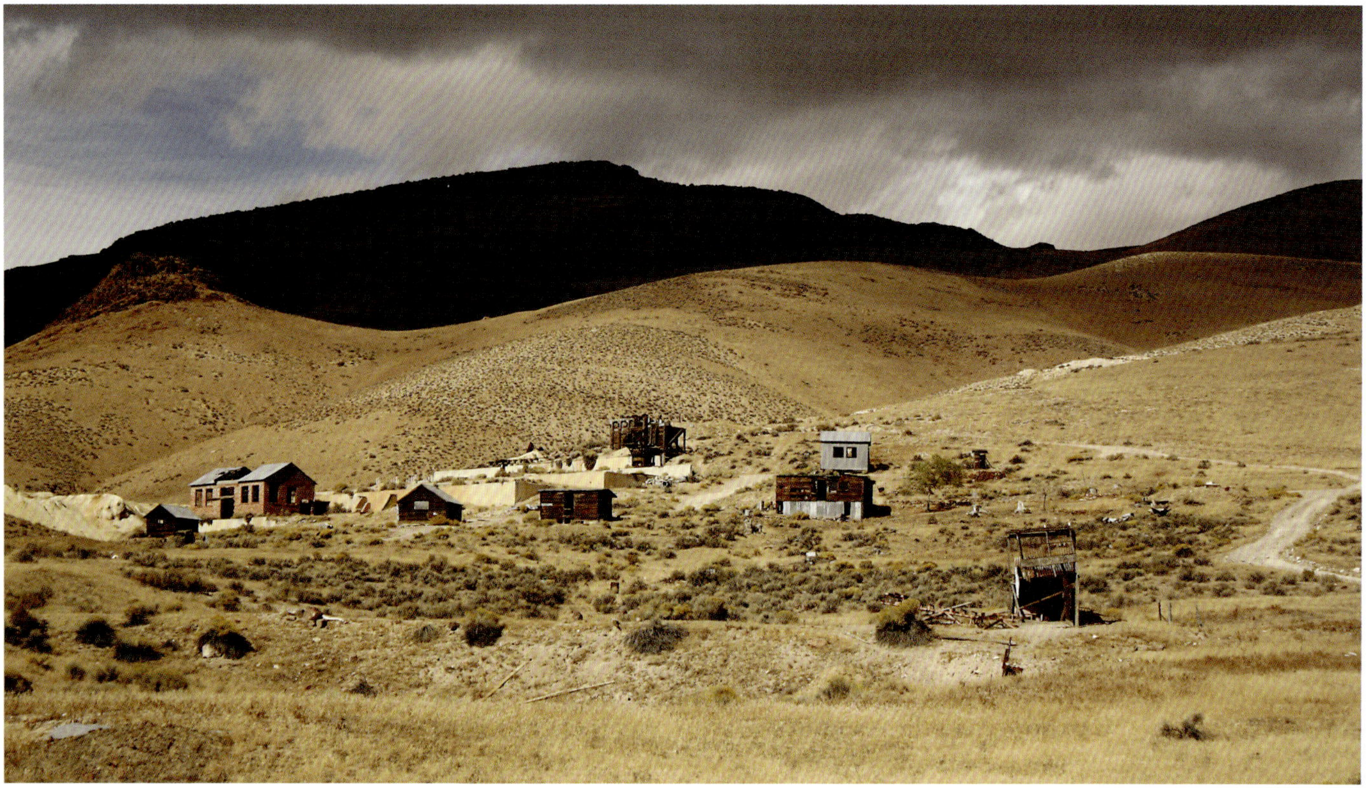

The abandoned Seven Troughs mining camp.

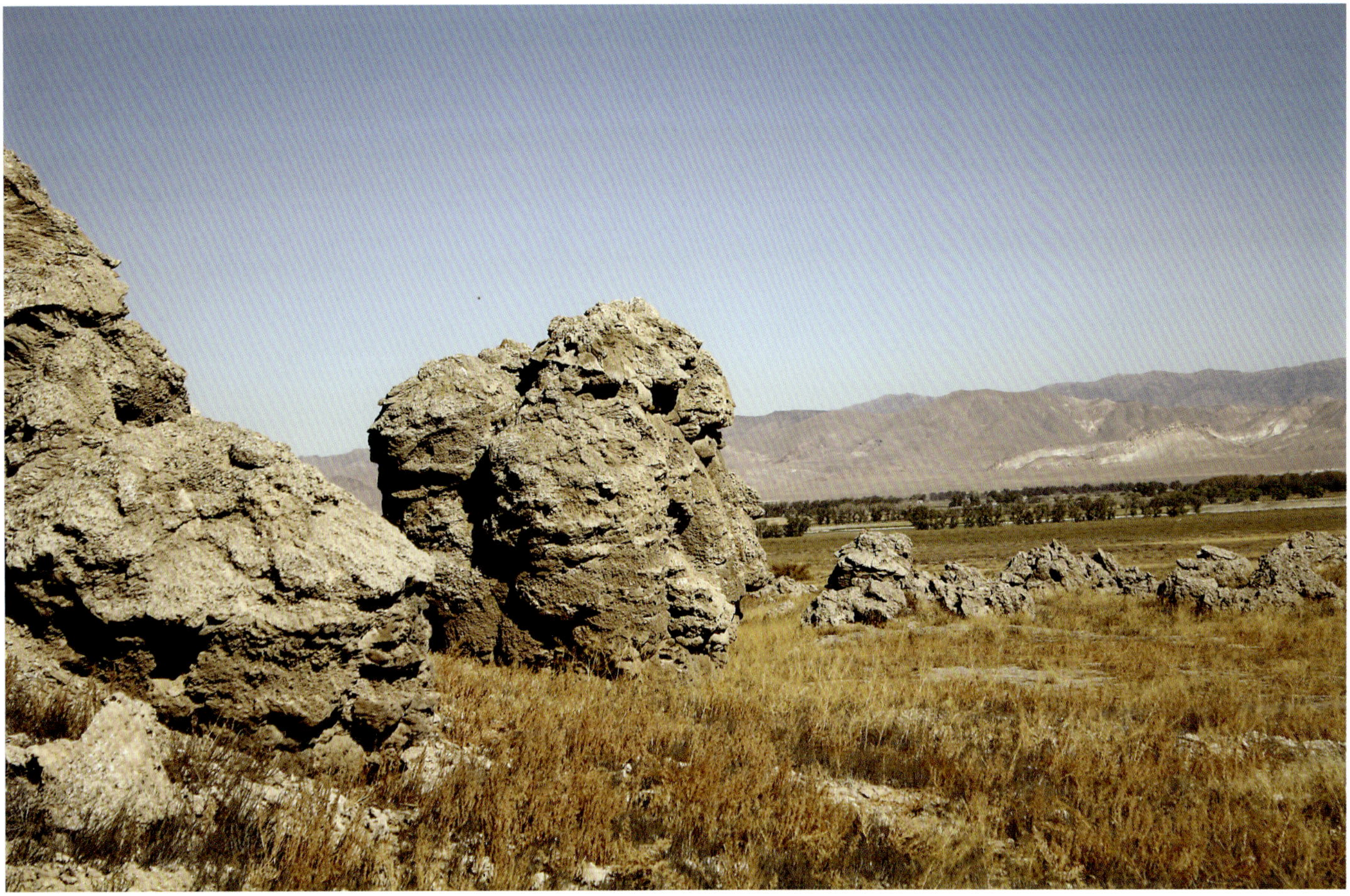

Tufa is a common rock formation in areas once covered by desert lakes and hot springs.

drying lakebed. These captivating natural sculptures can be found in abundance outside Lovelock, not far off Interstate 80.

The northwest corner of Pershing County embraces a major portion of the Black Rock Desert, a vast, barren plain enclosed by rugged mountains that stretches for more than a hundred miles in a southwest-northeast direction. The Black Rock is considered one of the major deserts of the world, although it is technically a playa, the dry bed of an ancient lake. Winter precipitation and spring runoff turn the plain into a broad, shallow sheet of water,

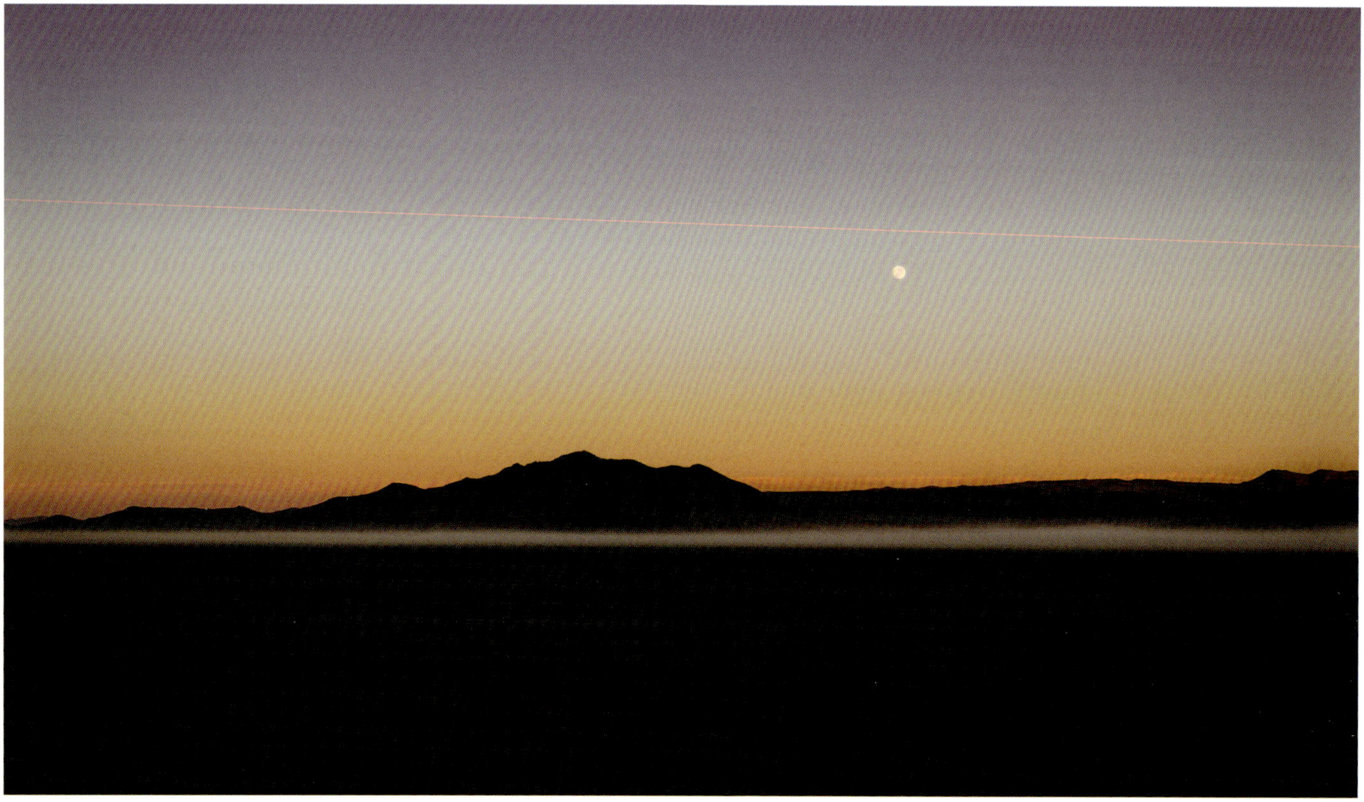

The Black Rock Desert in northwestern Pershing County each summer hosts the Burning Man gathering. Photo by Spencer Jones.

but when the water evaporates the playa clay hardens into a smooth, nearly impermeable surface, hot and dusty. The Black Rock is, however, home to many species of life, including birds, rodents, plants, insects, and amphibians that live both above and beneath the dry mud surface. This desert is also host to the annual Burning Man festival, where tens of thousands of people from all over the world congregate in the middle of the Black Rock Desert to celebrate art and community.

THE PEOPLE

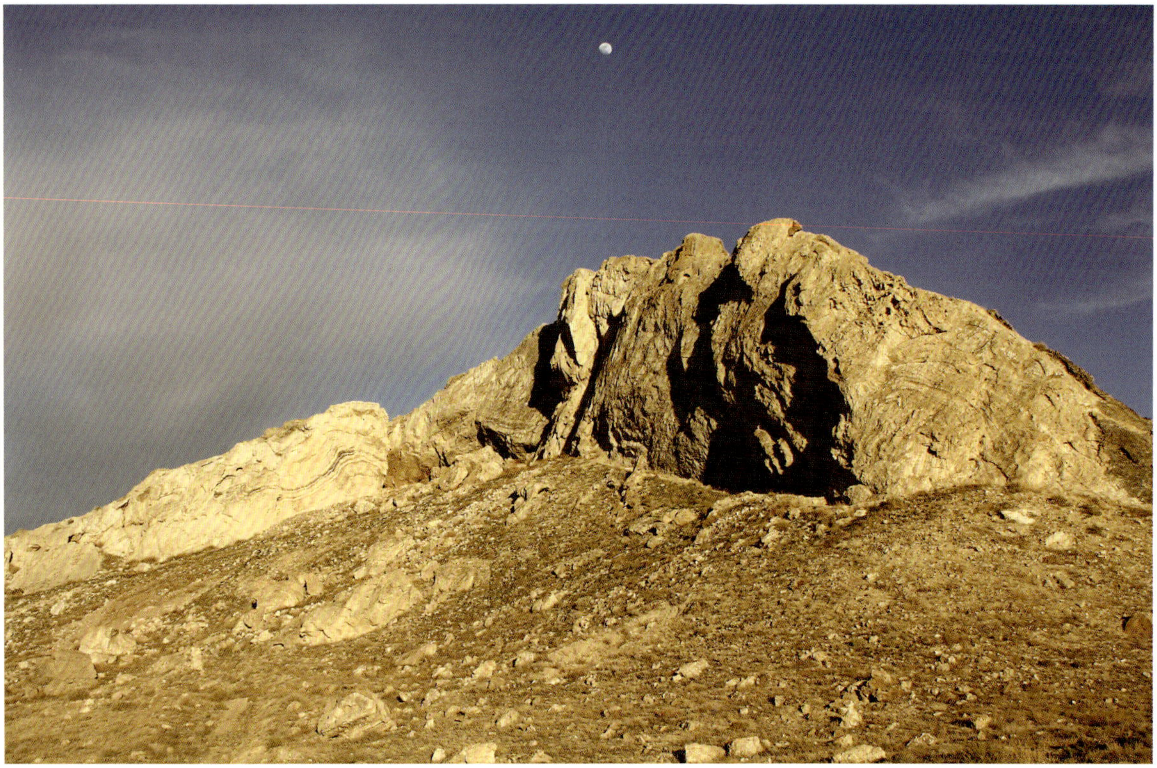

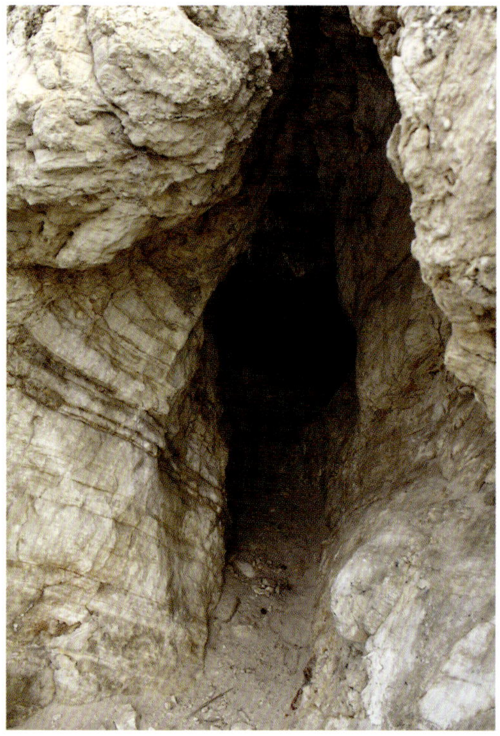

ABOVE: *For millennia, the Lovelock Cave sheltered some of Pershing County's earliest residents. Archaeologists have found thousands of objects left here by ancient people that give us information about their lives and skills.*

RIGHT: *The entrance to Lovelock Cave.*

North-central Nevada, including Pershing County, has been home to human beings for millennia. Over the centuries, various indigenous peoples made their homes here, adapting to the changes of climate—the region was far wetter ten thousand years ago—and eventually creating a rich spiritual culture and a unique material life based on the varied resources of their environment. Evidence of their earliest presence has been found in Lovelock Cave, which lies twenty-two miles southwest of Lovelock in neighboring Churchill County, on what was once the edge of ancient Lake Lahontan, and nearby at another site, the Leonard Rockshelter. Both caves were created by the wash of lakes undercutting the local rock.

Lovelock Cave is 150 feet in length, more than 30 feet in width, and 29 feet high. It was intermittently occupied by various peoples from as early as 3,000-2,000 B.C. until the middle of the nineteenth century A.D. The cave was first excavated in 1911 by men seeking bat guano. Later that year, after the guano mining had removed 250 tons of material, Dr. L. L. Loud of the University of California in Berkeley began an examination of the site that ceased when he ran out of money. In 1924 archaeologist and ethnologist Dr. M. R. Harrington joined Loud, reinvigorating the project with new capital, and they began further, more serious study.

The cave environment was so dry that even ancient hair and feathers were preserved, except for some insect damage. Deposits of man-made material varied from six to fourteen feet in depth. During Loud's first study of the cave, he catalogued about ten thousand artifacts, including bone, matting, bits of rope, atlatls (throwing sticks), nets, weapons, bird decoys, baskets, seeds, dried meat, nuts, dried fish, fur robes, moccasins, blankets of feathers, shell ornaments, and coprolites (fossilized human waste). When Loud returned to the cave in 1924 with M. R. Harrington, they excavated on six levels. This is when they found the now-famous eleven Lovelock Cave painted and feather-covered duck decoys.

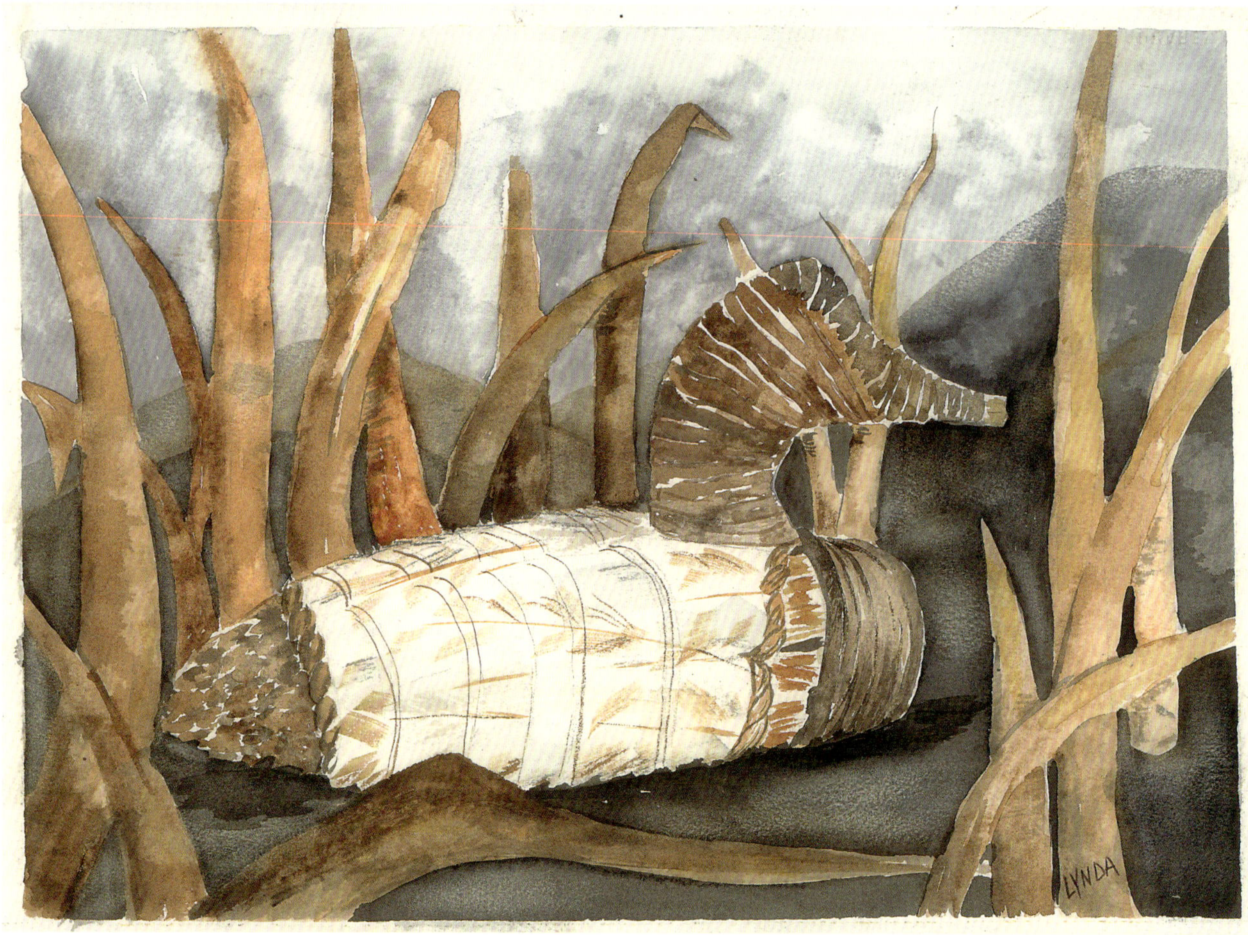

This duck decoy, one of several found in Lovelock Cave, reflects the skill of the ancient people who lived in the area. The decoys are many centuries old, preserved in the dry atmosphere of the cave. Watercolor by Lynda Quilici.

In 1949, 1950, and 1954 University of California archaeologist Robert Heizer visited Lovelock Cave and also excavated at the Leonard Rockshelter. There he found evidence of human occupancy dating back as early as 9248 B.C. He also found an atlatl foreshaft from about 5088 B.C. Over time, these prehistoric peoples evolved permanent societies and formal groups that identified themselves as Paiute.

According to *Numa: A Northern Paiute History,* the Numa, as the Northern Paiutes refer to themselves, who lived in the area near today's town of Lovelock called themselves *Koop Ticutta* (ground-squirrel eaters). Like other

Numa groups, they took their name from their area's most abundant food. The *Koop Ticutta* developed a clever way to force the squirrels out of their dens. First, they poured water down the squirrels' holes in the ground. When a squirrel appeared to escape the flood, they grabbed it behind the head, twisting and snapping its neck. Paiute storytellers offered another story that explained the origin of their traditional method of catching fish: "A natural dam southwest of Lovelock was built long before human beings existed. When *Itsa Pahtuma* (Coyote Dam) was created, animals spoke, thought, and acted like people. Coyote built the dam to catch fish."

The Numa continue to be the majority of the region's Native American population. In the nineteenth century, a local Paiute leader, known to history as Captain Truckee, was born somewhere in the area now known as Pershing County. The tribes of this region were all migratory, following the seasons and the game and plant foods that sustained them. At some point, Truckee's daughter, Tuboitonie, met a Shoshone named Poito and married him. As the son-in-law of Truckee, Poito aligned himself with the Numa and

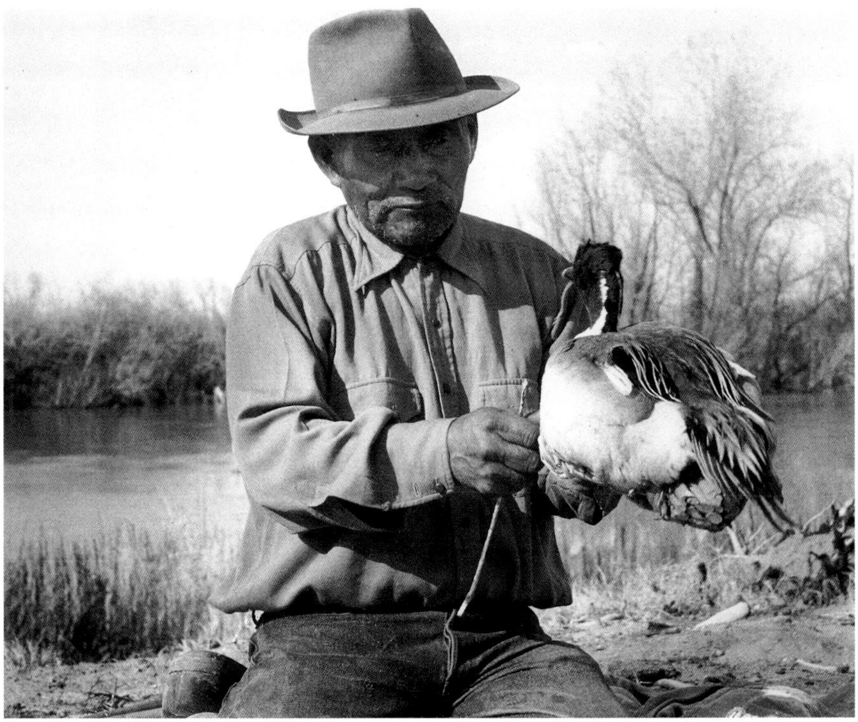

Well into the twentieth century, the Paiutes were still making duck decoys in the style of their ancient ancestors. Here, the decoy-maker is covering his decoy with the skin and plumage of a local duck. Photo by Margaret Wheat, courtesy University of Nevada Press.

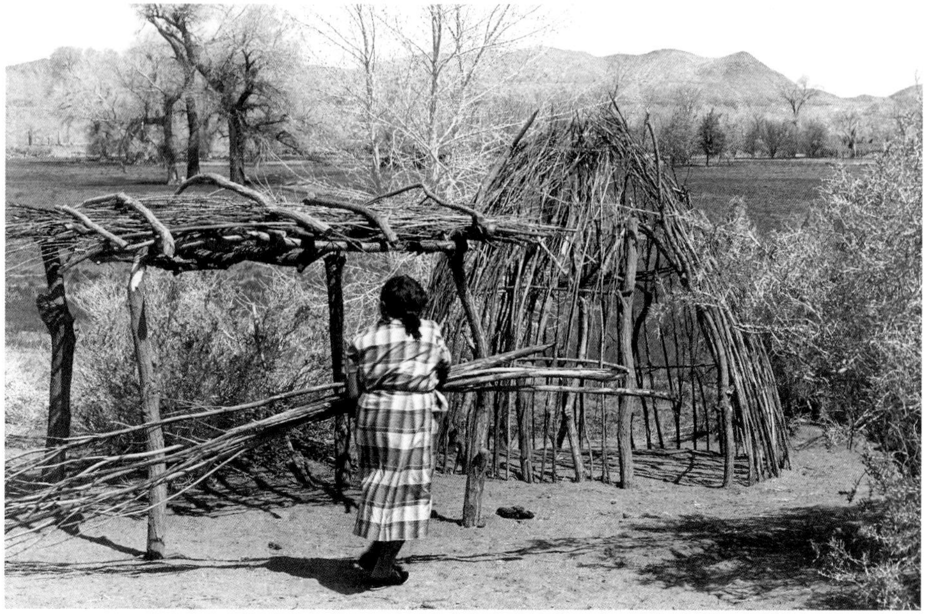

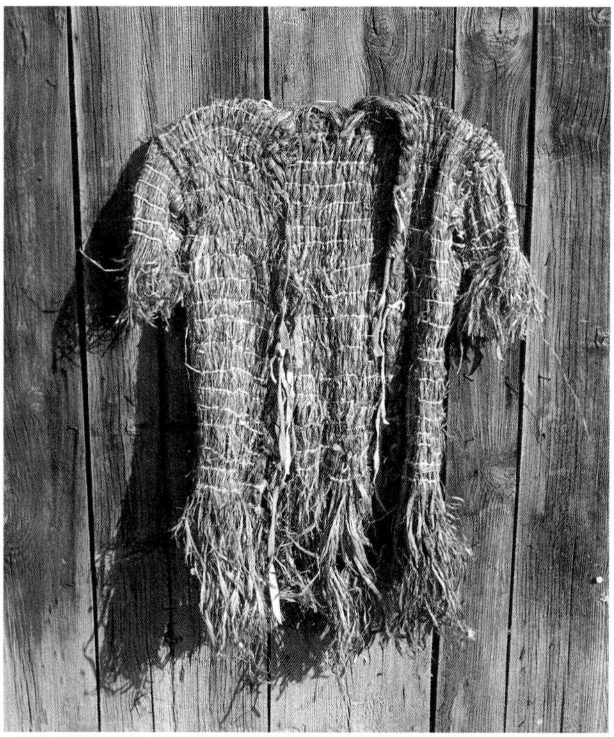

ABOVE: *The Paiutes used local materials to build their dwellings. Here, a summer house and shaded shelter are under construction. Photo by Margaret Wheat, courtesy University of Nevada Press.*

LEFT: *In addition to the skins and fur of animals, the Paiutes used plant materials to create their garments. This jacket, twine-knotted from the leaves of cattails, was a common garment in pre-contact times. Cattails, a common regional sedge, were an important plant in the Paiute culture. Their roots and pollen provided food and their stalks and leaves were used for building shelters and many other purposes. Photo by Margaret Wheat, courtesy University of Nevada Press.*

took a Paiute name, Winnemucca. Later known as Chief Winnemucca, he became an important leader of his people during the difficult years when their territory was being taken over by white settlers.

Winnemucca's daughter Thocmentony (Shell Flower) was born near Humboldt Lake (Sink) about 1844. She later acquired the Anglo name Sarah Winnemucca Hopkins. Her autobiography, *Life Among the Piutes: Their Wrongs and Claims* (1883) is the first book ever written by a Native American woman. It documents her remarkable life as an activist for the rights of native peoples and provides a great deal of information about the Paiutes of the area in the second half of the nineteenth century.

The Paiutes created a lifestyle based on hunting and fishing, and gathering the seeds, fruit, and tubers of plants. They were clever artisans, creating warm blankets and clothing from the hides and fur of the animals they hunted. They also developed a wide range of tools and implements from stone, bone, wood, and other natural materials. They were especially gifted basketmakers, using the willows, reeds, and grasses of their territory to make fine baskets decorated with intricate designs. Paiute baskets are still widely admired for their exquisite craftsmanship. These baskets have been included in private and museum collections around the world.

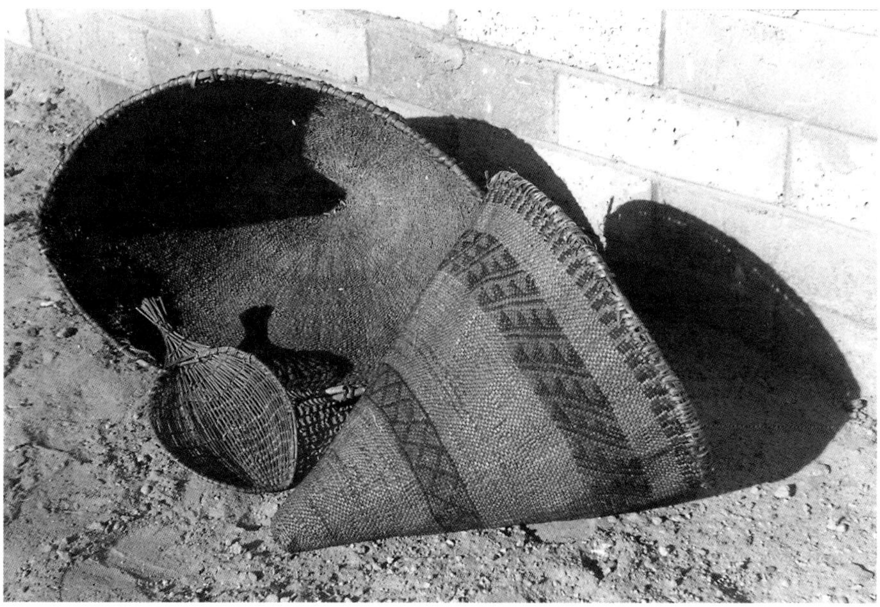

The Paiutes have been long known as expert basketmakers. These historic examples show the fine workmanship and exquisite design devoted to utilitarian objects. The modern Paiute community includes a number of basketmakers who are keeping the tradition alive and producing baskets that are eagerly sought by collectors around the world. Photo courtesy Special Collections Department, University of Nevada, Reno Libraries.

The Lovelock Indian Colony of the Lovelock Paiute Tribe was established in 1907. On November 1, 1907, the U.S. government bought two acres of land from William and Capitola Pitt, two well-established white settlers in the area. Then on November 17, 1910, the Pitts sold an additional eighteen acres to the government for three thousand dollars. These twenty acres southwest of the center of Lovelock are now the Lovelock Indian Colony of the Lovelock Paiute Tribe. The reservation is governed by a five-member tribal council, has its own tribal police force, and offers a range of social, educational, and medical services to tribal members.

After the arrival of Euro-Americans, some of the men of the Lovelock Paiute Tribe became agricultural workers. An interesting book by Lalla Scott—*Karnee: A Paiute Narrative*—is a first-person account of the life of a female member of the Lovelock Paiute Tribe, Annie Lowry. She was employed by Mrs. John G. Taylor and Mrs. George W. Lang as a housekeeper.

Today, members of the tribe can be found engaged in every aspect of the life of Pershing County. Families like the Summerfields, Panchos, Wassons, and Blisses have been prominent as tribal leaders in the Lovelock Indian Colony and also in the sports history of Pershing County High School. Perhaps the most famous Paiute athlete was Joe Bliss, who starred in five sports at PCHS and went on to greater fame as a boxer at the University of Nevada.

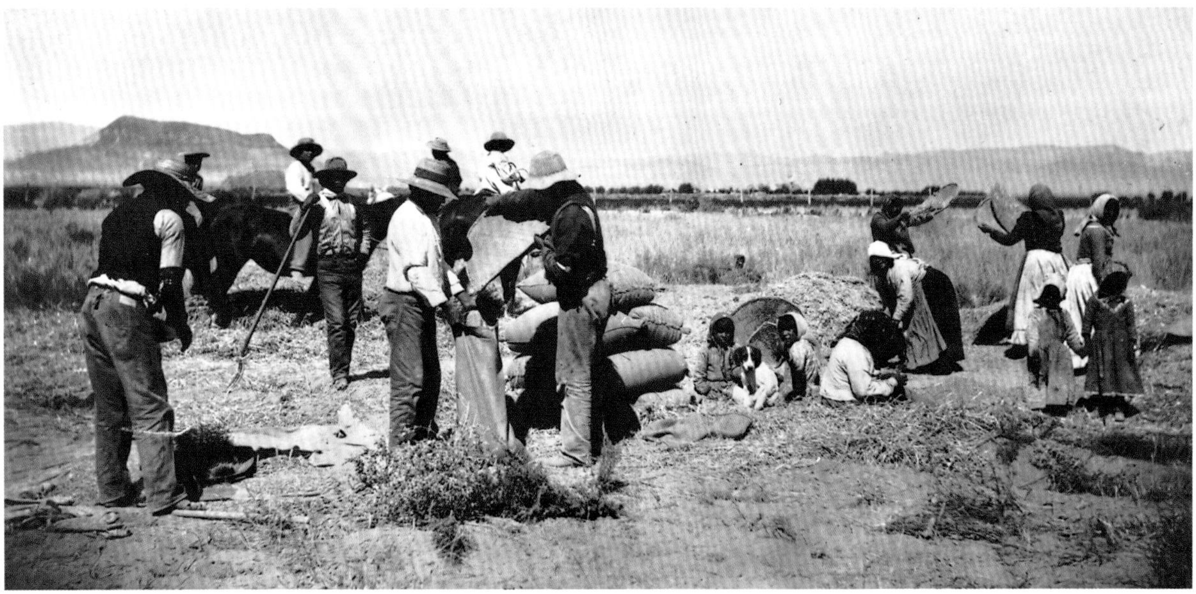

Paiute farm workers near Lovelock, 1897. Courtesy Nevada Historical Society.

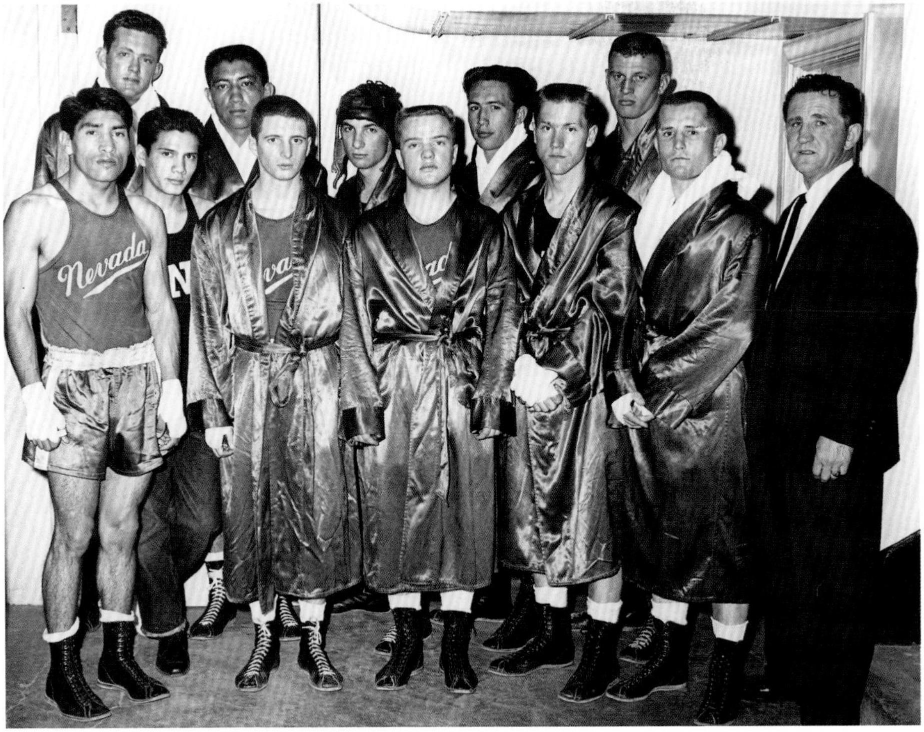

Joe Bliss (front left) with the 1960 University of Nevada boxing team. Photo courtesy Special Collections Department, University of Nevada, Reno Libraries.

In a July 1, 2014, article in the *Reno Gazette Journal,* reporter Chris Murray quotes from *Sports Illustrated*: "In 1959 a crowd of 4,500 filled the University of Nevada gym to capacity as an Indian lad, a Paiute from Lovelock, brought Nevada its first NCAA championship in school history. He went on to be one of the first thirteen athletes inducted into the Wolf Pack's Hall of Fame in 1973."

On Veterans Day, November 11, 2016, forty-three Native American veterans flew to Washington, D.C., as part of the first-ever all-Native American Honor Flight. Richard Wayne Carter Sr., tribal police chief of the Lovelock Indian Colony from 2011 to 2014, was among those honored. Carter had served in Desert Storm and was joined by his family when the flight returned to Reno International Airport.

• • •

The arrival in Pershing County of Anglo-Americans began with the fur traders of the early nineteenth century and grew exponentially with the flood of emigrants moving west to secure farmland and later to find their fortunes during the Gold Rush. Some of these emigrants settled in the area around

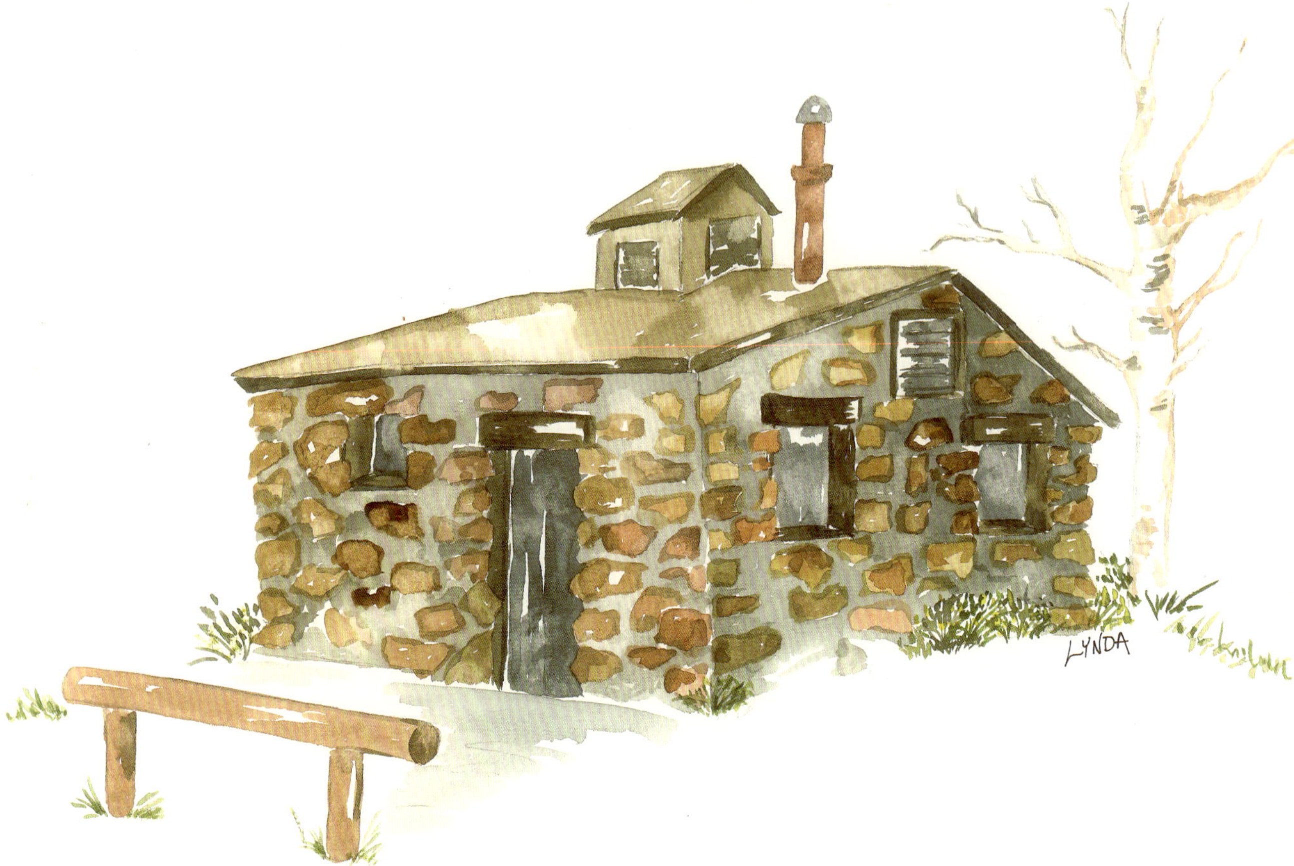

Early Euro-American settlers in the Big Meadows built simple dwellings and barns from readily available local materials, especially rock. Such structures are fairly common in rural northern Nevada, where there are few trees suitable for lumber. This old structure still stands on the Rye Patch Ranch. Watercolor by Lynda Quilici.

the Big Meadows and formed the nuclear community around which the town of Lovelock grew. Others homesteaded the open land and established the foundations of Pershing County's important agricultural economy.

But Anglo-Americans were not the only people who helped to settle and develop Pershing County. Another of the county's diverse ethnic groups were the Chinese, who played an important role in the construction of the transcontinental railroad. The first Chinese to enter the western United States arrived in San Francisco in 1848, and Chinese were known to be in

Nevada by 1854, working as miners in Gold Canyon, near what later became Virginia City. Statistics indicate that as many as 25,000 Chinese entered the U.S. in the 1850s and 1860s. Most came to the "Flowery Country" to earn money to send back to China to support their families and, ideally, to allow them ultimately to return to China with enough money to support themselves.

Thousands of Chinese workers helped to construct the western end of the transcontinental railroad. After the railroad was completed through what became the town of Lovelock in the fall of 1868, some of the Chinese railroad workers remained in the area. Many found employment as cooks on the local ranches or headed into the Humboldt Range where they reworked older placer operations on mining sites abandoned by the original miners. There are rock ruins in American Canyon where artifact hunters have found objects left behind by Chinese miners, and newspapers from 1863 mention Chinese placer miners working in the Unionville area along Buena Vista Creek.

The Chinese who remained in Lovelock operated restaurants, laundries, and pharmacies that specialized in Chinese traditional medicines, and worked as employees in a number of other local businesses. They tended to live close to the railroad around 9th and Amherst, according to the 1923 Sanborn map of Lovelock's downtown area.

One prominent Chinese family, the Changs, owned the Wing Lee store next to the Arobio Hotel between 9th and 10th streets. Even as late as 1936, Jim Chang On owned the Elite Hotel, where both Chinese and non-Chinese lived.

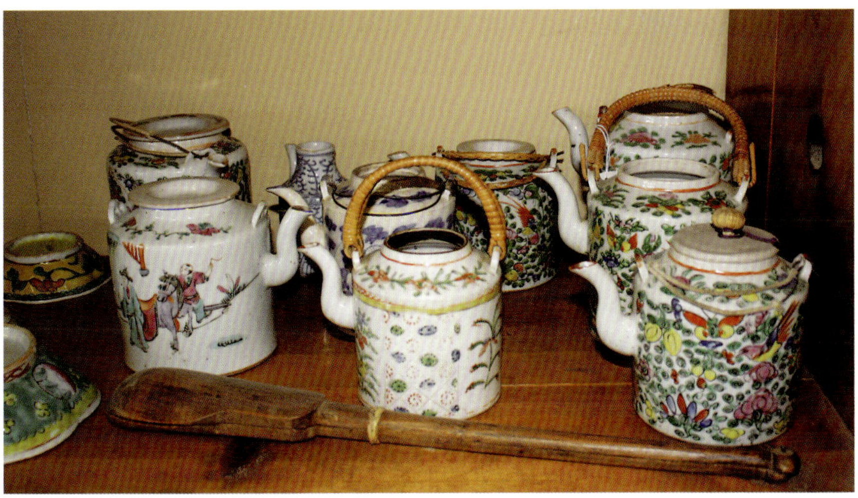

These Chinese teapots are part of a collection of artifacts left by Chinese railroad workers and the Chinese miners, ranch workers, and merchants who succeeded them.

Today there is a small building at 875 Broadway Street that houses the Chinese Museum. The museum is open only by setting an appointment with its owner, Larry DeLeeuw, a Lovelock businessman. However, the window collections give a fine view of Chinese artifacts from the county's past, and inside the door is an old mannequin that guards the collection.

• • •

The development of the sheep industry in the American West during the late nineteenth and early twentieth centuries was largely responsible for the arrival in Pershing County of two other important ethnic groups. Within a very few years, millions of sheep were roaming the mountains and valleys of the West, providing wool and meat for the nation's growing population. Their owners needed herders to stay with the flocks as they moved into the

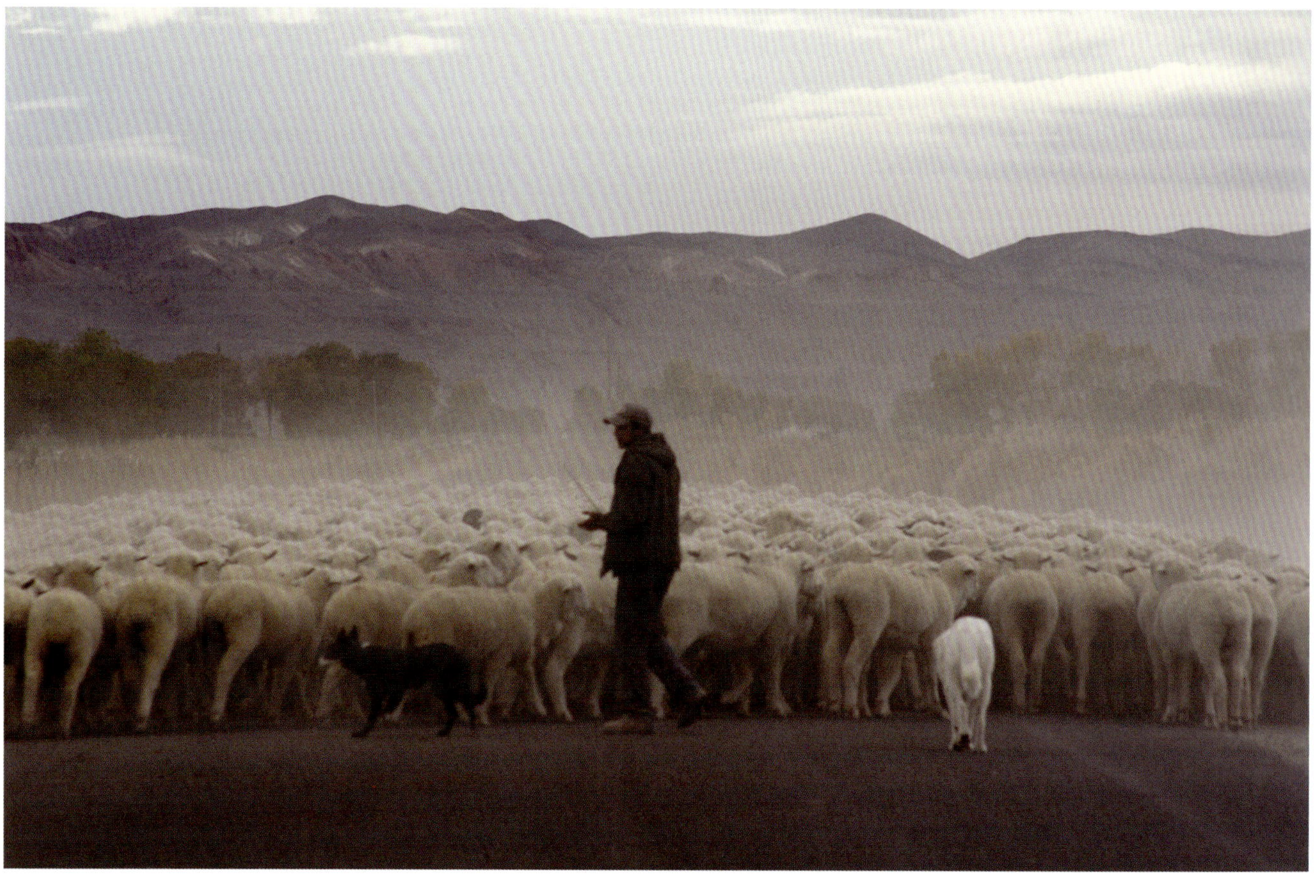

At the end of the nineteenth century, millions of sheep grazed the sparse grasslands of the American West. Today, sheep remain a vital part of Pershing County's livestock industry.

mountains for summer grazing, and most of these herders were found in the Iberian Peninsula, where poverty and politics drove many Basques and Portuguese to emigrate. Soon there were hundreds of Basque sheepherders following their flocks around the West, including many in Pershing County. Some of the herders took their payment in sheep rather than cash, a practice called hiving-off, gradually building herds of their own. Many of these herders chose to settle permanently in the U.S., bought land, and eventually established families here.

Two such Basque herders were José Zabalbeascoa (later known as Joe Saval) and his older brother John from the Basque province of Bizkaia (Viscaya) in northeastern Spain. They were hired by John G. Taylor, who developed an enormous sheep empire that ran from Humboldt County to northern Idaho in the last quarter of the nineteenth century, with his office in the Pershing Hotel in Lovelock. At the time of his death in 1929, Taylor owned 250,000 acres, valued at more than $2,500,000. With inflation, this equals just over $35,000,000 today, and included 75,000 sheep and 10,000 head of cattle. The Zabalbeascoas "hived off" sheep until around 1900, when they began to buy land and created their own hugely successful business. Today, the sheep holdings of another Basque, John Espil, and his wife, Carolyn Gottschalk Espil, stretch from Modoc County, California, to Lovelock and are vital to Pershing County's economy.

The Basques of Lovelock have contributed greatly to the development and economy of the county, as other Basques have to the entire state of Nevada. Families like Landa, Prida, Turillas, Gandiaga, Bengochea, Urriola, Zubieta, and others have played important roles in agriculture, commerce, education, and politics.

Miss Urriola

"Donde està el teatro?"
I said to our Spanish teacher over the phone.

"The opera? Why are you asking me about the opera?
Aren't you going fishing in Mexico?"

Everyone practiced on Miss Urriola,
our new Spanish Basque teacher from Battle Mountain.

In the night she translated
for new mothers at Pershing General Hospital.

At the police station she pleaded
for old sheepherders who ran the solo stoplight.

Miss Urriola at twenty-four was a necessity.
As Mrs. Fundis at fifty-four, she's an institution.

She set up a school for wives of Mexican garlic pickers.
"They, too, have a right to know."

—PAT FERRARO KLOS

Portuguese immigrants were also drawn to Pershing County by the sheep industry. Many of them came from the Azores, an island chain in the eastern Atlantic that suffered from overpopulation and poverty during much of the nineteenth century. Sheepman John G. Taylor met the transcontinental trains in Golconda and hired the Portuguese as they disembarked to work on his various ranches. Likewise, Frank Mancebo Sr. immigrated from the Azorean island of Flores and was met by John G. Taylor. Starting as a sheepherder, he eventually became Taylor's flockmaster and later owned several ranches of his own. When the Great Depression severely limited the market for agricultural products, including wool and meat, Mancebo, like many of the other Portuguese, discovered that he could make more money in business, so he opened the Azores Mercantile on Broadway Street, and later the Big Meadow Market with several different business partners.

Another prominent Portuguese family is that of Tom Moura. The Mouras originated on the island of Santa Maria in the Azores and came to the U.S. because of drought and a failing economy in that island chain. Tom's maternal grandfather, Manuel Moreira, was recruited by John G. Taylor to work on his ranches. Manuel was later able to buy the original family homestead in Lovelock Valley. Tom's father, Manuel Moura, immigrated to Golconda from the Azores and worked for the Miller & Lux cattle operation. According to Tom Moura, "Manuel Moura moved to Lovelock to work on several ranches in the valley, including the ranch that his future father-in-law, Manuel Moreira, managed for John G. Taylor. He met and married Virginia Moreira and eventually took over the Moreira ranch and farming operation in order to continue the legacy of agriculture for both families." The Moreiras and Mouras are now one family, and they continue to be important to agriculture in the valley. Tom and Darlene Moura have extended this ranch property to include the site where they live on the Humboldt River. Tom Moura is one of the few Portuguese ranchers in the Lovelock Valley because so many others have turned to other businesses.

The Portuguese community has always been influential in Pershing County, partly because it is so large. It includes many families—Mancebo, Moura, Mateas, Costa, Texeira, Santos, Rodriques, Souza, Alves, Hendriques, Tenente, Nunes, Amarant, Penque, Andrede, and others.

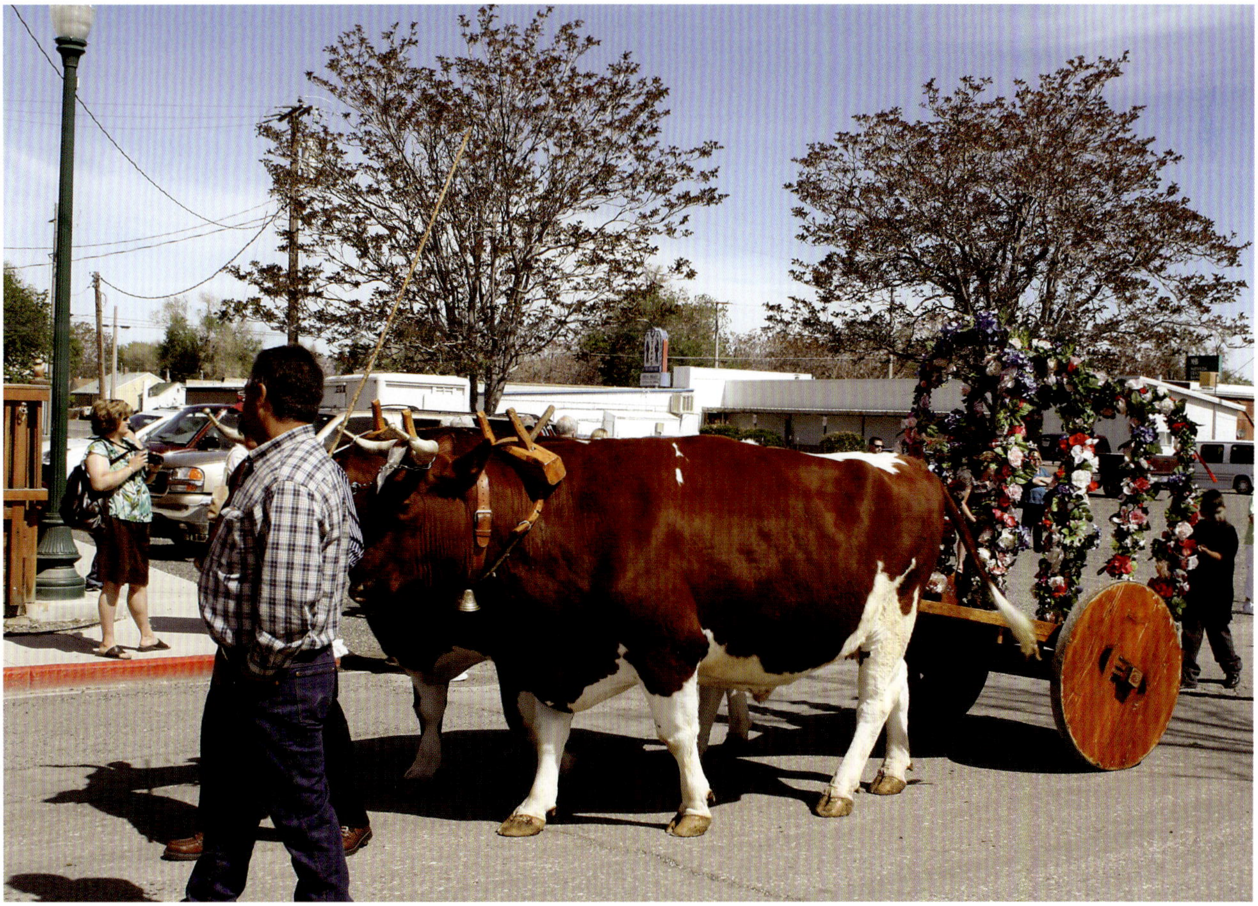

Pershing County's large Portuguese community continues to celebrate its annual Pentecostal Festa, a traditional festival of thanksgiving dating from the fourteenth century. This ox-drawn cart is part of a large parade that is part of the celebration.

The annual I.D.E.S. Pentecostal Festa, or Holy Ghost Festival, brings together many of the area's Portuguese as well as other members of the community. This traditional Azores *festa* of thanksgiving, dating back to 1323 A.D., began to be observed in Lovelock around 1934. It starts with a parade from the Lovelock Depot and ends at the Catholic church with the crowning and blessing of the festival queen, followed by a free dinner of the traditional *sopa*, or soup of beef, broth, and bread. An auction to finance the next year's celebration culminates the festivities, and a bid of a hundred dollars for a loaf of Portuguese bread is not uncommon.

The cultural diversity of Pershing County is illustrated by the names of settlers in the county during the past one hundred years. Besides the Chinese, Basques, and Portuguese, Italians came to work on the railroad and stayed to build stores, hotels, halls, and restaurants and to mine and farm the county. Names like Arobio, Dericco, Cerini, Guisti, Fialdini, Marcucci, Menicucci, Quilici, and Stephanini fill the pages of the tax rolls and the phonebook. There are also Scandinavians. From Denmark came the Ankers, Munks, Hansons, Markers, and Nelsons—many from the Isle of Bornholm. From Finland came the Holmstrom, Hostman, Nordman, Jorgensen, Sund, and Montrose families. The Swiss are represented by the Aufdermaur and Parietti families. Pershing County has been a traditional American melting pot. The invaluable *Lovelock Centennial 1868-1968* booklet includes stories about many of these families. Curiously, the Catholics seemed to settle either in town or to gravitate toward Upper Valley, whereas the Protestants migrated toward Lower Valley. There are exceptions, of course, but language and religious faith played a role in determining settlement choices.

There were few Hispanics among the earliest settlers of northern Nevada, but they soon arrived to work the ranches, mines, and railroads. A Spaniard, Manuel San Pedro, prospected in Humboldt County in the 1860s and discovered several new veins of ore on which he established mines. Later, he was responsible for organizing the Union Mining District around Grantsville. According to the 1875 census, 11 percent of the population of Humboldt County was Hispanic. Many of these residents were Mexican, including Mexican miners in Unionville.

In the decade between 1910 and 1920, World War I left workers in short supply in many parts of the United States. The opportunities for better, higher-paying jobs beckoned young Mexicans to Nevada for available railroad jobs. One such very young man was Joaquín Sambrano from Zacapo, Michoacán, Mexico. When Joaquín arrived in Lovelock in 1916, he had to lie about his age to get a job, but he prevailed and worked on the railroad for most of the rest of his life. After several years in Pershing County, Joaquín returned to Mexico, married his Maria, had two children with her, and finally moved his growing family back to Pershing County in the Oreana-Humboldt area outside of Lovelock. Joaquín and Maria went on to have eleven more children, and the Sambranos were established as a well-known, hard-working family. Daughter Angie Sambrano Pommerening remembers that there was no TV in their home in Oreana and how excited everyone was when one of the older brothers moved to Lovelock and bought a TV for all to enjoy.

After 1942 another labor shortage in the West fostered the *bracero* program. From 1942 onward, through an agreement between the U.S. and Mexican governments, Mexican *braceros* worked on farms and ranches in the West, including many in the Winnemucca and Lovelock areas. *Bracero* is the Spanish word for "one working using his arms."

Alicia Arias Dyer recalls that her father, José Arias, left Jalisco in 1950 and went to Fremont, California, to work as a *bracero.* José had grown up on a ranch in Jalisco, but after his father's death the ranch was divided and parts were sold. José Arias was able to hang on to his share of the land, but to maintain this land he needed more money. This is why he became a *bracero*. He later had his family join him, and they moved from one place to another, because José never found work that he liked. Through a friend in Fremont, he heard about a ranching job outside of Lovelock, on a ranch owned by Leonard Silvey. This work was what he knew and preferred. Later the Silvey ranch was sold to the McDougals, and after many years of hard work, José Arias and his wife Graciela were able to purchase several acres of this property, including a house for their family.

By the 1960s, these seasonal agricultural workers had become essential to the economy of Pershing County. Many of them liked what they saw and stayed, just as others had done before them. It seems that wherever Mexicans settle, their restaurants spring up to satisfy the Norteamericano craving for Mexican food. Lovelock is no exception. A longtime favorite local eatery, Andy and John's, is now a Mexican restaurant called La Casita, and gathering there is still a local tradition.

SOME HISTORY MAKERS

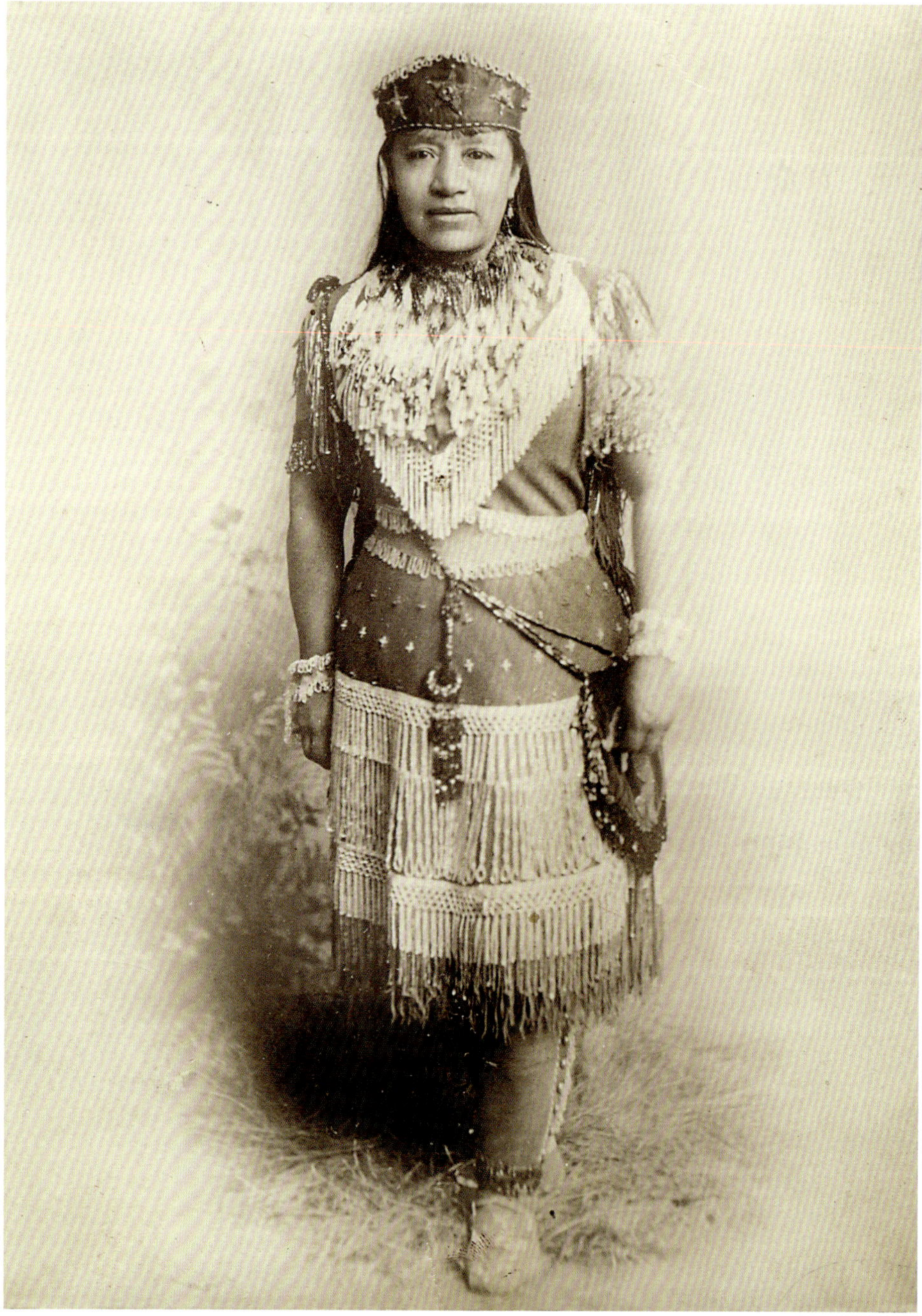

Sarah Winnemucca. Photo courtesy Nevada Historical Society.

Despite its relatively small population and largely rural economy, Pershing County has produced its share of people who have made significant contributions to the county, state, nation, and even to Hollywood history. The determined and resilient spirit of the diverse peoples who settled this area seems to have survived among their descendants into the present.

Sarah Winnemucca (ca. 1844–1891), the daughter of Chief Winnemucca, became an important early activist for Native American rights. She studied at a Catholic school in Santa Clara, California, where she learned English, and later moved from California back to Nevada. As a young adult, she became an interpreter for the U.S. Army at Camp McDermit (1869), then an assistant teacher at the Malheur Reservation school in Oregon.

Life Among the Piutes: Their Wrongs and Claims, published in 1883, is both Sarah Winnemucca's personal memoir and a history of her people in the forty years following their first contact with Euro-Americans. Following publication of the book, she traveled widely in the eastern United States and gave over three hundred speeches advocating for better treatment and rights for Native American peoples. She was encouraged by two Boston women, Elizabeth Palmer Peabody and Mary Tyler (Mrs. Horace) Mann, to open the Peabody Indian School in Lovelock on land belonging to Sarah's brother Natchez. Since Numa children were not admitted to the area's public schools, Sarah's purpose in establishing her day school was to teach the English language to Numa children. The school, although it lasted only a few years (1885–88), became a model for the education of Native American children, focusing on teaching the children near their own homes and families, rather than in distant boarding schools as was then the policy. The school, and Sarah Winnemucca's tireless efforts to better the lives of her people, secured her place in Nevada and Pershing County history.

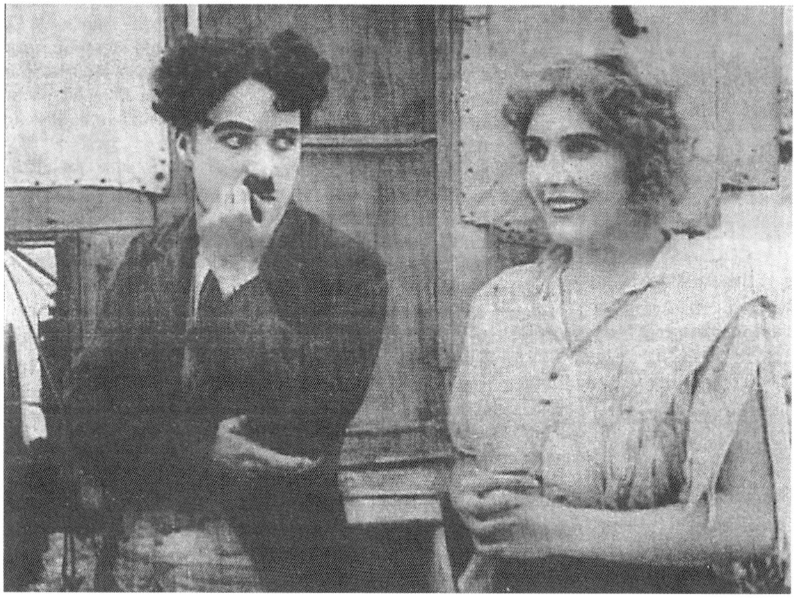

Edna Purviance with Charlie Chaplin. Photo courtesy Lovelock Review Miner.

Edna Purviance (1895–1958) was a star of the silent-film era. She was born in Paradise Valley, in Humboldt County, but moved to Lovelock as a child when her parents bought the Singer Hotel in 1900. Her parents divorced two years later, and her mother took possession of the hotel. By 1911 Louise Purviance had changed the hotel to a boarding house called the Central House. It was one of many small residential hotels where miners, railroad workers, and visitors stayed for short periods of time. An article in the *Lovelock Review-Miner* in 2016 calls it the Workingman's Hotel, and it was indeed a workingman's lodging. However, the correct name of the business was the Central.

As a young girl, Edna often performed in Lovelock as a dancer and pianist. She graduated from Pershing County High School in 1913 and moved to San Francisco where a sister was living. Through a chance meeting in San Francisco with the great silent-film star Charlie Chaplin, Edna decided to move to Hollywood in 1915. Ultimately Edna made thirty-seven films, thirty-four of them with Chaplin. She was a petite, very pretty natural golden blonde who maintained close family ties throughout her life. She died in Hollywood in 1958.

Today Edna Purviance Road runs through the Humboldt River Ranch area northeast of Lovelock as a memorial to this actor. In 2016 Lovelock also sponsored a film festival celebrating her career.

One of Nevada's finest statesmen, Charles Hinton Russell (1903–1989) served in state and federal offices. He was born in Lovelock to parents who were both born in Nevada. His father, James Russell, was a cattle buyer for the W. H. Moffat company. Young Charlie attended Lovelock schools until he was nine years old, when his family moved to Deeth. Russell recalled in his oral history, "The first school that I remember was in Lovelock. I attended first and second grades there. I remember that my teacher was Bessie Keith, who was of a pioneer family from Elko. I remember her because she wore her hair all fluffed up and we called her Miss Tumbleweed." A true son of Nevada, Russell started life in Lovelock, graduated from high school in Elko, later owned the *Ely Daily Record* newspaper, and represented White Pine County in both the Nevada state assembly and the state senate. A Republican, he served one term in the U.S. House of Representatives from 1947-49, then served as governor from 1951 until 1959. Russell died in Carson City in 1989 and is interred in the Dayton, Nevada, cemetery.

Another prominent Nevadan, Alan Harvey Bible (1909–1988), was born on a ranch just outside Lovelock. His father, Jacob "Jake" Bible operated a grocery store as well as a cattle ranch. His mother, Isabelle Bible, taught school. Jacob had come to Nevada from Ohio, and he worked at the mining camps of Vernon and Seven Troughs, where he was postmaster in both places. The Bibles lived on the ranch outside Lovelock until 1919, when a fire destroyed their home. They then moved to Fallon, where Jake again ran a general merchandise store.

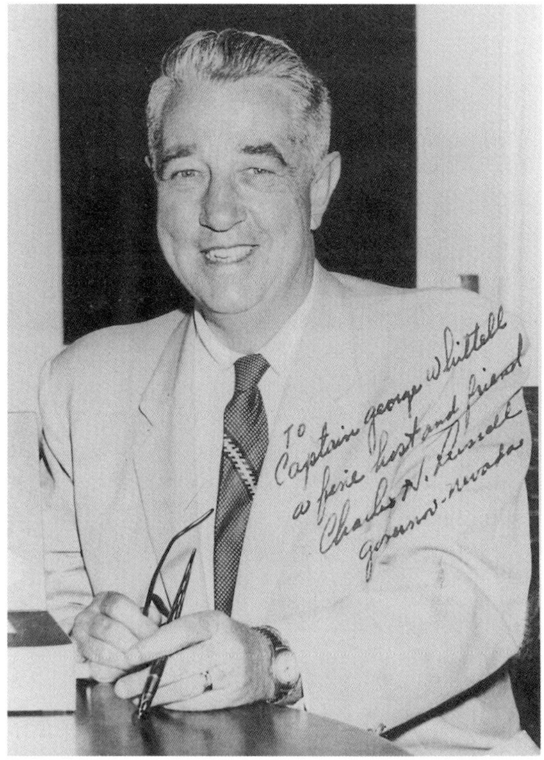

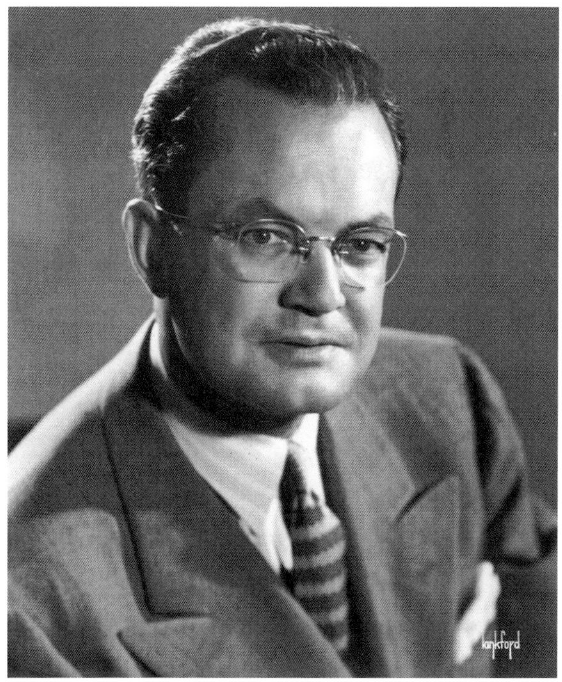

TOP: *Charles Hinton Russell. Photo courtesy Special Collections Department, University of Nevada, Reno Libraries.*

BOTTOM: *Alan Bible. Photo courtesy Special Collections Department, University of Nevada, Reno Libraries.*

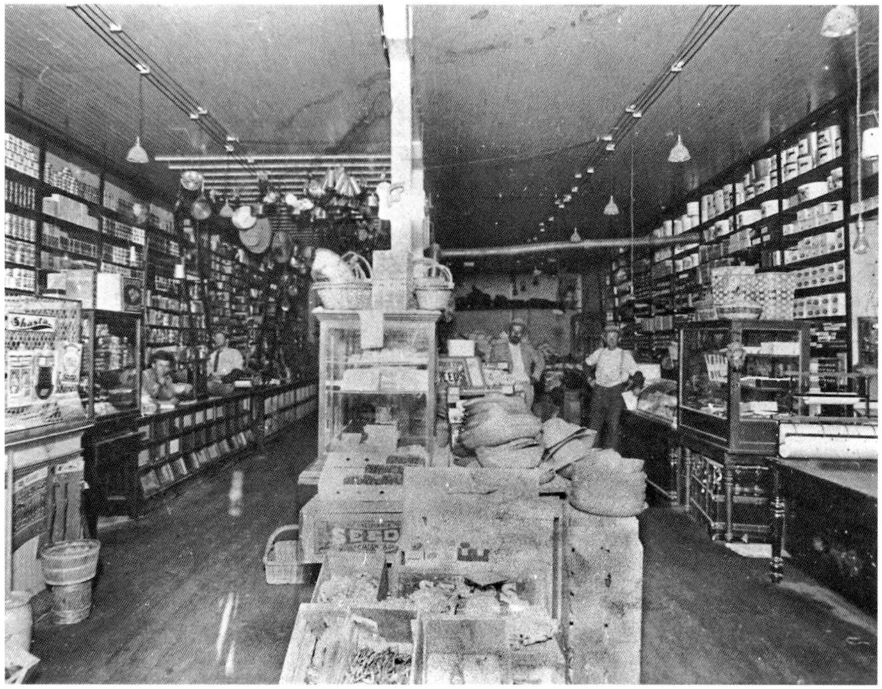

Stephen R. Young's Enterprise store was important to the economy of Lovelock for many years. Photo courtesy Nevada Historical Society.

After graduating from the University of Nevada, Alan Bible went to Washington, D.C., to study at the Georgetown University School of Law. He graduated in 1934 and was admitted to the Nevada Bar in 1935. Shortly thereafter he was appointed to serve as district attorney of Storey County, then appointed to serve as deputy attorney general of the state. In 1942, at age thirty-two, he was elected attorney general of Nevada. He served until 1950, becoming an expert on water law. He also worked to regulate the state's gambling industry. In 1950 he retired to private practice and was elected to the U.S. Senate in 1955. He served as Nevada's Democratic senator until 1974, when he retired.

The Young family represented three generations of distinguished Nevadans. Stephen R. Young and his wife arrived in Unionville in 1873, and he soon discovered pay dirt in Spring Valley. Later that year he was in Lovelock, where he spent the rest of his life. The Youngs had four children, all born in Nevada. Son Leland became mayor of Lovelock; daughter Blanche married into the Goodin family and daughter Mary into the Marker family. Son Clarence was born in Lovelock in 1885; he became an engineer, rancher, and finally a Pershing County attorney. He married Florence Anker of another early Lovelock family. They had three children. One son, Llewellyn Young, became a district court judge; the other son, Clarence Clifton Young, was a Republican representative to the U.S. Congress from 1953 to 1956.

Perhaps the best-known member of the Lovelock Paiute Tribe is writer Adrian C. Louis (b. 1946), one of Nevada's and the contemporary West's most distinguished and admired poets. He was born in Lovelock, later attended Brown University, where he received a B.A. and M.A. in creative writing, and he subsequently worked as a journalist and as editor of four tribal newspapers. He has published ten books of poetry, two novels, and numerous short stories. He has also won several literary awards and fellowships, including two Pushcart Prizes, and his work—some of which reflects his Pershing County roots—has been widely published, anthologized, and translated for publication in foreign editions. His first novel, *Skins,* was recognized as "the first major novel of reservation life to be written from inside the reservation." In 1999, Louis was inducted into the Nevada Writers' Hall of Fame. He lived on South Dakota's Pine Ridge Reservation for many years, taught at the Oglala Lakota College and was a professor in the Minnesota State University System. He is now retired from teaching but still actively writing.

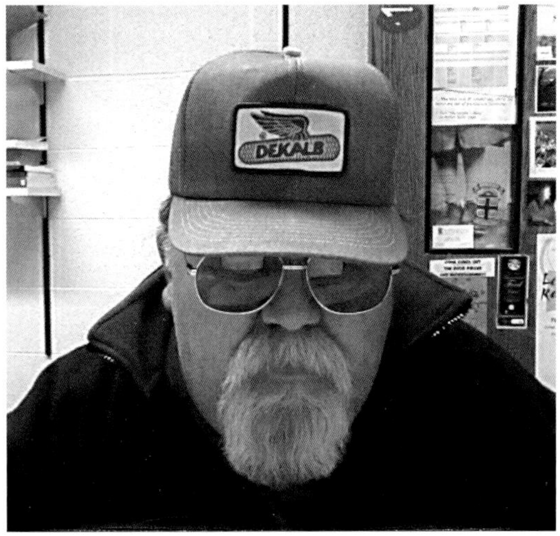

Adrian Louis. Photo courtesy Adrian Louis.

Today, Pershing County's Hispanic population is involved in every aspect of the county's economy and life. Some of them have established and run successful businesses that benefit the entire community. Alicia Arias Dyer is the daughter of a *bracero,* José Arias, who came to the U.S. in 1950. Alicia was a young girl when she moved to Lovelock with her family, one of four girls and six boys. She speaks proudly of her older brothers—one graduated from the University of Nevada-Reno, another from Chico State University, and two others completed Truckee Meadows Community College. Alicia graduated from Pershing County High School, belongs to the PCHS Alumni Association, and has been an active participant in the community. During high school, she began working in the kitchen at Sturgeon's Log Cabin Restaurant and decided then that she really liked cooking. She worked at the restaurant for thirteen years, most of those years with her sister Maria.

In the early 1980s, Sturgeon's opened a part of the restaurant as a "dinner house" called La Fiesta. The owner asked the Arias girls to work in the

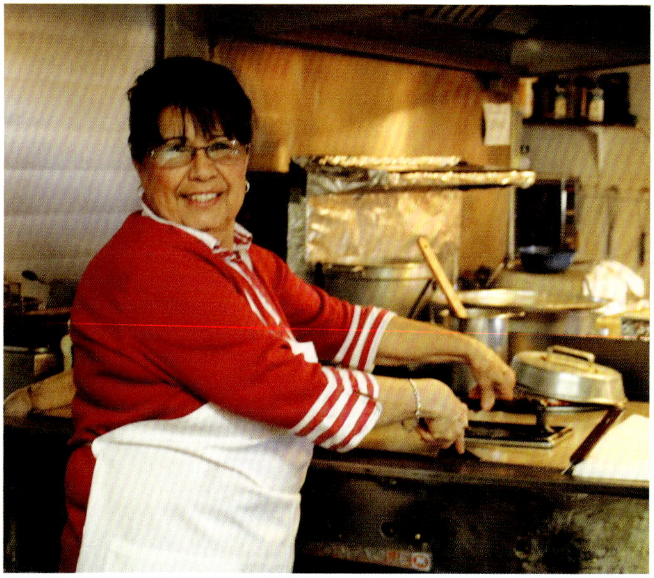

Alicia Arias Dyer.

dinner house and design a Mexican menu using their family recipes. La Fiesta featured Mexican food but also offered steaks, lobster, and other specialties. "The prison was opening, and we frequently served one hundred people a night," says Alicia. However, when the ownership changed, Maria stayed only three months and quit and Alicia stayed six months.

At just that time, a favorite Lovelock café came on the market, Andy and John's at the opposite end of town from Sturgeon's. José Arias encouraged his daughters to buy it, so Alicia and Maria, and Maria's husband, Jorge Guerrero, with funding from the family and a ten-year loan, opened La Casita. Alicia's husband, Robert Dyer, a mining man, supported her in her new enterprise. Alicia reminisces about ten- to eighteen-hour days, but they paid off their loan in six years and owned one of the most popular spots in town. One of the specialties at La Casita is La Graciela, a combination plate named for her mother, and a second one is Alicia's Taco Salad.

Alicia says she married a *gringo* and with a laugh says, "the *gringo* boys liked the Mexican girls." The cultures were blending as they always have in the United States. Alicia Arias Dyer, now a widow, is the sole owner of La Casita, having bought out Maria when Maria's health began to fail.

These are only a few of Pershing County's distinguished citizens. The history of the county is full of individuals of many cultures and occupations, most of them known only to their families and friends, whose hard work and vision brought the county into existence and made it thrive. They have taken the abundant natural resources of the area and prospered, and they have put deep roots into the county's history and legend. In the next hundred years, no one doubts that this kind of courage and tenacity will continue to move the county forward.

LOVELOCK AND IMLAY

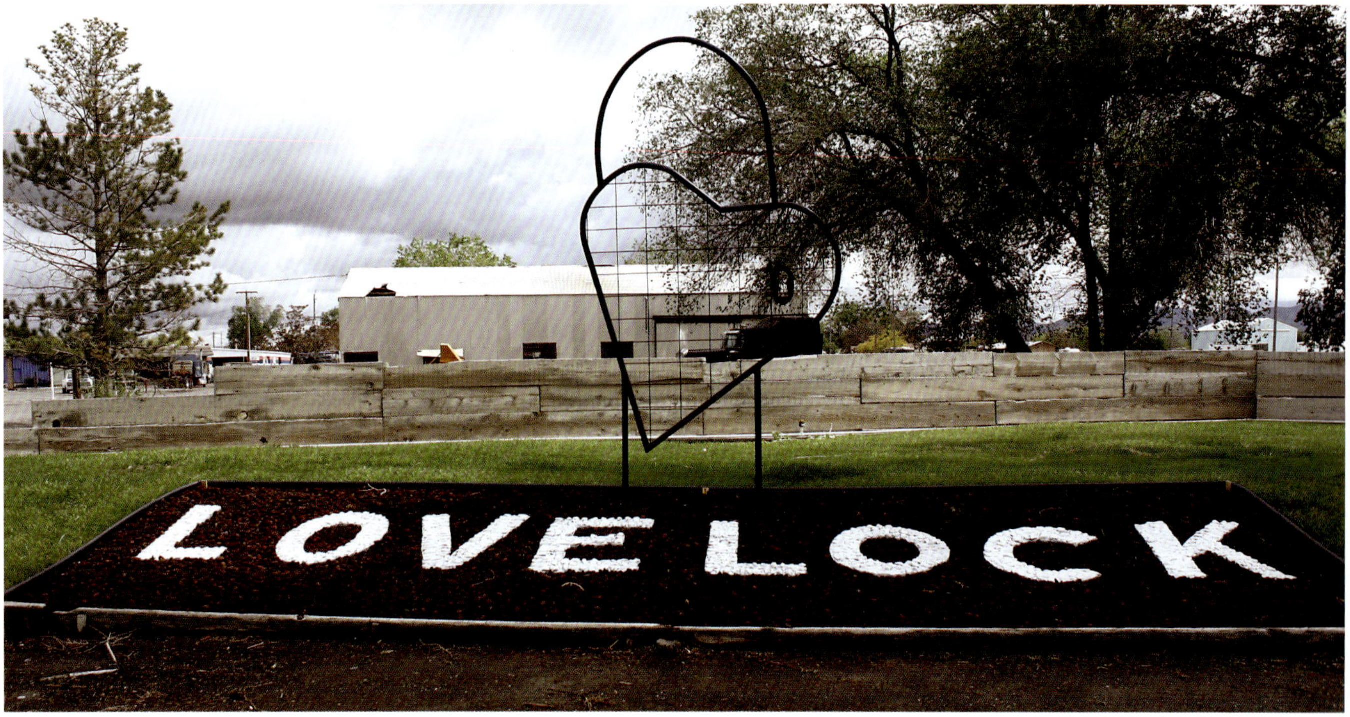

The Lovelock sign greets drivers as they enter the town.

Lovelock, the seat of Pershing County, has been an important community both now and in the past. It is also a visual reminder of a bygone era. Never having faced serious gentrification and dramatic change, Lovelock continues to be a farming-ranching town with many residents claiming ancestors who settled in the area over a hundred or more years ago. Pride runs as deep here as family roots. As Lynda Quilici said, "It is the people who give Lovelock a special sense of place."

Entering Lovelock from the west, one encounters bold lettering and entwined hearts. Originally, the letters welcomed people disembarking from the train at the Lovelock railroad station, but they were removed when trains no longer delivered passengers to Lovelock. In the early 1980s, Fundis Trucking Company owner Pete Fundis rescued the letters from oblivion and moved them to the edge of town, onto land that he had donated to the city.

In 1919, the newly elected Pershing County commissioners contacted well-known Reno architect Frederic DeLongchamps to provide a design for a courthouse, a design they requested "be of something different." DeLongchamps presented a circular design that he felt would set the structure apart from other courthouses in the state. He drew inspiration from Thomas Jefferson's design for the library at the University of Virginia. His design achieved its purpose, so much so that tourists today leave Interstate 80 to visit "the round courthouse," eat lunch in the park, lock their love on the plaza, and take a walk around town.

The courthouse is one of five buildings in Lovelock listed on the National Register of Historic Places. Across from the courthouse is another listing, the 1938 U.S. Post Office in a style called Starved Classicism. Inside the post office is a 1940 mural entitled *The Uncovering of the Comstock Lode*, by Danish painter Ejnar Hansen. The National Register listing says, "The building and the mural are significant as legacies of the massive public works programs

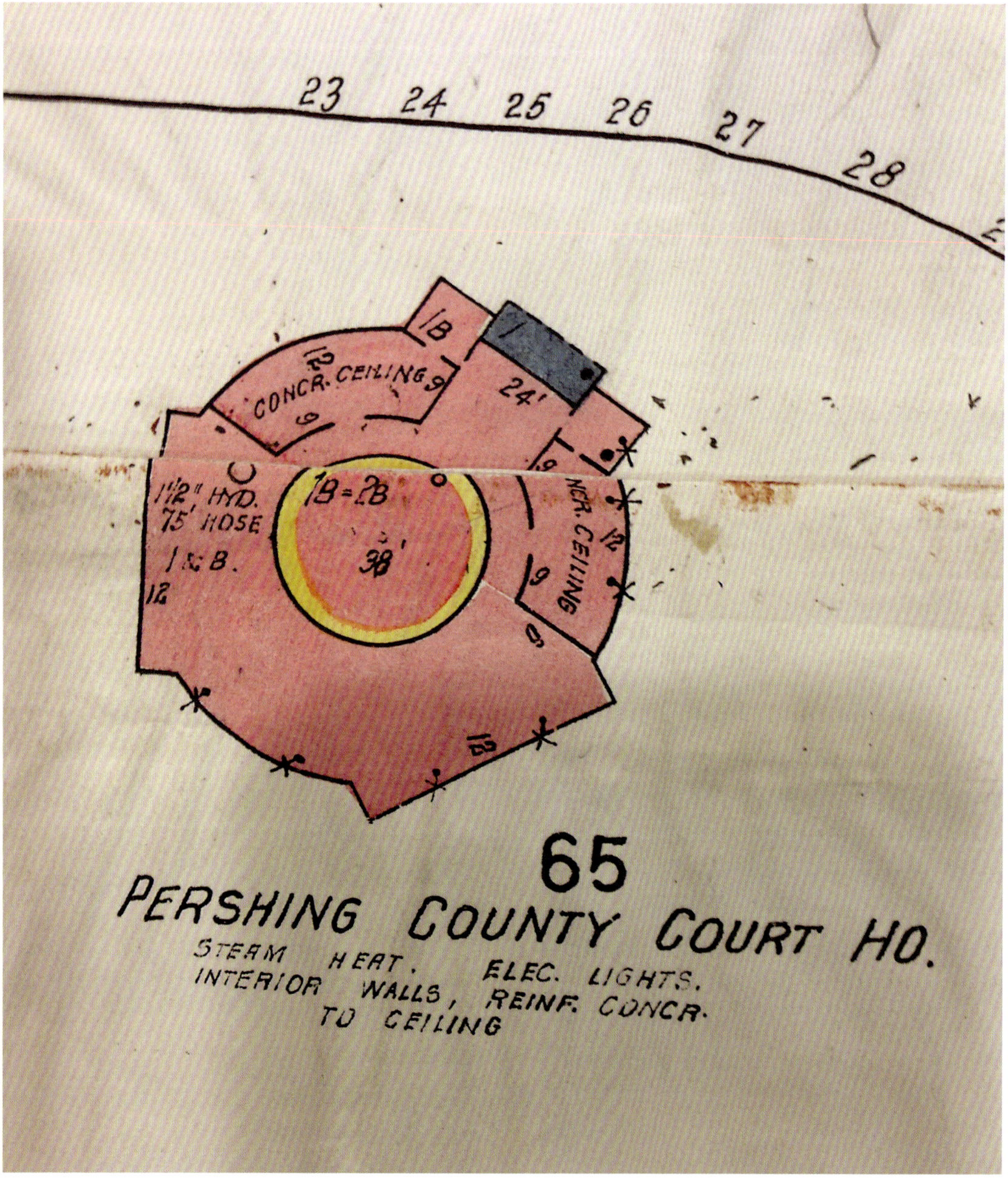

This floor plan for the Pershing County Courthouse comes from a 1923 Sanborn map.

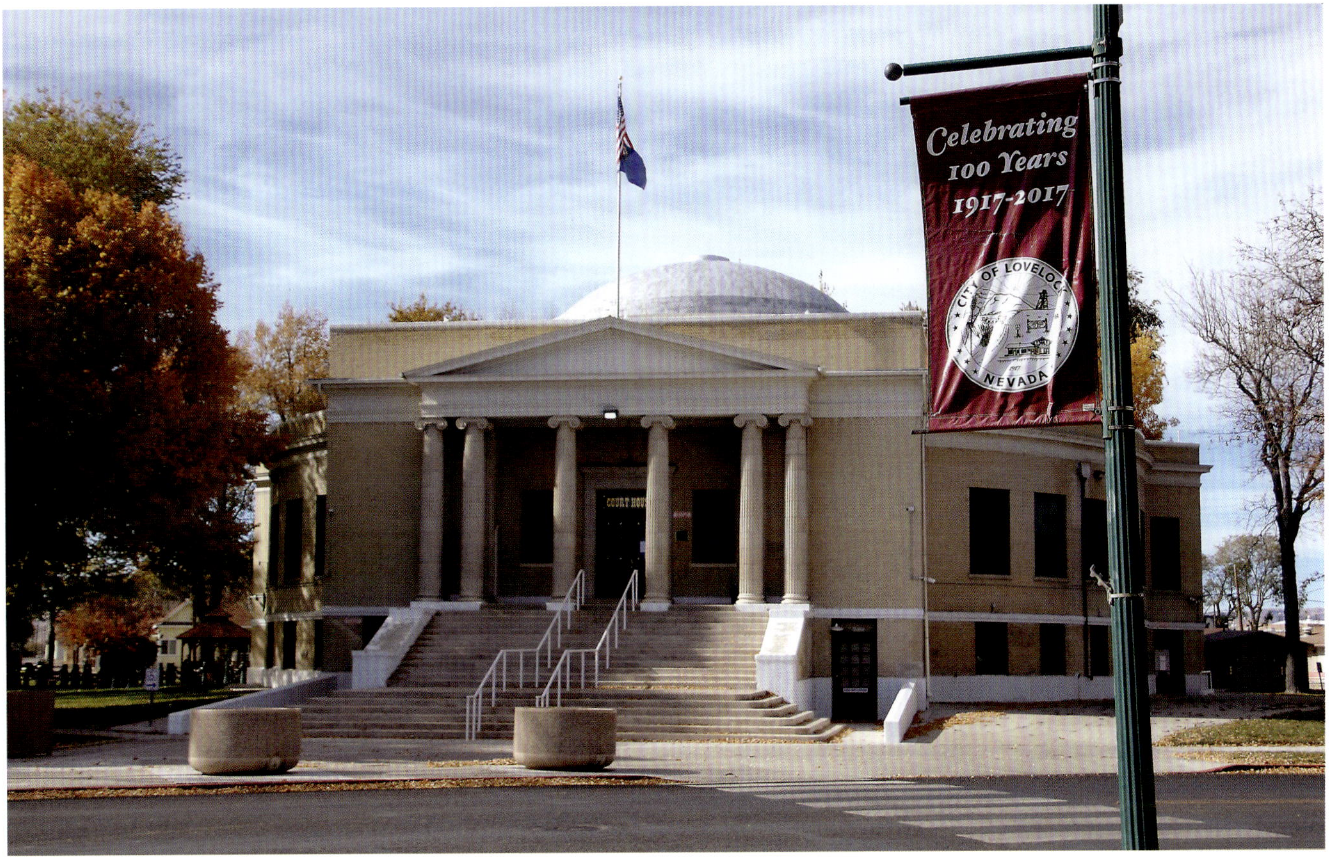

The Pershing County Courthouse. The novel circular design was chosen to distinguish this building from other county courthouses in Nevada.

undertaken by the federal government to bolster the economy during the depression." The Lovelock Post Office mural is one of three in Nevada sponsored by the Works Progress Administration. The other two are in the Yerington and Winnemucca post offices, painted by Polly Duncan and Adolph Gottlieb, respectively. All three murals are oil on canvas, and approximately five feet by twelve feet in size.

Upon completion of the Lovelock mural to the satisfaction of the townspeople, Postmaster Art Gottschalk wrote to artist Hansen that the many admirers of the mural included "the old prospectors and miners of this state, who as a class, are about the hardest people in the world to please."

Other buildings in Lovelock that are listed on the National Register of Historic Places are the 1880 Eastlake-style railroad depot, the 1941

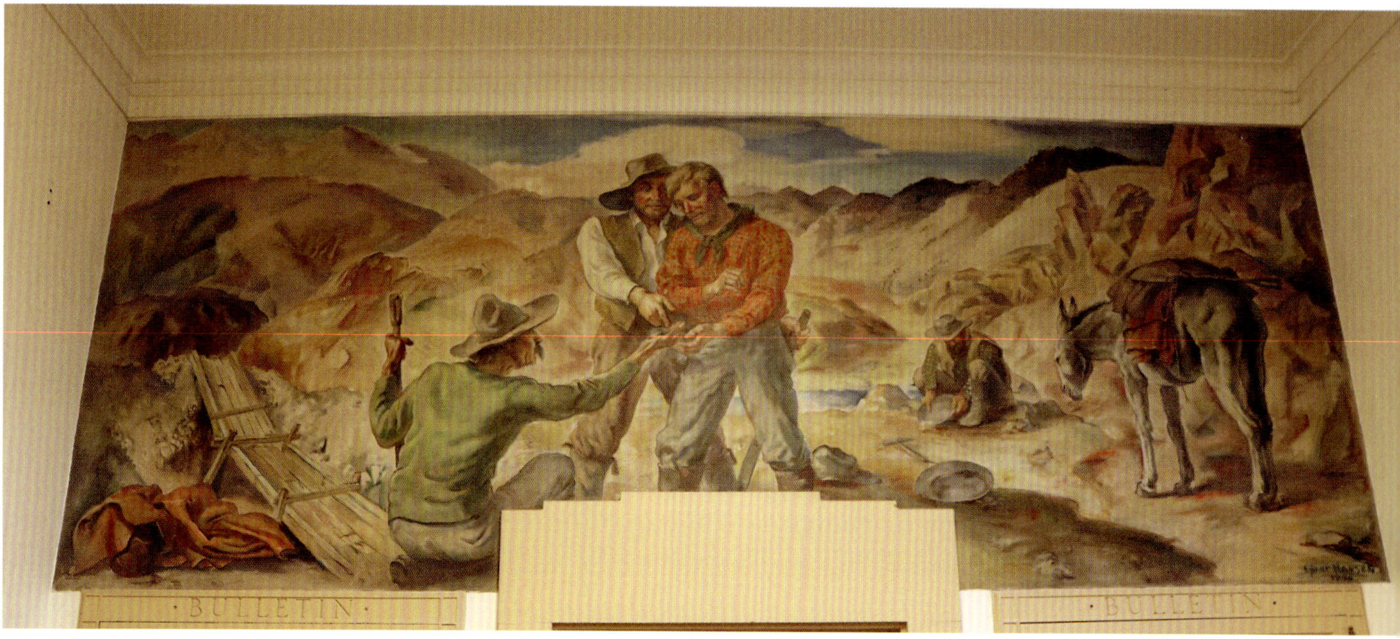

The Uncovering of the Comstock Lode *by Ejnar Hansen has graced the U.S. Post Office in Lovelock since 1938. The WPA, a New Deal program, commissioned art for public buildings as a way to bolster the economy and support artists during the Great Depression.*

vocational agriculture building in the school complex, and the iconic Marzen House Museum on the western edge of town. The 1874 Italianate Marzen House is "a two-story symmetrical building topped with a low-pitched hipped roof and decorated with ornate jigsaw cutout window moldings and cornerboards," according to the National Register listing. The house originally belonged to Colonel Joseph Marzen, a butcher, farmer, rancher, and politician. Later the building belonged to Pershing County Senator Ray Knisley, then to Walt Brinkerhoff, before it was donated to the county for use as a museum. The museum site offers visitors a wide variety of experiences, as Scotty's Assay Office is on the grounds nearby, along with a revered fire truck in its own special building.

George Lovelock gave his name to the community that would become the county seat of Pershing County. He also gave the history of the area a saga seldom equaled among the town's founding fathers. He was born in Swansea, Wales, a mining town, on March 11, 1824. George learned the mining trade, but he had an adventurous spirit that took him and his young

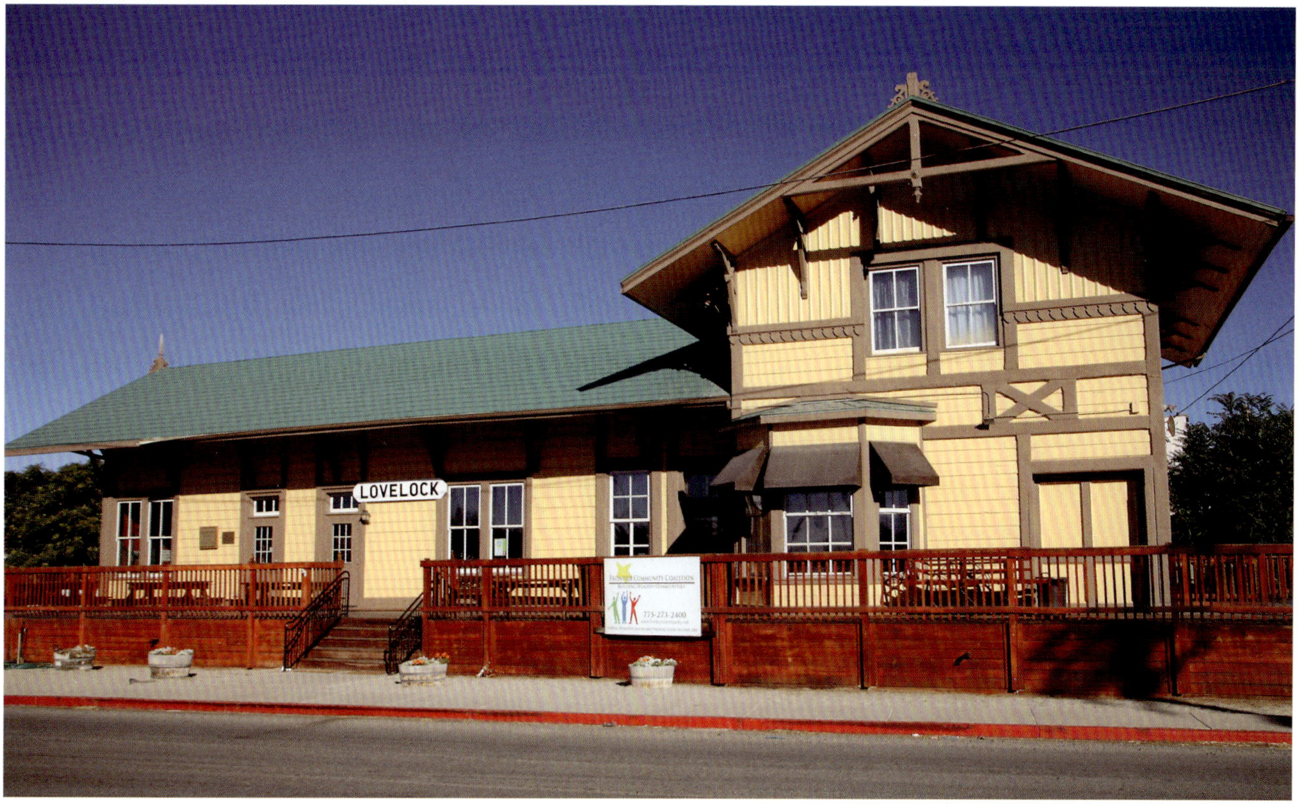

The Lovelock train depot, built in 1880, is one of several buildings in the city listed in the National Register of Historic Places.

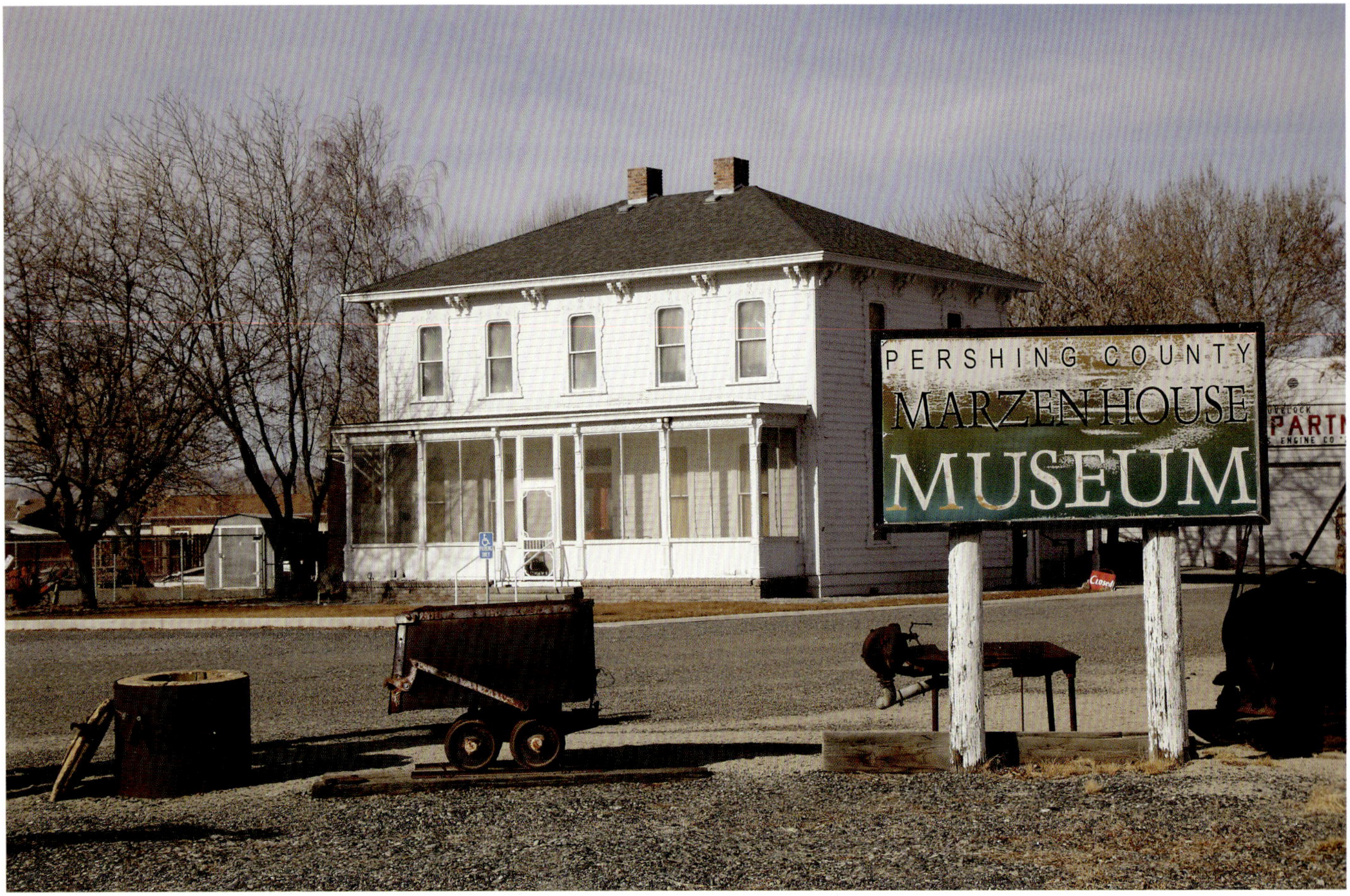

The Marzen House, built in 1874, is today a popular museum. It is an elegant example of the Italianate style and is listed in the National Register of Historic Places.

family away from Wales to Australia, the Hawaiian Islands, and several mining camps in California. At some point, he sold his California holdings and moved to Rocky Canyon in what was then known as Humboldt County in Nevada. The first mention of George Lovelock in Humboldt County records is dated April 13, 1863, and lists him as a miner in Rocky Canyon. He is later identified as the owner of a toll road and a bridge at Oreana, then as the owner of homes in Alpha and Unionville. He remained there for five years with his wife, Mary Forest Lovelock, and sons Fred and Thomas. In 1866, he bought 320 acres from local rancher James Blake at Big Meadows on the west side of the Humboldt River. Blake owned several ranches in the area, as did J. L. Hart, James Mallon, Edmund C. Asher Sr., and two men named Slavan and Eddinger. The 1866 county tax rolls indicate that Lovelock also operated Lovelock's Hotel, which at various times had been called Blake's Hotel, Blake's Station, Lovelock's Station, and the Big Meadow Hotel.

In his 1984 *Reno Gazette-Journal* article on George Lovelock, Phillip Earl tells us that Lovelock donated eighty-five acres to the Central Pacific Railroad in 1867 for a town site, right-of-way for the railroad, and a depot. In return, he was promised a block in town, but later he had to pay $500 for a half block. For a number of years the railroad depot was called Lovelock's Station.

Following the history of the hotel is fascinating. In a *Humboldt Register* of 1866, there is an ad indicating that George Lovelock is operating the Big Meadow Hotel, a hotel previously owned by James Blake, from whom Lovelock purchased his ranch land. Another ad two weeks after the first one states that this is the same hotel as Lovelock's Station. Tax rolls show Lovelock operating Lovelock's Hotel in 1866.

In 1887, Lovelock bought additional land, which included the Ruddell Ranch complex, from Antonio and Louisa Feliz. He paid $2,250 for the land and held the first water rights on the Humboldt River. William C. Ruddell's name first appears in record books in the 1880s. In 1882 Ruddell married Jennie C. Lovelock, George and Mary's fourth daughter. Through the purchase of land from George and Mary, by 1901 Jennie and her husband eventually owned all of the Lovelock family land.

George Lovelock worked as a rancher, farmer, businessman, and miner, but he never really struck it rich. Eight children were born to George and Mary Forest Lovelock: Frederick, Thomas, George Jr., Daniel, Stephen, Nellie, Jennie, and Ellen. George

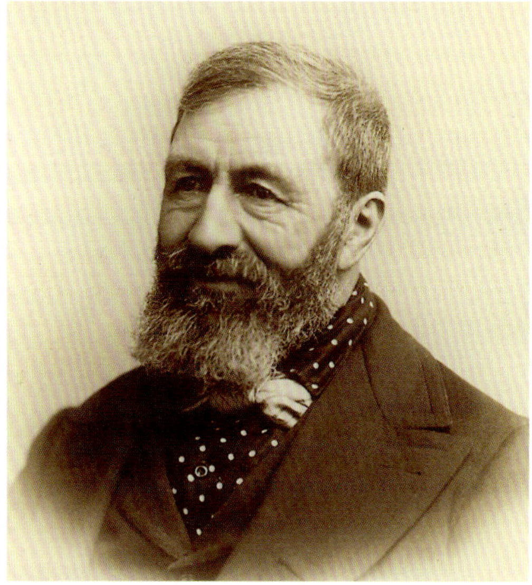

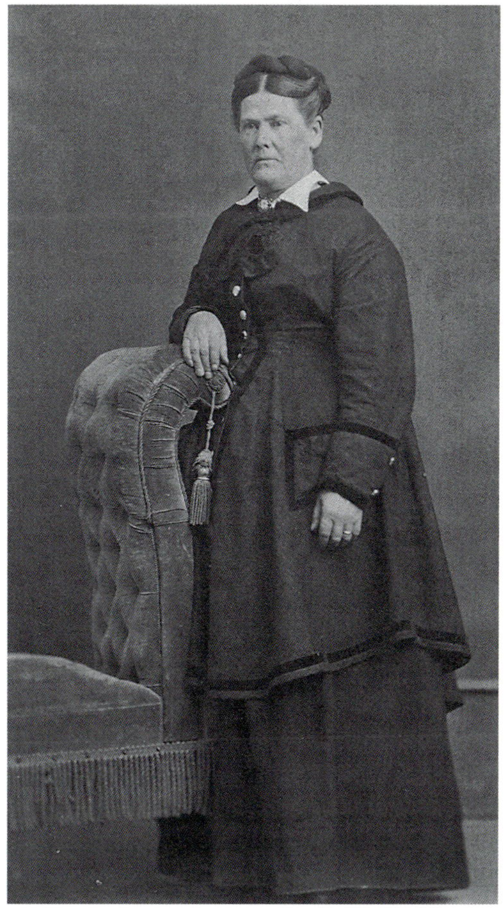

TOP: *George Lovelock, after whom the city is named, was a Welsh miner who was one of the first residents of the settlement that became the town of Lovelock. Photo courtesy Elaine Pommerening.*

BOTTOM: *Mary Lovelock, wife of George Lovelock. Photo courtesy Elaine Pommerening.*

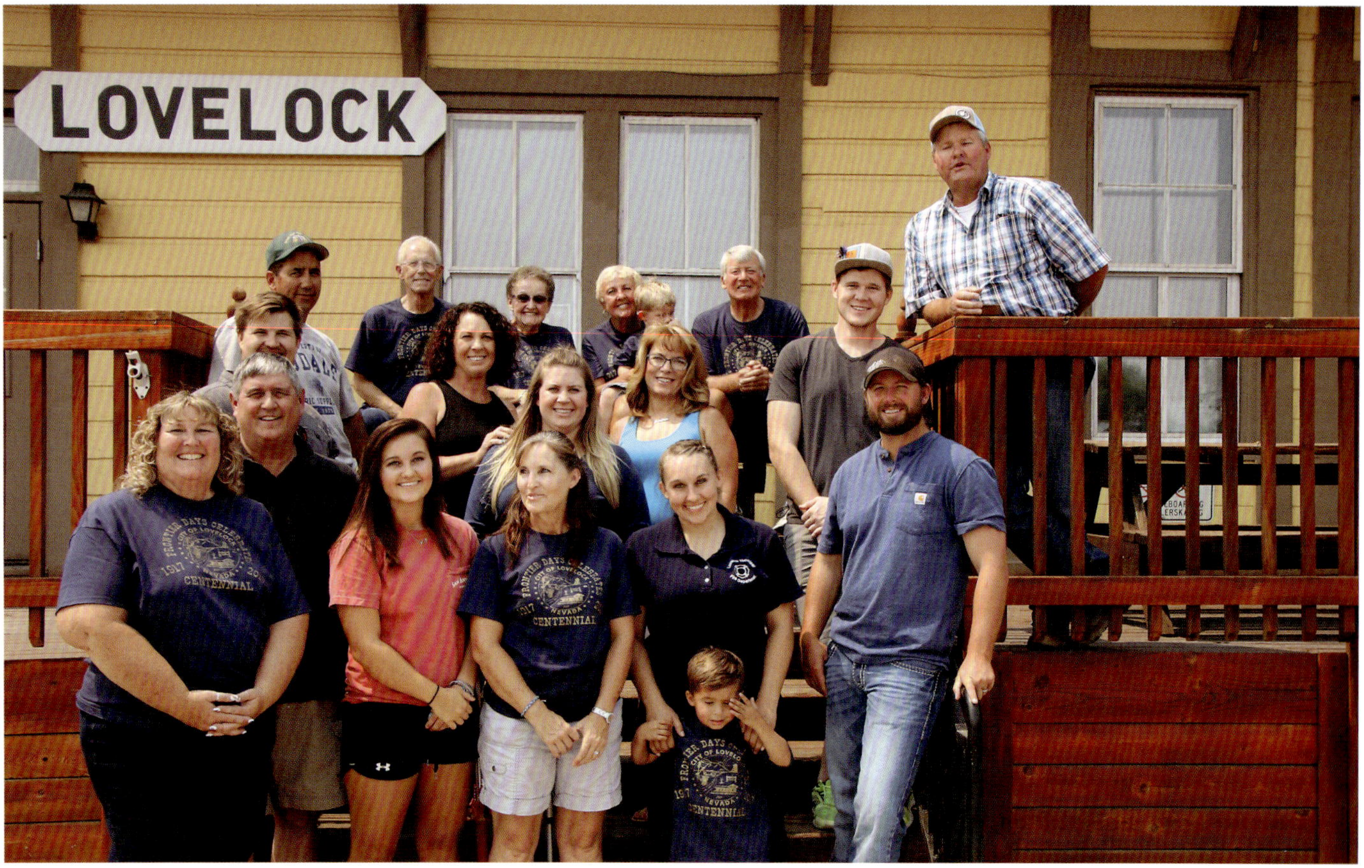

Descendants of George Lovelock standing in front of the Lovelock Depot. Family roots run deep in Pershing County.

died of pneumonia on March 21, 1907, the result of catching a cold while prospecting in his eighty-third year.

In the 1970s Leona Munk and her brother-in-law Lester Munk bought the Ruddell Ranch property, and for a number of years Deanne Munk Davidson and her husband Paul Davidson lived on the ranch with their family. Today it is owned by the Frank List family.

• • •

In the era before the automobile dominated life, walking to church on a Sunday morning was the custom. Lovelock's churches are not in cookie-cutter

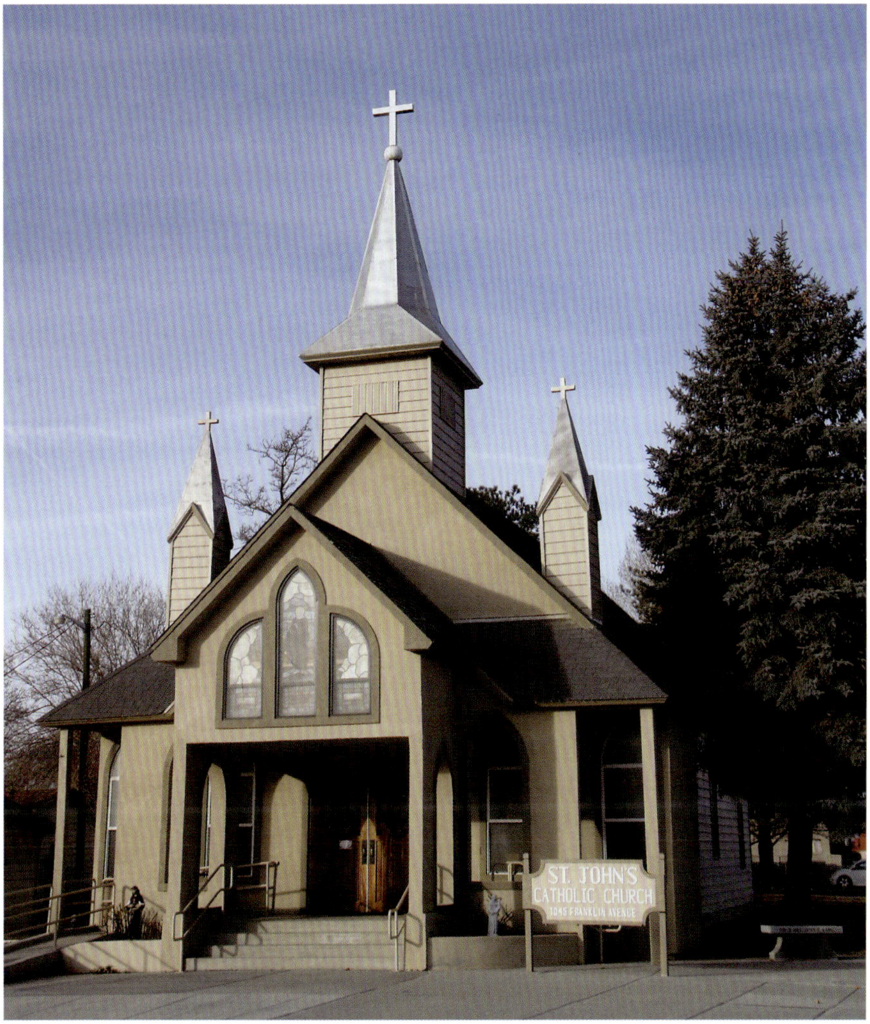

St. John the Baptist Catholic Church.

residential neighborhoods but rather on streets where each home is different from its neighbors. Walking these blocks is like opening a book of domestic architectural design over the last hundred years.

Churches are always symbols of community strength, continuity, pride, and public involvement. Lovelock is no different. St. John the Baptist Catholic Church was organized as a parish in 1875, and the Gothic-style church was constructed in 1900. The land was donated by sheepman and rancher John G. Taylor and Nevada State Senator and Mrs. John O'Kane of what was then Humboldt County. Initially the parish consisted of Catholics born

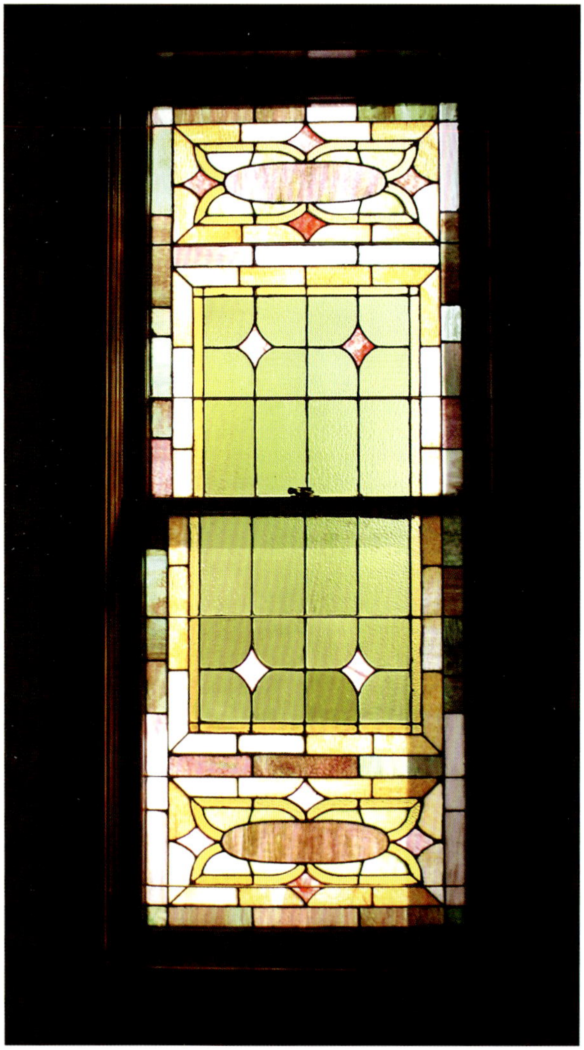

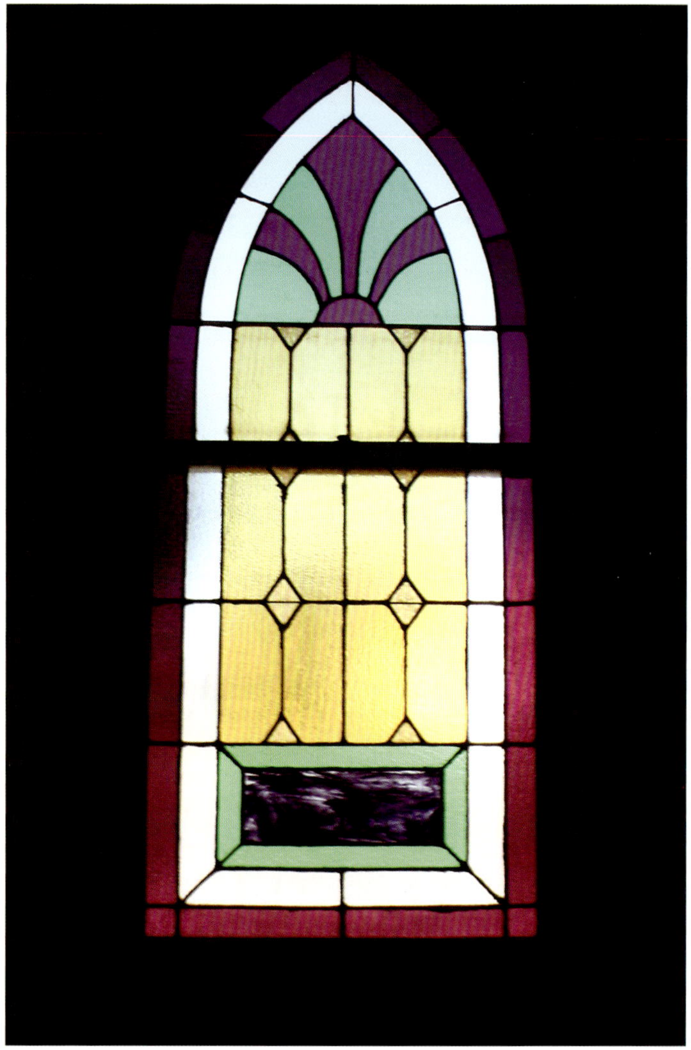

Stained-glass windows in the Methodist Church.

in the United States and immigrants from Portugal, Spain, France, Italy, and Switzerland.

The original Methodist Church was moved to its present location on Cornell Avenue in 1886 from Washoe City, a former railroad stop between Reno and Carson City. That original building was destroyed by fire in 1922; arson was suspected because of a political dispute. The current building caught fire in 1983 but enough was saved that it could be restored. Fortunately, the jewel-like stained glass windows were undamaged.

The Mormon Church has a more clearly defined history in Nevada than many other religions. In 1861 the Church of Jesus Christ of Latter Day Saints (LDS) in Salt Lake City sent LDS groups to various Nevada areas deemed suitable for agriculture in order to establish new Mormon communities. Mormon Station (later called Genoa) in Douglas County was a prime example. This was the first Euro-American settlement in Nevada. However, such centrally planned migration and settlement was not the case in Lovelock

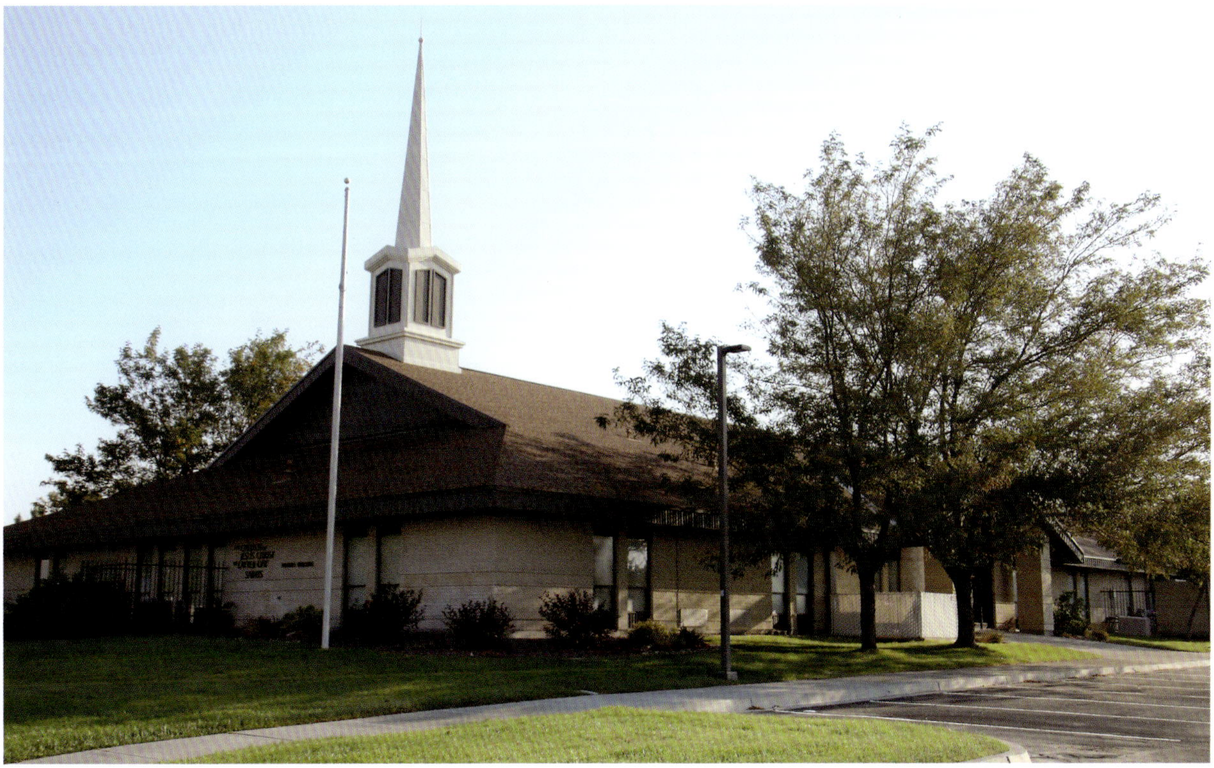

Church of Jesus Christ of Latter-Day Saints.

Valley. Instead, LDS settlers drifted into the area along with other migrants, establishing their farms and ranches independently of Salt Lake City direction. The Mormon settlement in Douglas County did not long endure as an LDS outpost, but by the end of the nineteenth century the Mormons had established a permanent presence and church in the Big Meadows.

About fifty years after these first Mormon settlers arrived, Walt and Viola Brinkerhoff moved from Millard County, Utah, to Winnemucca, and then to Lovelock. Walt Brinkerhoff, a fur trapper, left Utah during the Great Depression. In the early 1930s he saw trapping possibilities along the Humboldt River in Winnemucca. He had as many as seven thousand traps there until the price of fur dropped. He then moved his family to the fertile Lovelock Valley on February 5, 1945, and that has been the home of this large, prominent Mormon farm family ever since. Their contributions to the county include encouraging the county to move the Marzen House one and a half miles from the Brinkerhoff ranch property to its current location and then donating it to Pershing County to house a county museum.

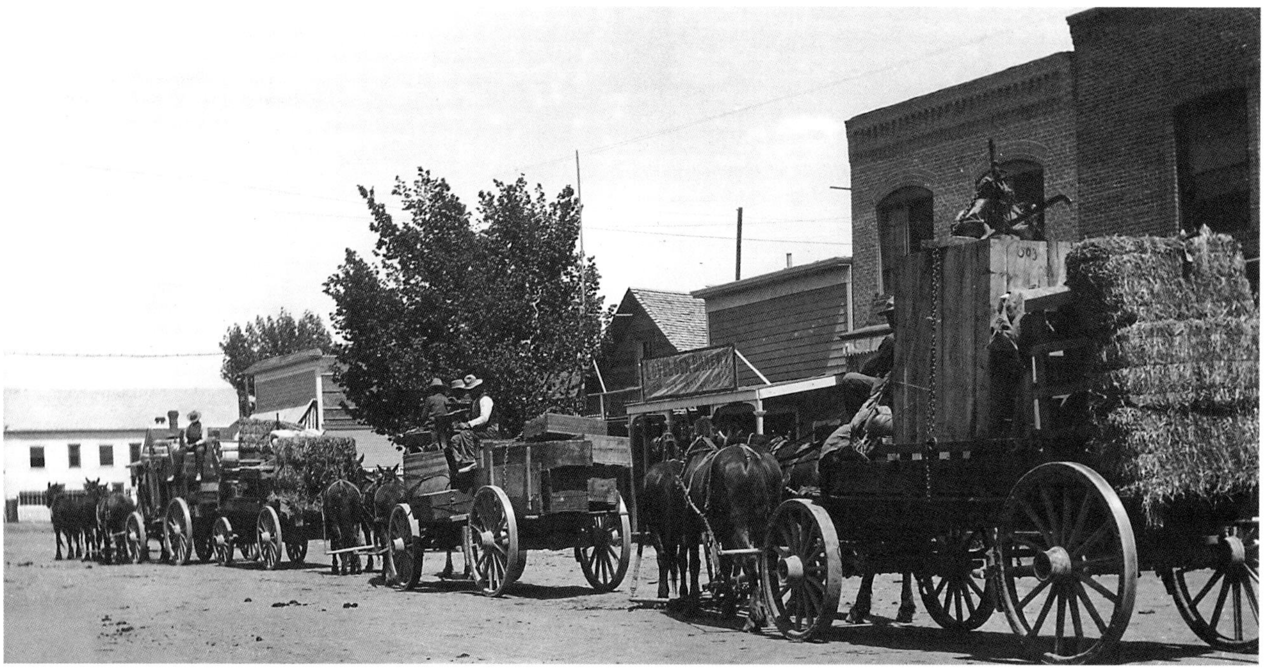

Freight wagons leaving Lovelock, 1907. Courtesy Nevada Historical Society.

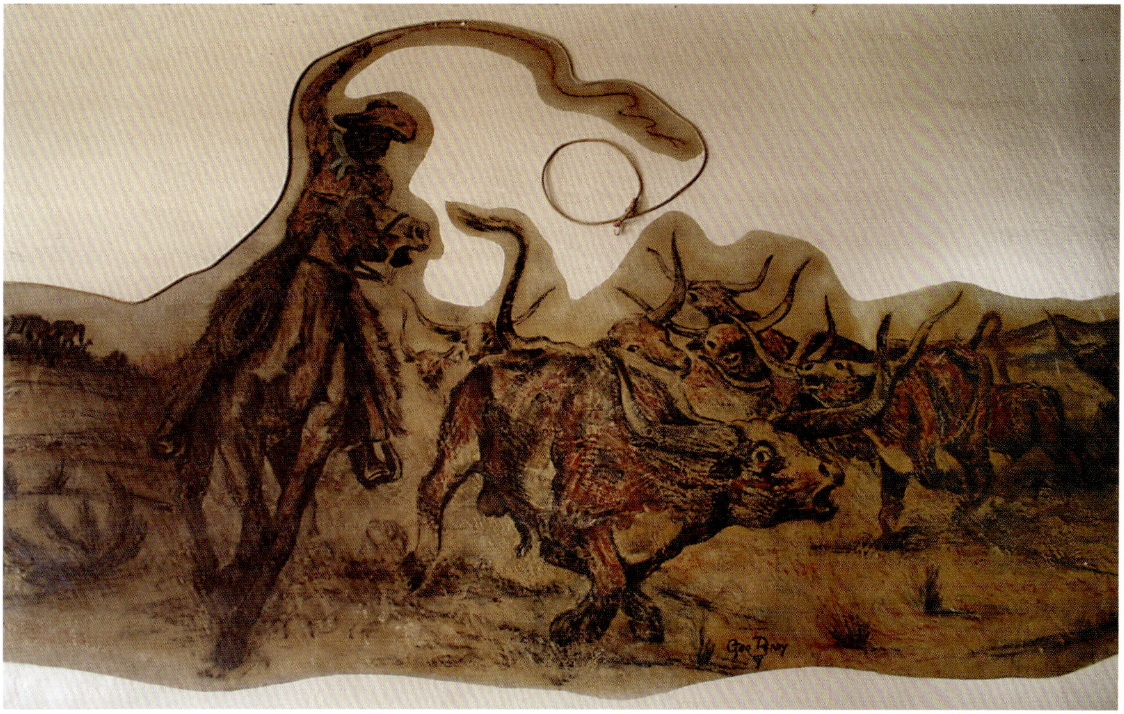

Detail of the Longhorn Bar chalk mural by George Perry.

Lovelock's shops, markets, drugstores, laundries, bars, restaurants, and service stations offered all the services of a small town. Many of the original buildings are gone now or see life under different names and services, but some haven't changed for years. In 1907, across from the railroad tracks, a watering hole provided spirits for travelers. Today it is the Longhorn Bar, which houses a unique cattle-drive mural of longhorn steers, cowboys, bucking broncos, a chuck wagon, and even a few saloon girls. The chalk mural has been shellacked for protection and is signed Geo. Perry.

Geo. Perry turns out to be George Perry, eldest of five children born to Frank and Alice Perry, who homesteaded near the California-Nevada line between Modoc County and northern Washoe County. They lived on Cottonwood Creek northeast of Gerlach on the tip of the Black Rock Desert, and some detailed maps indicate a Perry Spring in that area. Later, they lived in Cedarville, so when the famous massacre of three Basque sheepmen and a cattleman occurred on January 19, 1911, in Little High Rock Canyon in northern Washoe County, Frank Perry joined the posse tracking the killers suspected of the crime. The final conflict occurred at Kelley Creek north of Golconda, when Shoshone Mike and his cohorts were apprehended.

George Barton Perry (1916–82) was not born until several years after this famous incident, but family stories exist along with Frank Perry's journal of the event. George's life was as interesting as his father's. He was an itinerant carpenter and artist known to pay his bar bills by painting murals, thus the mural in the Longhorn Bar in Lovelock and a second mural dated 1942 at Cheers Bar in Winnemucca. As a young man, George was recognized as an accomplished artist in California, and his sketch of San Francisco's Palace of Fine Arts hangs in a gallery there. Family members have paintings and sketches he did while traveling in Cuba and Haiti. At the time of his death, he was living in Fallon.

Several blocks east of the Longhorn was one of Lovelock's more famous businesses—LaBelle's Lounge, the location for "the working girls." LaBelle's was close to the railroad tracks, not far off the transcontinental highway, and an easy stop for hunters and travelers who wanted to spend a little leisure time in Lovelock. The Lounge is gone now but not forgotten by its former habitués.

When Highway 40 was completed through downtown Lovelock, the heart of Lovelock's business center surrounded the only stoplight in town, at the intersection of the highway and Main Street. The four corners of the intersection consisted of the Lovelock Mercantile Building, constructed in 1909 and severely damaged by a 1950s earthquake, leading to the ultimate removal of the second floor. Felix's Bank Club and Cocktail Lounge, purchased by Felix Turillas in 1953 and closed by the Nevada Gaming Commission in 1977, occupied the southwest corner. The Lovelock Pharmacy building was built in 1905 to house the Lovelock Commercial Company and later several other businesses. It was remodeled in 1940. On the fourth corner, the southwestern corner, was the Victory Motor Service, a Ford dealership operated by D. E. Winchell, according to Pershing County High School yearbook ads from the mid-1950s. These four corners saw changes over the years, but residents remember them for their importance to the community.

Just a stone's throw from Felix's was the iconic Two Stiffs Selling Gas service station, started by Henry Lawrence Stiff in 1935. H. Lawrence Stiff, born in Lovelock in 1900, leased the property that was his first "gasoline station," the Victory Service Station, in 1923 when he was twenty-three years old and "had $500 in his jeans and could pay $75 a month for the leased site."

Lawrence Stiff later moved across the street, and the business became Two Stiffs Selling Gas when in 1933 he hired his father to work with him. Edward Lawrence Stiff, known as Ed Stiff, was a carpenter by trade but joined his son in the venture, which eventually included a motel and a gift shop.

Few travelers passed through town without stopping at one or the other of these businesses. The original businesses were gone by 2000, and the town's commercial nexus moved to new enterprises located just off Interstate 80—Steve Young's Chevron Casino and Food Mart and Nanny Jo's Antiques just down Main Street at the stoplight in the former Mercantile building.

Pershing County's stately 1920s courthouse dominates its Lovelock neighborhood and is surrounded by the county library, the 1937 post office, and the Pershing County administrative offices located in the former Spouse Reitz store. A coffee bar and deli currently occupies the 1920 Valley Equipment building, which formerly housed the Nevada National Engineering Guard armory, the location for drill and target practice during World War II.

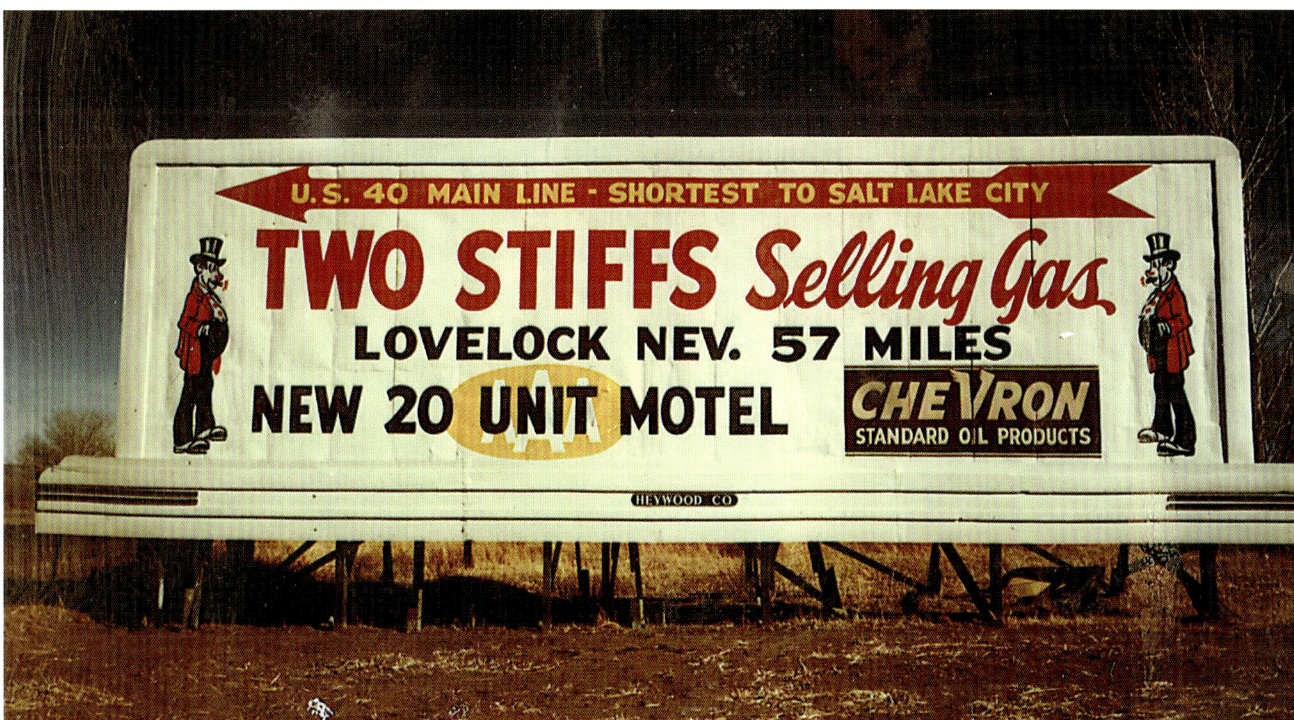

Road sign advertising the Two Stiffs gas station. Photo courtesy Sharon Stiff Calvert.

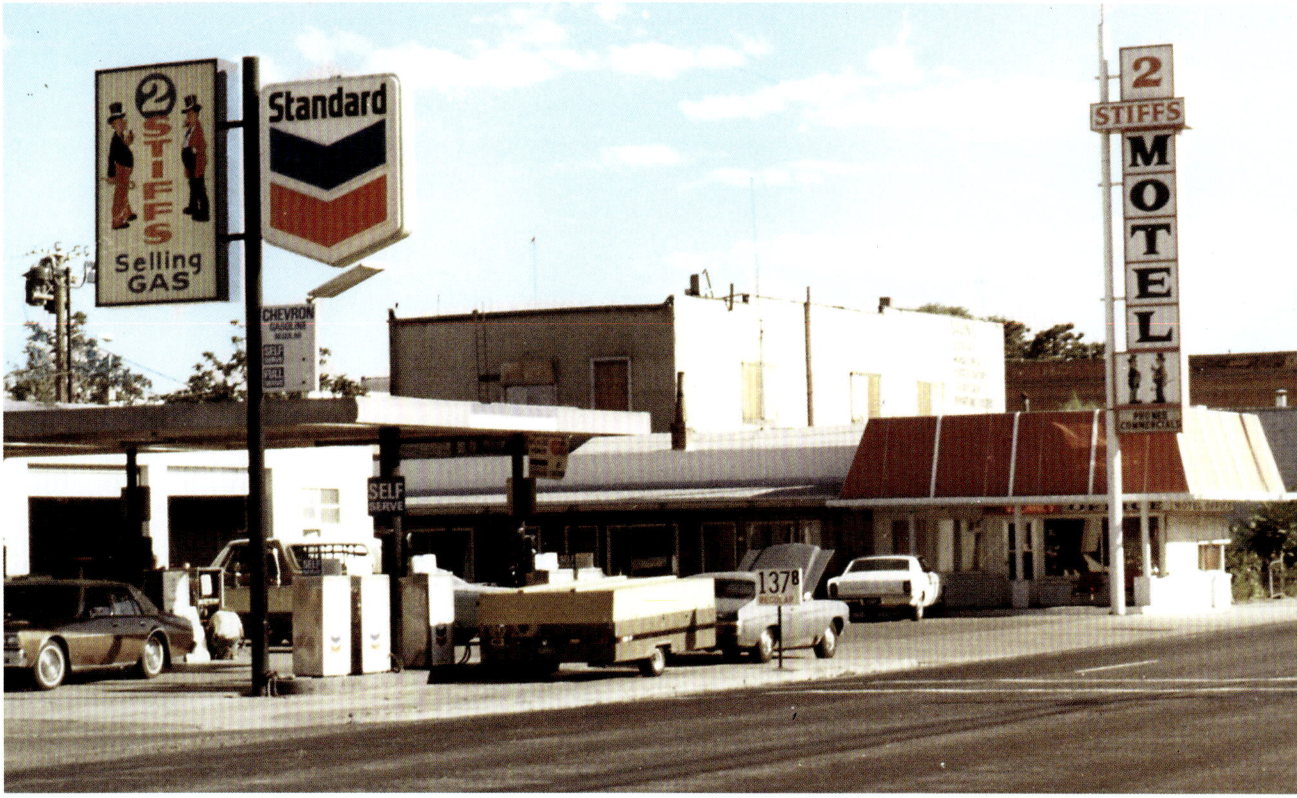

Two Stiffs gas station. Photo courtesy Sharon Stiff Calvert.

To the north of the courthouse on the periphery of the park is the mid-century-modern Pershing County Public Library. Built in 1970 and designed by Edward S. Parsons of Reno, the library became so vital to the city that a 1987 addition almost doubled the space. The addition was designed by George Trowbridge, who is known for his design of legislative buildings in Carson City.

The library provides a learning center for school children, senior citizens, and a public eager to gather in this welcoming environment. The Nevada Room and the collection of Pershing County and Lovelock materials, especially mining books, maps, and periodicals, complement the large collection of audiobooks. But the library and the staff headed by Kathie Brinkerhoff also provide outstanding programming—art shows both local and traveling from the Nevada Arts Council; performances from Reno's Pioneer Center for the Performing Arts; as well as puppet shows and other children's events.

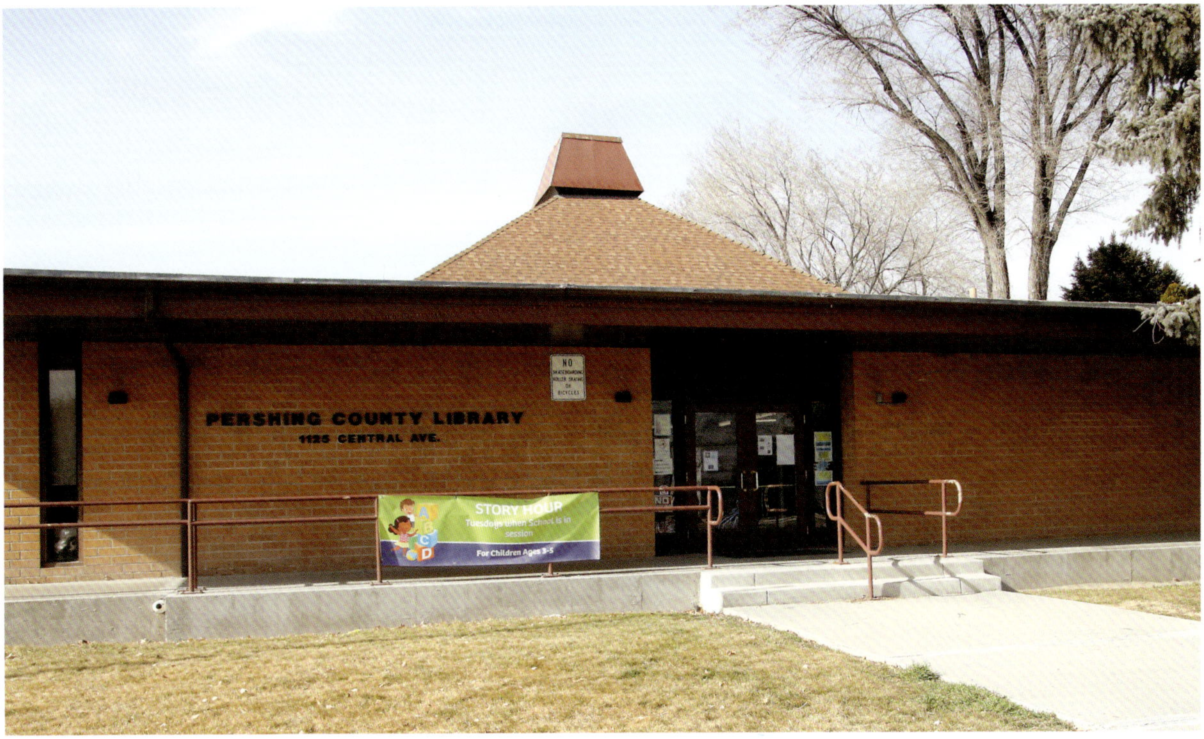

Pershing County Public Library.

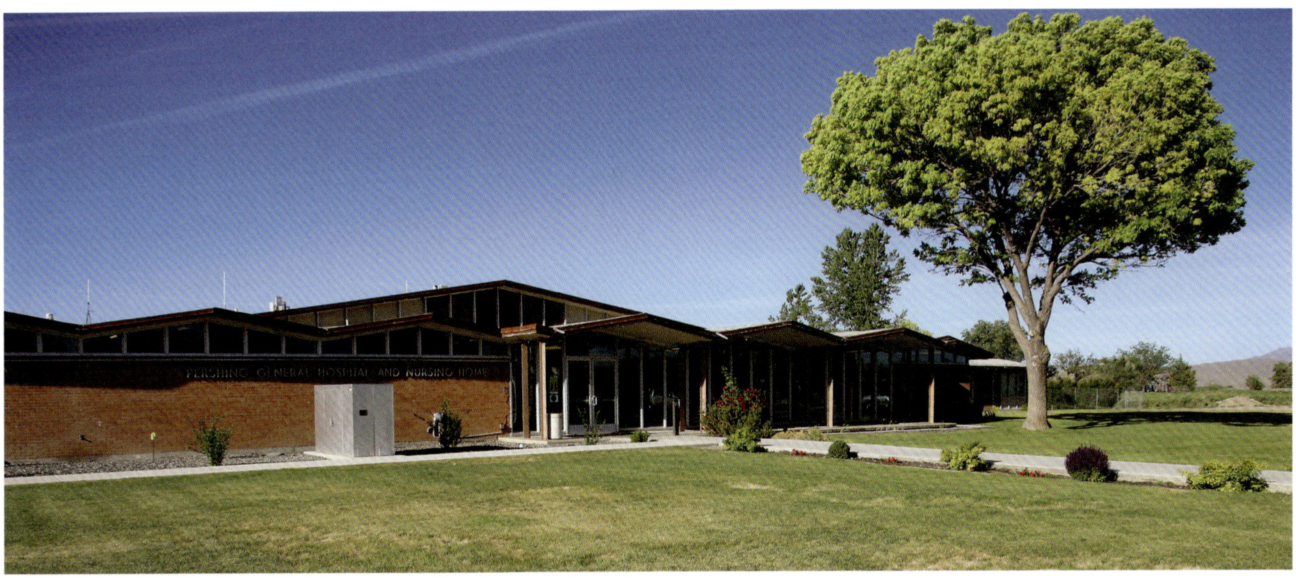

Pershing County General Hospital.

Another important section of Lovelock, albeit off the beaten path, is the Medical Complex comprised of the hospital, nursing home, clinic, and community center. Today's Pershing General Hospital and Nursing Home, built in 1962 and designed by Deseret Architecture and Engineers from Salt Lake City, serves over 6,900 people from the community, the county, and the surrounding area. The vitally important medical center has thirty-eight beds; the long-term nursing home has twenty-five.

The original Pershing County General Hospital started as an old-folks' home on Dartmouth Avenue in Lovelock on December 31, 1921. In her notes as historian for the hospital's Pink Ladies' Auxiliary in the 1970s, Norma Arobio wrote, "It had become clear by 1944 that Pershing County needed a general hospital, so remodeling of the Nursing home was started. After the addition of an O.B. ward and delivery room, operating facilities and a new nursing home ward, the Pershing General hospital was established."

The hospital has been fortunate in enjoying the services of a series of commendable physicians, beginning with Dr. F. M. West in the 1920s, Drs. J. R. Gill and West in the 1930s and 1940s, and then in 1942 Dr. Joseph M.

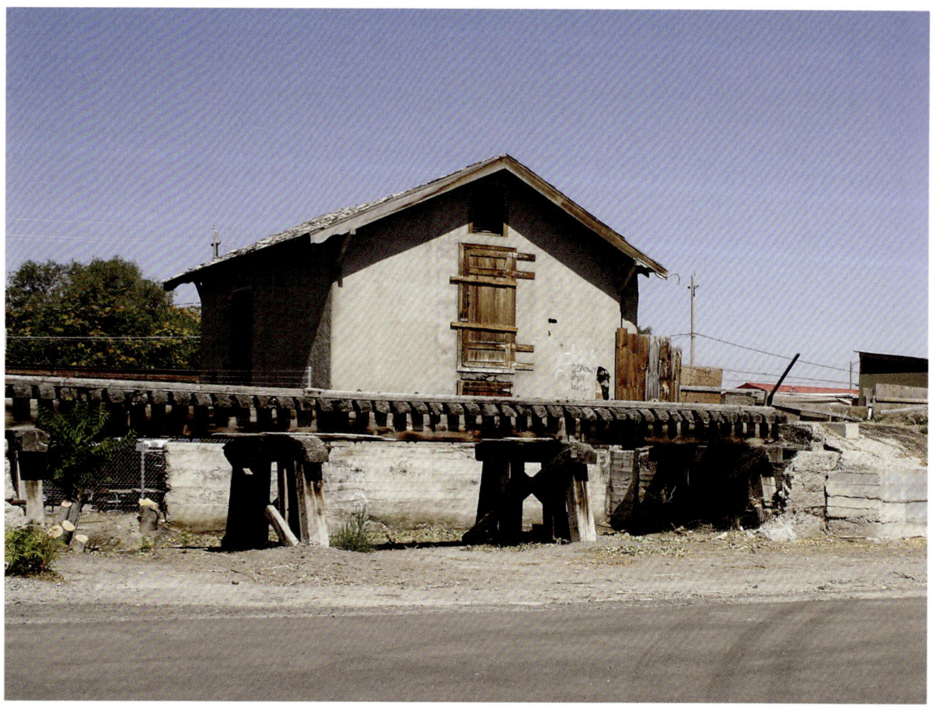

The Pitt Mill Ice House.

Presti arrived from New York. During the decades Dr. Presti practiced medicine in Lovelock, his medical expertise went above and beyond what he was formally asked to do.

The governmental entities, churches, downtown businesses, and medical facilities give life to Lovelock, but agricultural enterprises have been a backbone for decades. One cannot read about Lovelock or Pershing County during its first one hundred years without finding references to William and Capitola Pitt. An August 21, 1925, article in the *Review-Miner* gives today's reader a look at this primary agricultural business in Lovelock Valley:

> P. A. Quigley, Pitt Mill manager, is making arrangements to start the annual flour manufacturing campaign shortly and in any event in advance of September 1. A grinding mill for chicken feeds and custom milling is being installed. Wheat crops from the Hans Westergaard and Pitt ranches have been bought at $50 per ton although the market shows signs of weakening at this time. It is Mr. Quigley's belief that Lovelock Valley wheat production approximates 1500 tons this year which is about an average crop.

Pitt's White Rose Flour was a completely local product and a popular one as well. Today, however, the once-prominent Pitt Mill and Elevator Company has fallen to the wrecking ball, razed to the ground in 2016.

A year and a half before Pershing became a county, the city of Lovelock became an official community. On September 26, 1917, the city charter was signed, and in the same week baby Irva Hanson was born at home. Irva was born to Celia and John Hanson on September 22 and was four days old when Lovelock was born. She married Floyd Marcucci on October 9, 1938, and she and Floyd gave a lifetime of service to their family and their community. Floyd passed away in 2008 at age ninety-four, but when the city celebrated its hundredth birthday on September 26, 2017, a dinner was held to honor Irva Hanson Marcucci on her hundred years as a Lovelock native.

• • •

Lovelock has always been the largest population center in Pershing County, but other communities, including Imlay, have had their time in the sun. Imlay had its beginnings in the early 1900s as an important stop for the Southern Pacific Railroad and was home to a twelve-stall roundhouse, a power house, and a machine shop that formed the heart of this rail-line community. The railroad complex included a three-story Employees Club House, and it was here that the author's grandfather, Christopher Cameron

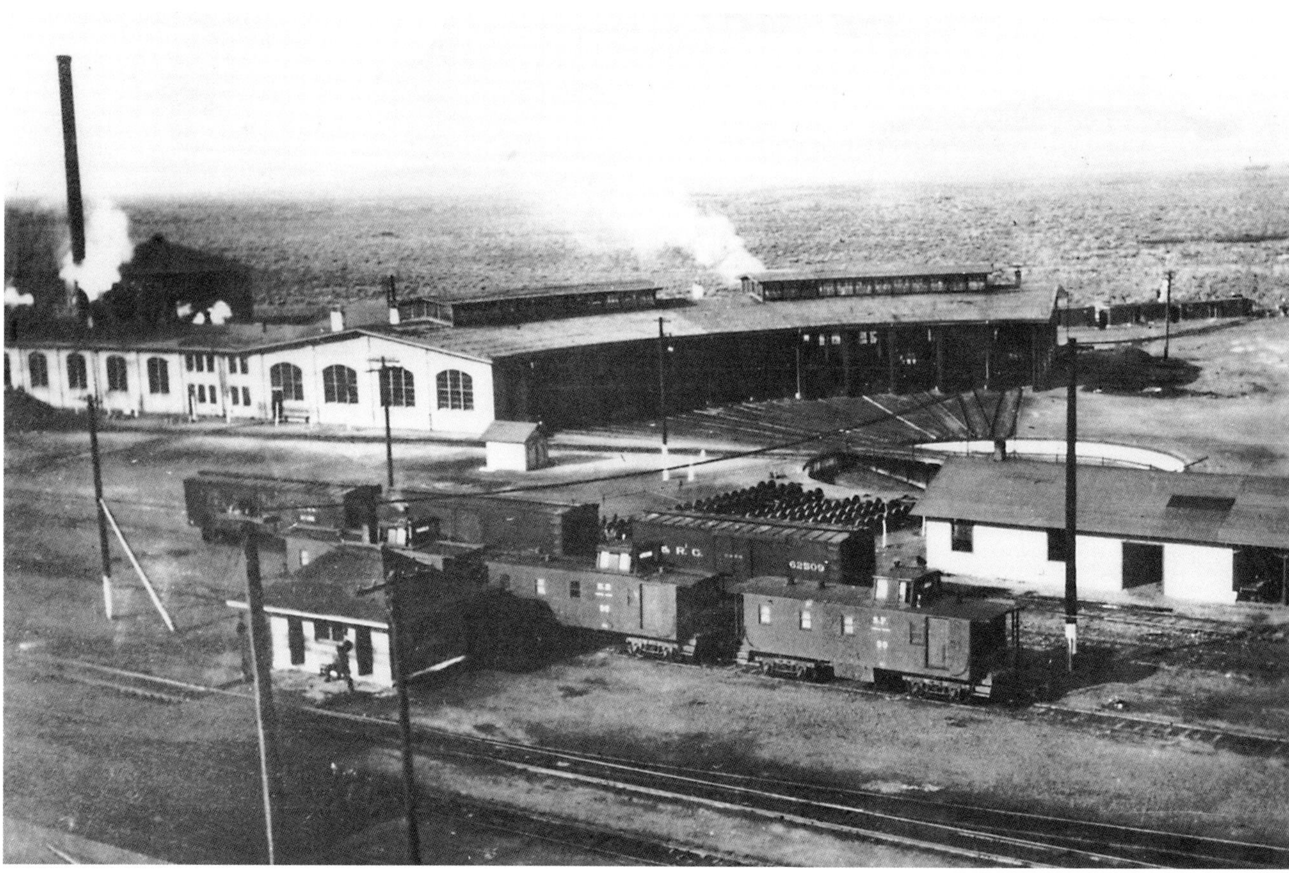

The Southern Pacific Railroad roundhouse, Imlay. Courtesy Nevada Historical Society.

Walker of Eureka, Nevada, who worked for the Southern Pacific Railroad, met his future wife, Ann McKenna of Wadsworth, at a dance at the Club House where she was working as a waitress.

Imlay's importance, along with the importance of all America's small communities, is illustrated by this historic anecdote:

> At seven-twenty-eight on the morning of September 22, 1948, the president's sixteen-car train pulled into Imlay, a tiny railroad town in the middle of Nevada. As soon as the train groaned to a stop, a slight man with thin hair, a polka-dotted bow tie, and thick glasses jumped off. About 150 people stood around the depot. By presidential standards it was a pathetic crowd. Harry Truman didn't care. He was in the fight of his life and needed every vote he could grab. "You folks," Truman said, "must have gotten up before daylight."

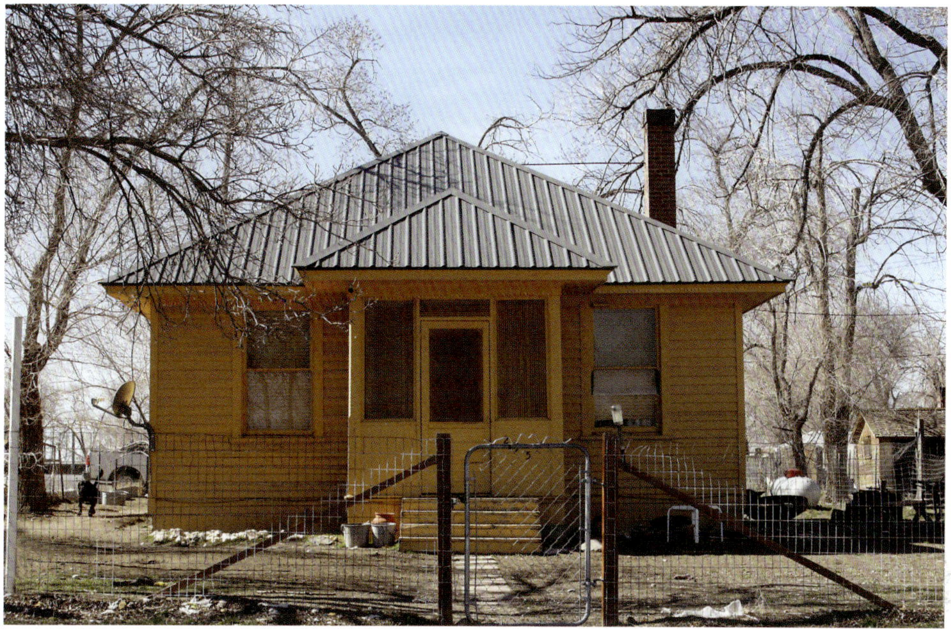

Typical railroad worker's house, Imlay.

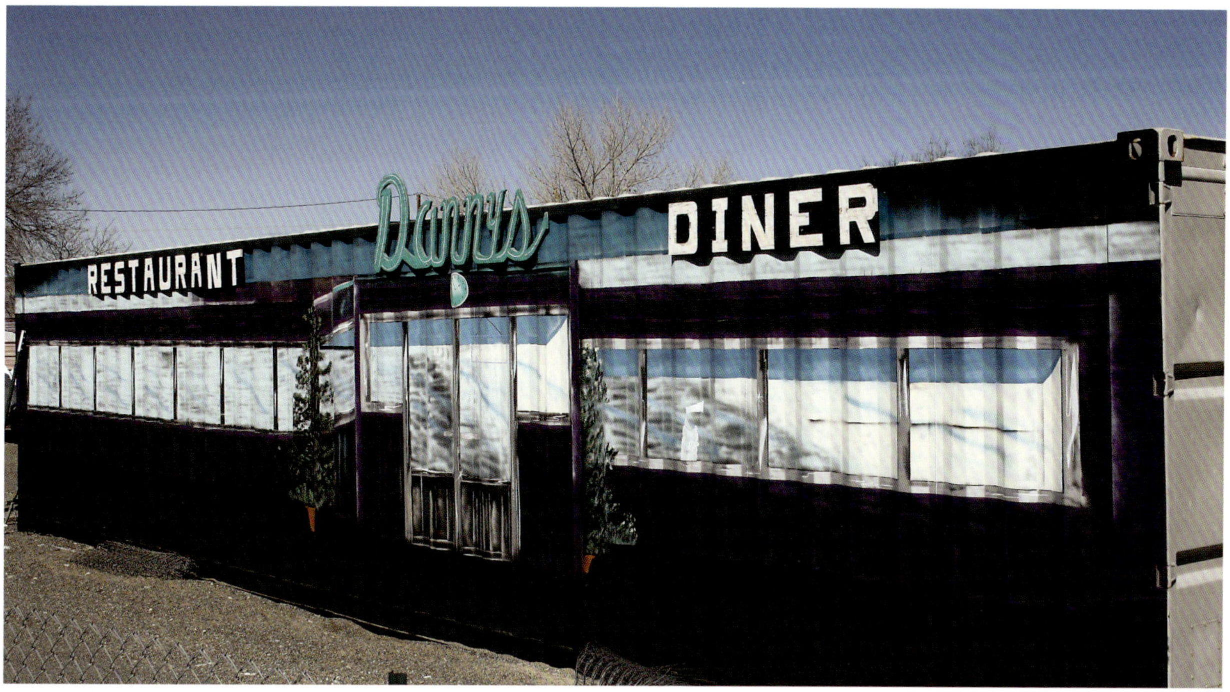

This trompe-l'oeil diner in Imlay is actually an empty cargo container.

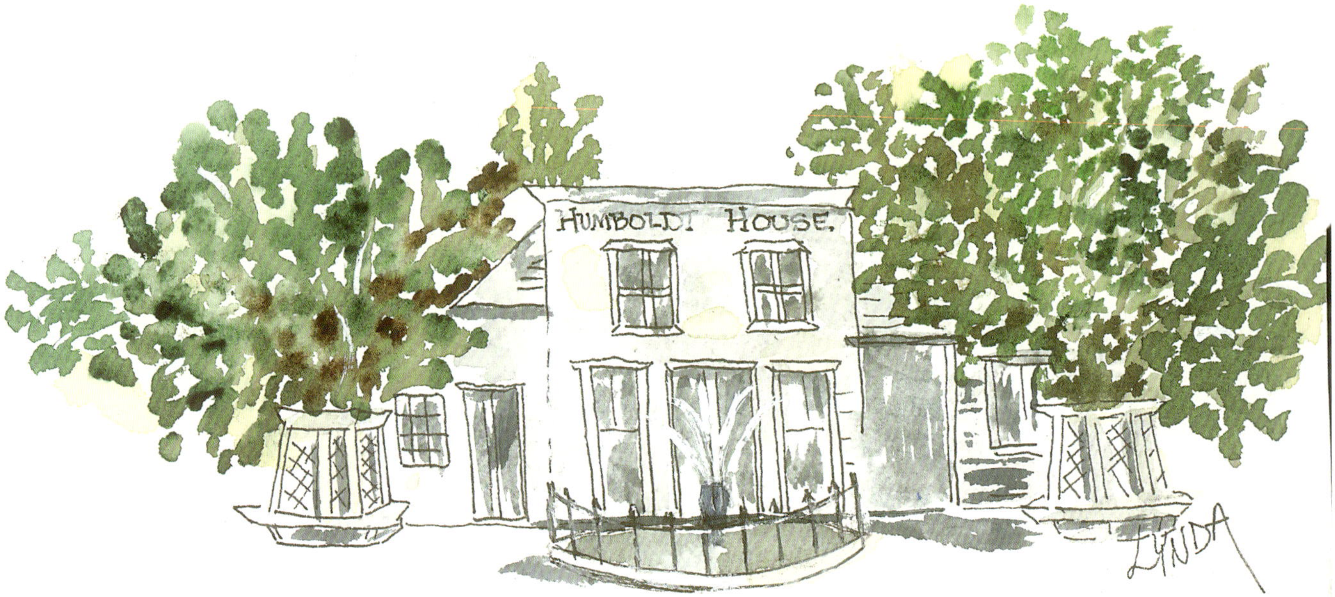

The Humboldt House, a hotel located about thirty-five miles northeast of Lovelock, was originally a point of departure to the mines in that area. In 1866 it became a stage stop. The Central Pacific Railroad reached here in 1868, and from then until 1900 it was known as one of the best eating places on the railroad line. Set in the middle of a lush oasis, the hotel provided fresh fruits and vegetables and pure water to weary travelers. Waterclor by Lynda Quilici.

Today, Imlay is an even smaller town than it was in 1948. The town was platted in 1907–1908, and a visitor can still see the two-story Victorian-era homes on Main Street and the hipped-roof houses that dot the rest of the small community. Many railroad towns in the West that developed after the 1900s include houses like these. Undoubtedly the railroad companies were encouraging this style of architecture. But Imlay has no sign of the old roundhouse, hotels, or any other reminders of its history as a major railroad town.

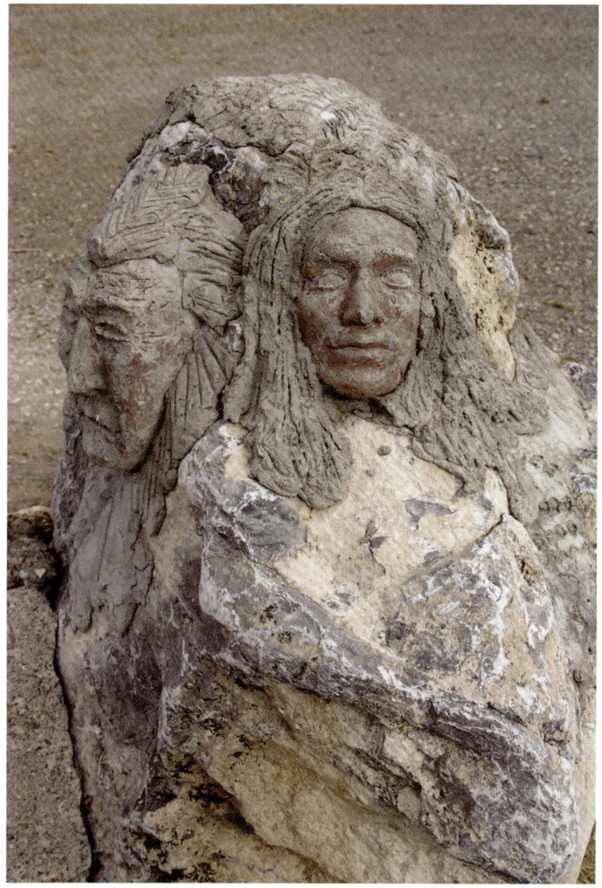

A statue of a Native American in the Thunder Mountain Monument.

Just outside Imlay on U.S. Highway 80, a curious monument springs from the land. The Thunder Mountain Monument began in 1968 when Frank Van Zant's truck broke down and he decided to stay put. The internet site Spaces says, "Visitors may walk through at their discretion for their own self-guided tours."

Frank Van Zant believed himself to be a full-blooded Creek Indian who lived a unique life after leaving his home in Okmulgee, Oklahoma, at age fourteen. He served in World War II, studied to be a minister, worked in the Sutter County, California, sheriff's office, and with his third wife headed east after retirement. It is likely that when his truck broke down, he camped at the spot. At some point, the owner of the land made him an offer, and for the next twenty years Van Zant worked on the fanciful creations that comprise Thunder Mountain Monument.

Van Zant called himself Rolling Mountain Thunder and tried to live in what he saw as the "Indian way." On his five acres he began his constructions by covering his travel trailer with rocks and concrete, and over the years he built a three-story monument, statues of Native Americans, colorful arches, paths, walls, and ultimately seven buildings. To achieve all of this, he covered chicken wire with concrete and a wide variety of rock, and for the buildings he used "daub and bottle" construction. Possibly he had seen the bottle house in Rhyolite. The property has undergone years of decay since Van Zant's death in 1989. In 1992 Thunder Mountain was entered into the State of Nevada's Registry of Historic Sites. It is now a State of Nevada Historic Site Restoration Project.

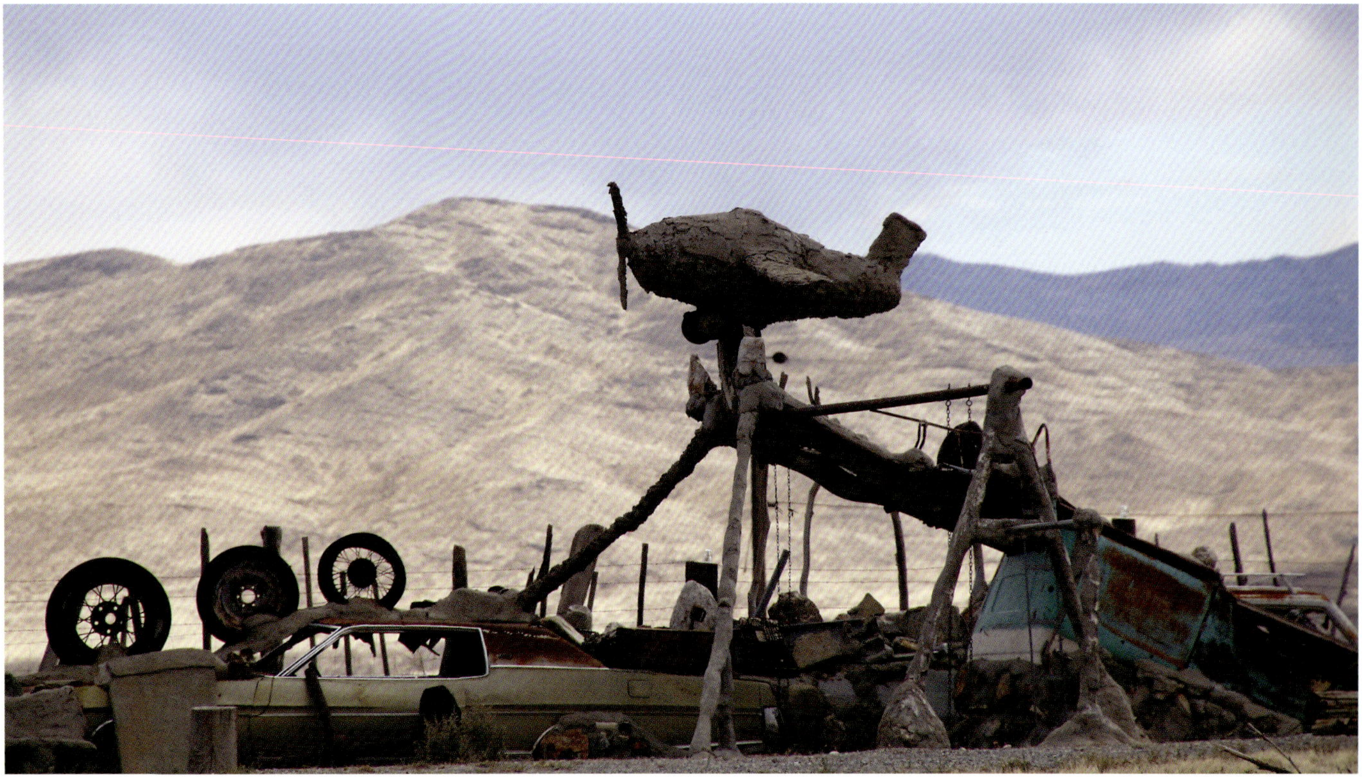

A construction built from found materials at the Thunder Mountain Monument.

BUILDING AN ECONOMY

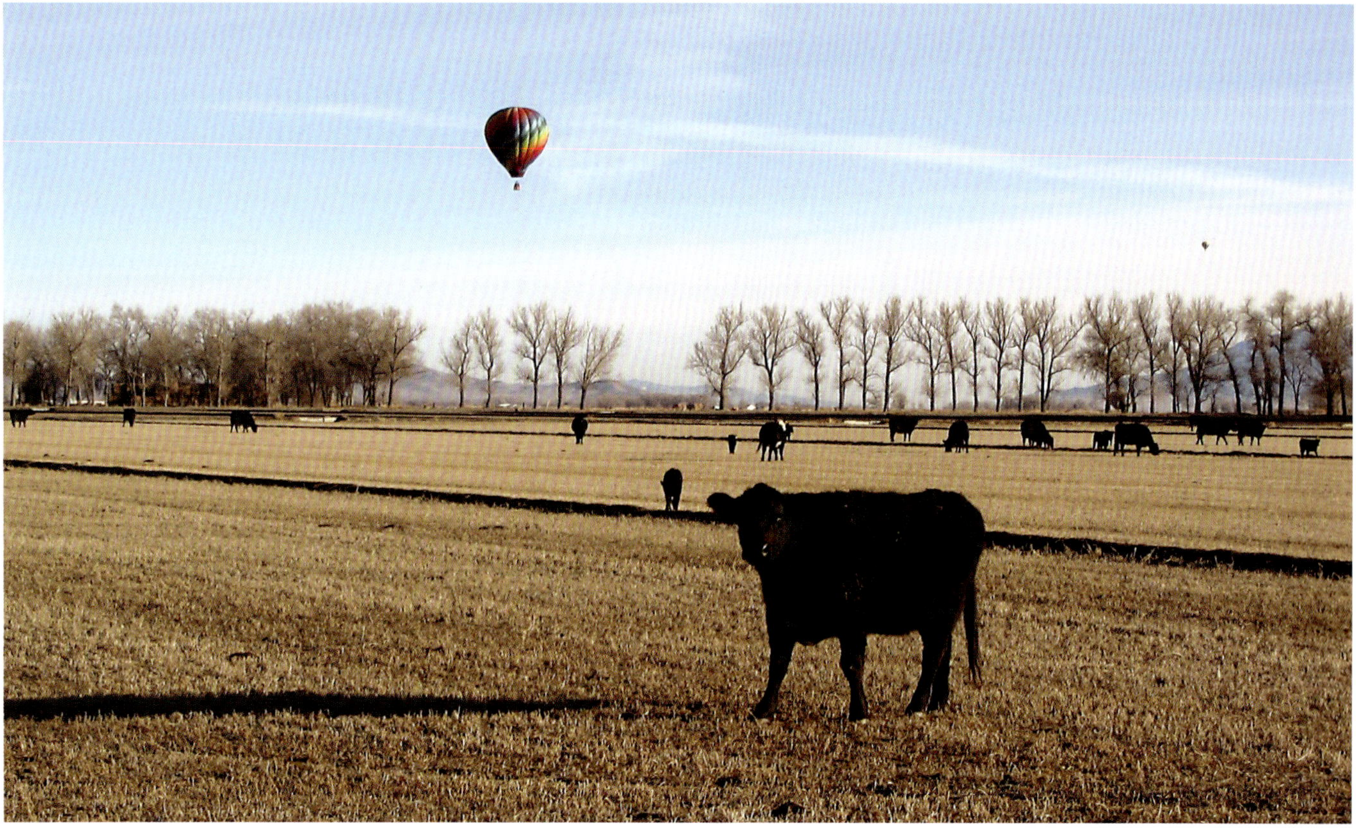

Black angus cattle and hot-air balloons in Lovelock Valley.

Water is essential to the agricultural economy of Pershing County. Because the Humboldt River tends to be undependable—in wet years it can flood, but in droughts it often runs dry—as early as 1909 a few small reservoirs had been constructed outside Lovelock to capture water. In 1911 a group of local farmers constructed the Upper and Lower Pitt-Taylor Reservoirs as a private venture, intended to store water from the high-water flow of the Humboldt River. In 1933 Nevada Senators Pat McCarran and Key Pittman, along with Congressman James Scrugham and State Engineer George V. Malone, negotiated with the U.S. Bureau of Reclamation for the purchase of land and water rights to build a dam on the narrow part of the Humboldt River northeast of Lovelock and create a large reservoir to provide a reliable source of water for the region's farmers.

The dam, constructed between 1935 and 1936, was a New Deal project, one of many created by the federal government during the Great Depression to provide employment. In this case, the workers came from the Civilian Conservation Corps. By July 1936 the reservoir stored 17,000 acre-feet of water, and within three more years, 183,000 acre-feet of water were available for local farms and ranches, as well as providing recreation, habitat for fish, and an important stop for migratory birds. In 1975–76, the dam was raised three feet to provide more storage capacity. Located northeast of Lovelock, the Rye Patch Reservoir, as it is called, stretches along the Humboldt River for twenty-two miles. Its current capacity is 231,000 acre-feet of water, covering an area of 11,970 acres.

But water remains an enduring and vexing problem. In good years, the Rye Patch Reservoir provides water for the farms and ranches of southern Pershing County as well as important recreational opportunities for people from all over northern Nevada. But in periods of drought, the reservoir's water is required to sustain local agriculture, and down-river agricultural

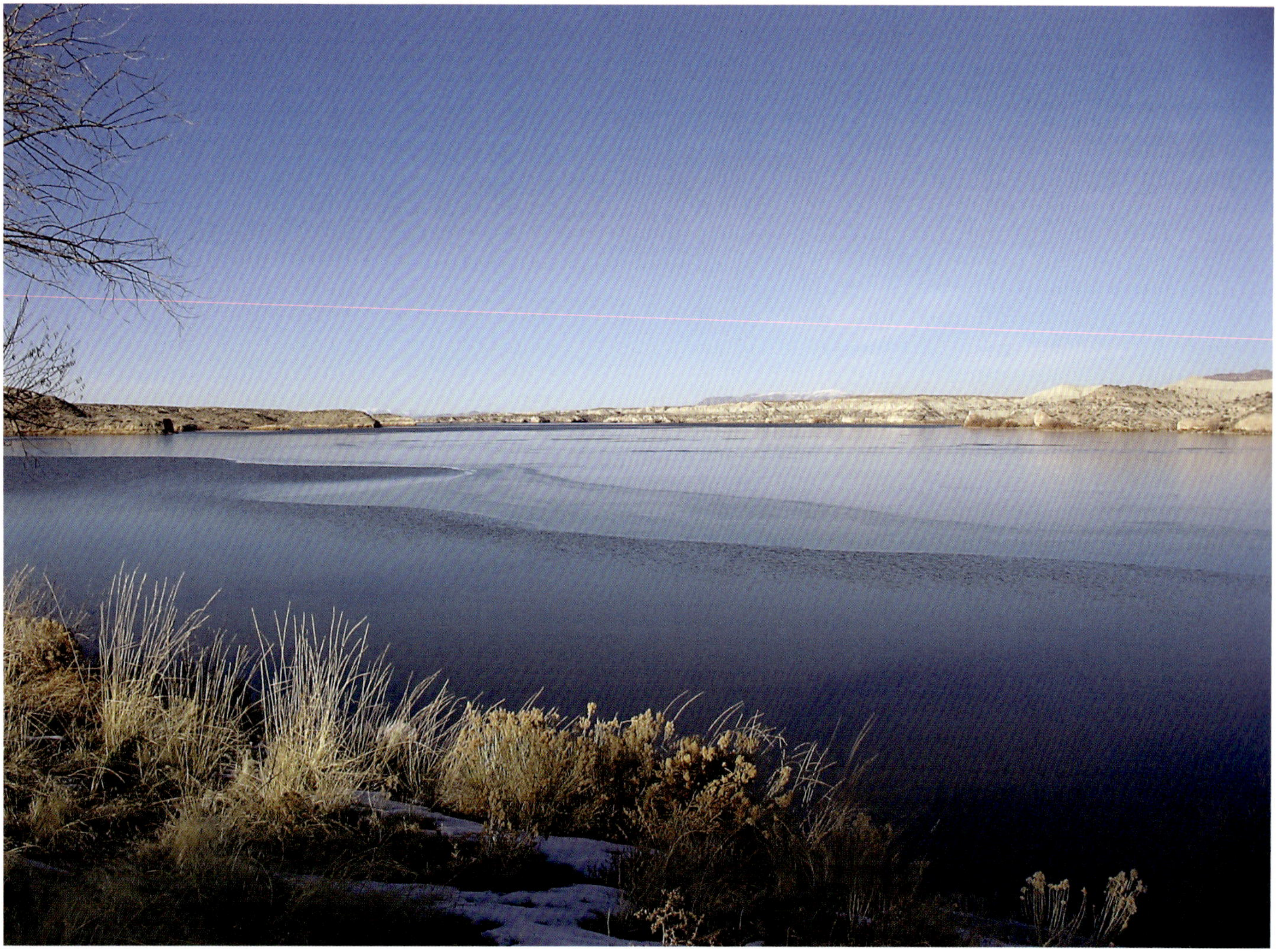

Rye Patch Reservoir.

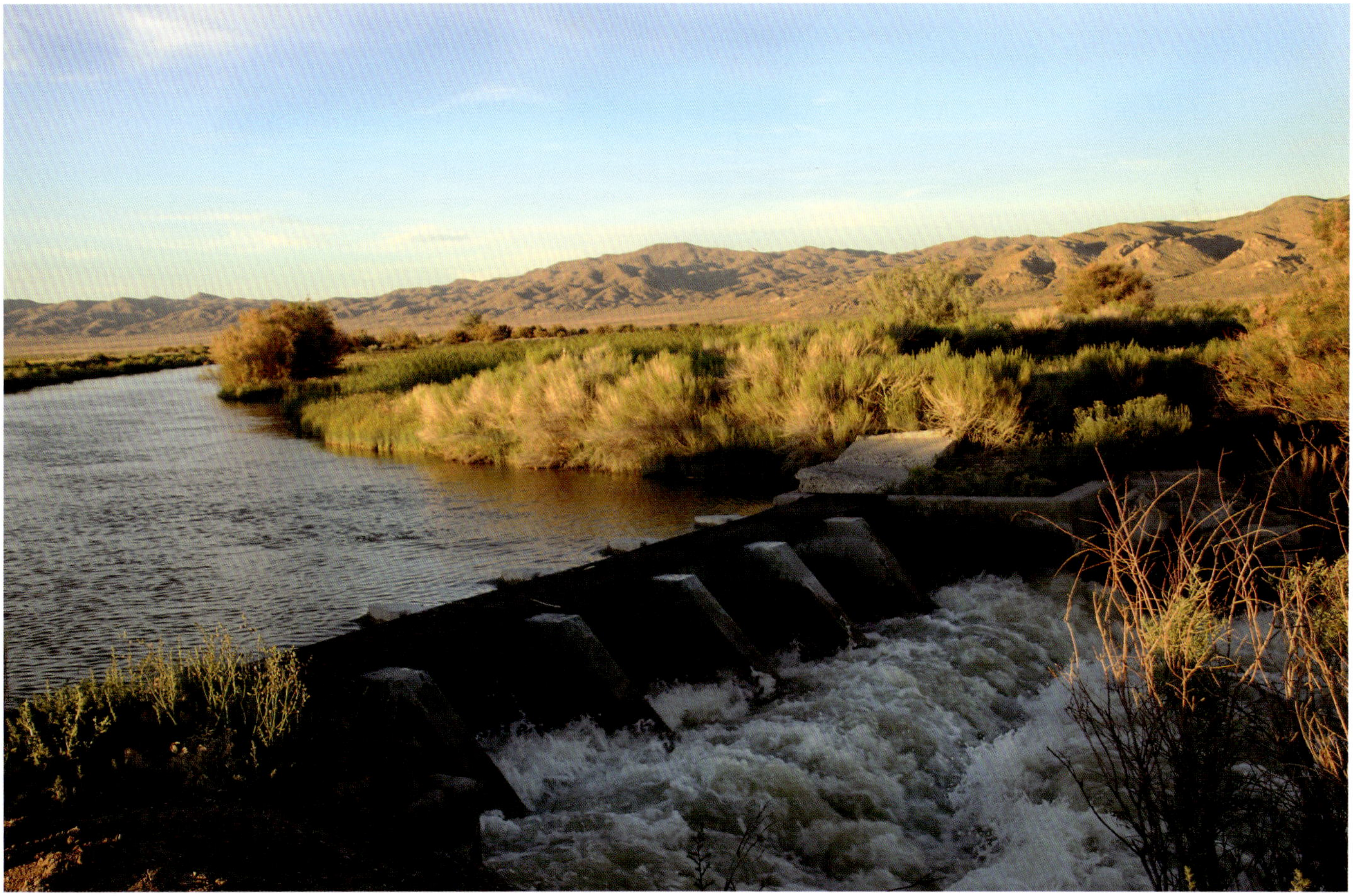

Rye Patch Dam.

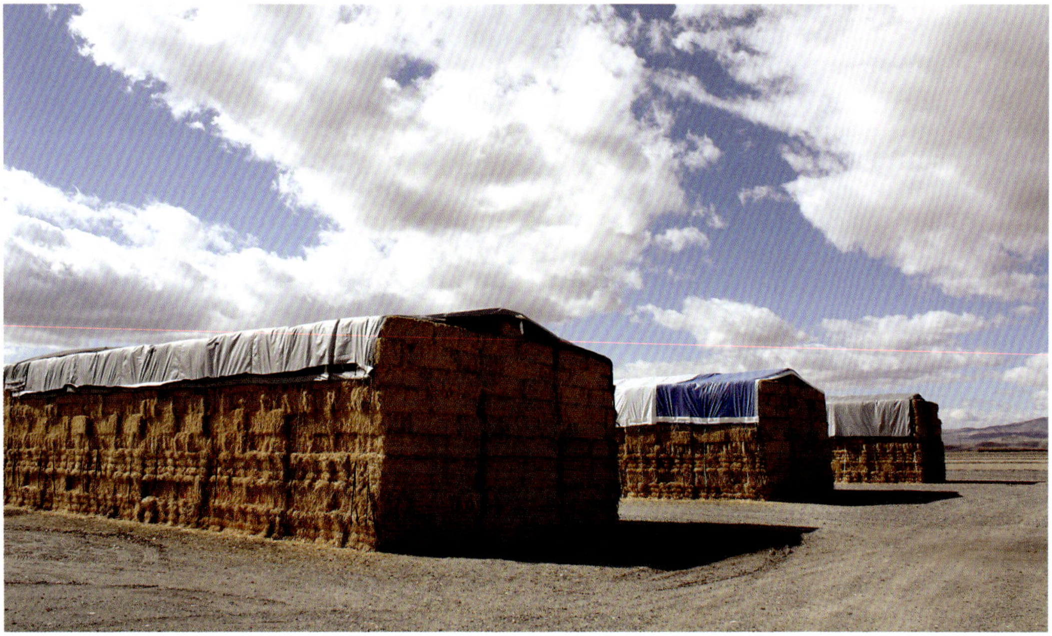

Hay is an important crop in Pershing County. It feeds local livestock during the lean months of winter and is also sold as an income crop.

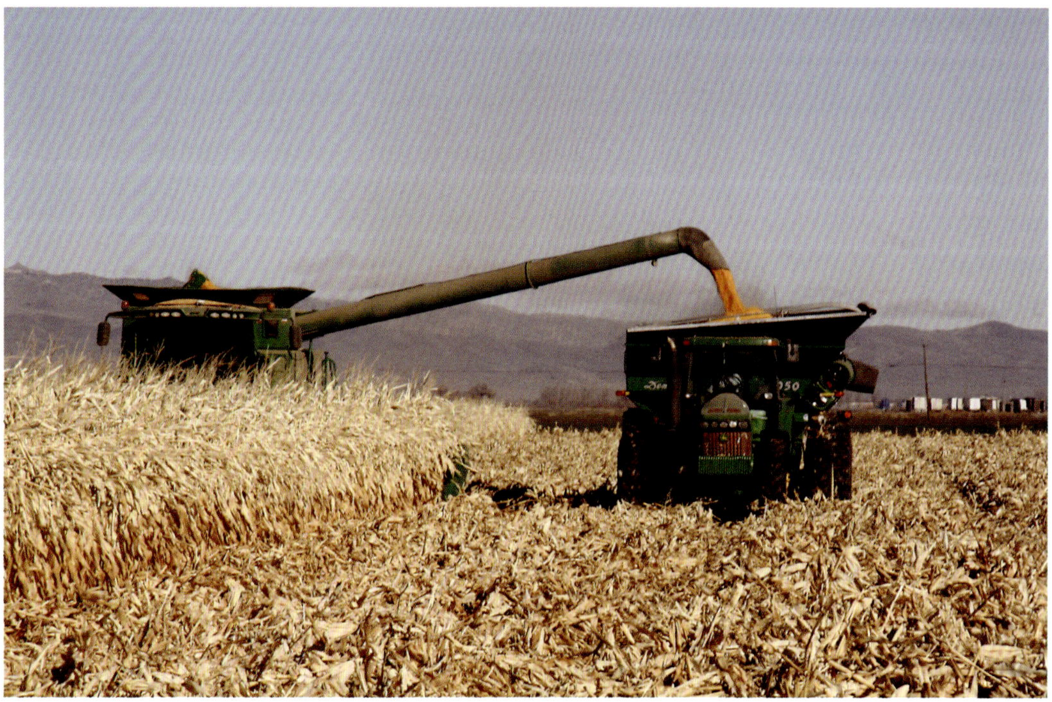

Corn is another important crop. Most of it is used to feed livestock.

interests, recreationists, and wildlife enthusiasts sometimes resent the loss of adequate water to sustain their needs.

In 2017, Pershing County Water Conservation District Manager Bennie Hodges told the *Lovelock Review-Miner* that "we seek to deepen our collective understanding of what sustainable and respectful water management means and how we (all farmers and ranchers) can work together." He added that some of the oldest water rights on the Humboldt River dated back to the late 1800s and had been consolidated into a cooperative irrigation system that was organized to end disputes over the valley's limited water resources.

Today, according to Pershing Country Agricultural Extension Agent Steve Foster, there are about 135 farms in Pershing County, primarily family-owned, with only a small scattering of corporate enterprises. These farms cover almost 40,000 acres, all of which are irrigated when water is available. Crops change as demands change. Formerly the region produced primarily alfalfa hay, then massive amounts of corn for feedlots. Today, production is more varied: farmers grow some alfalfa hay, winter wheat for crop rotation, field corn for dairies in the Fallon area, and teff—a high-yield, gluten-free grain native to Ethiopia that is particularly rich in protein and calcium.

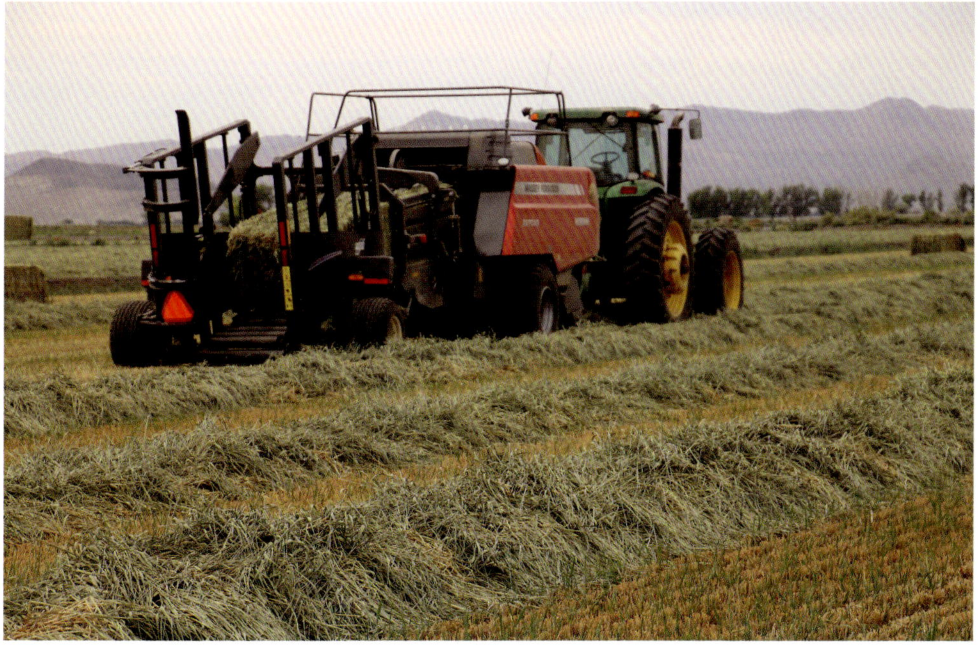

Nutritious alfalfa hay is another valuable crop.

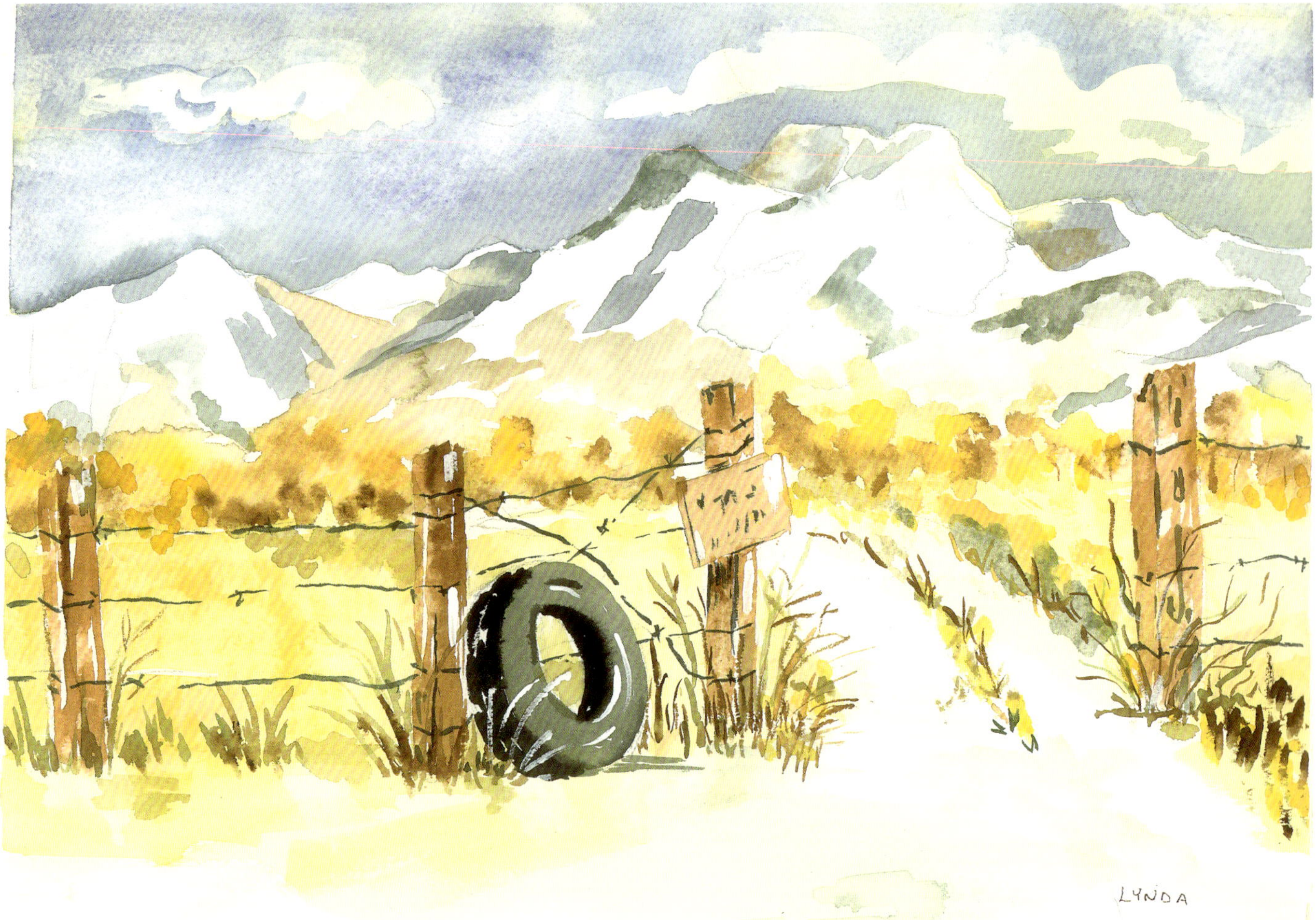

Pershing County landscape—grasslands, autumnal trees lining a riverbank, and snow-covered mountains. Watercolor by Lynda Quilici

Two historically well-known agricultural enterprises in Lovelock Valley are the Nevada Nile and Circle L ranches. The Nevada Nile was developed by Norman Biltz and his wealthy business partners in the 1930s. As Biltz recalled in his oral history, "Lovelock was in a disastrous condition" in the early 1930s. "Almost half of Lovelock Valley had been returned to the county for tax delinquencies . . . and a large portion was being held by the receivers." Biltz and his associates had little trouble getting a two-thirds vote in the Nevada legislature that would allow them to take over large pieces of land to rehabilitate the ranches.

Norman Biltz's Nevada Nile enterprises changed hands in the 1960s when Harvey McDougal and his son Richard began to buy land in both Upper and Lower Valleys. In 1963 the McDougals also bought the Lucky Livestock Feedlots, originally owned by the Lucky Lager Beer company. The newly formed Nevada Nile Ranches, or NNR, consisted of 12,000 acres of farmland in Lovelock Valley, and by 2017 NNR held 8,000 total acres, 7,560 of which hold water rights.

In recent years, farming has utilized state-of-the-art swathers, bailers, rakes, and even GPS-equipped tractors to cultivate the land and harvest its crops. Irrigation, however, remains labor-intensive, according to Robert McDougal, who oversees all NNR operations today, but the effort is well worth the toil. As a third-generation farmer and Pershing County commissioner, McDougal works with NNR and its stockholders and sees firsthand the products of this fertile Pershing County land.

Another major farm operation began in 1947 when Errett Lobban Cord, also known as E. L. Cord, bought 3,500 acres of alfalfa land in Lovelock Valley. Cord was a successful businessman and engineer with many interests. He was perhaps best known for his development of the Cord automobile, an innovative luxury vehicle manufactured between 1929 and 1941. During World War II he wanted to get his family away from the California coast, where he feared the threat of a Japanese invasion. Back in 1936, when he was flying his plane over the Sierra Nevada to his Silver Peak Mine, he had spotted "a green oasis with a lake" in the middle of Fish Lake Valley, and it included a handful of man-made structures. It was Dyer, Nevada, about seventy miles from Tonopah, and in May 1940 Cord bought this "oasis" of 2,200 acres for $66,000

This was the first of three Circle L ranches in Nevada. The second was in Jiggs, in Elko County, and the third was the Lovelock ranch. Cord brought

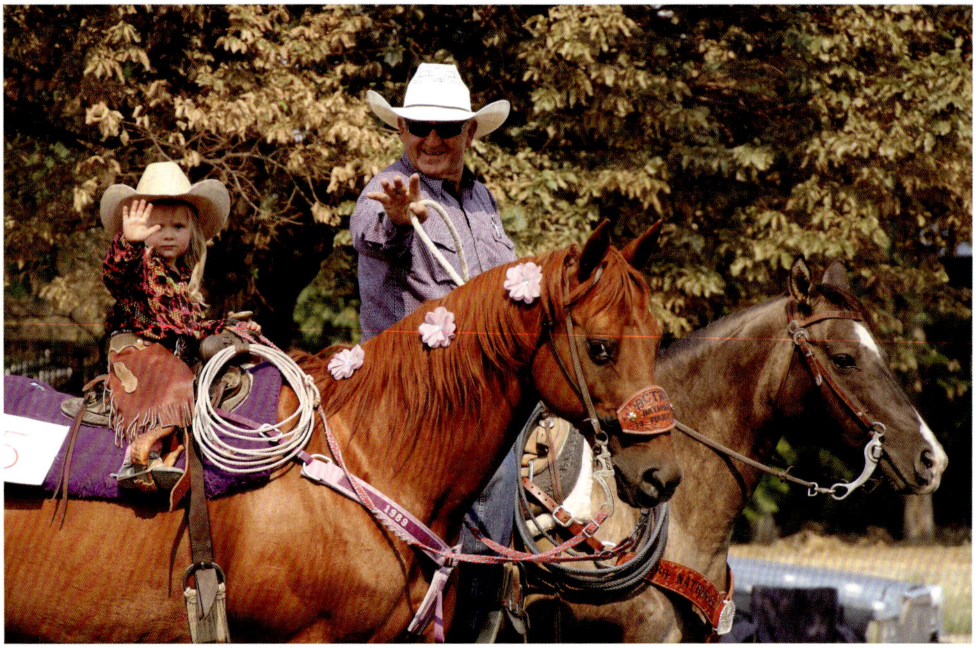

Dan Duncan is a rancher whose family has lived in Pershing County for several generations. In 2017 he rode in the annual Lovelock Frontier Days parade, accompanied by his granddaughter, Oneice Edmunds. That year, the Frontier Days festival celebrated Lovelock's hundredth anniversary as an incorporated town.

the well-known Los Angeles architect Paul Revere Williams to both Dyer and Lovelock to design the Circle L ranch houses and bunkhouses. Remembered in Reno for his design of the First Church of Christ the Scientist on Riverside Drive, and in Los Angeles for his design of the original terminal of the Los Angeles Airport, Williams used slump-stone blocks for the ranch buildings. Later he designed the Lovelock Inn using the same material.

The Circle L Ranch property was sold in 2004 to Louis Damonte Jr. and David Stix, and is now known as DNS. There are two DNS sister companies in Lovelock Valley—the Western Nevada Cattle Feeder LLC and the DNS Land & Livestock Company. According to Louis Damonte Jr., these holdings consist of almost 4,000 acres, 3,500 of which have deeded water rights.

• • •

Besides water for agriculture, Pershing County is rich in a variety of minerals, many with important commercial value—gold, silver, copper, tungsten, iron, gypsum, diatomite, and lithium. When flecks of gold were found in Nevada in 1850—in the Carson River in a place that came to be called Gold Canyon—Nevada became part of the gold-hunting madness that drew thousands of people to California. By 1861 fortune-seeking prospectors were finding silver and gold in the Humboldt Range and a few years later in the Trinity Range. The boom-and-bust cycle had arrived in what was later to be Pershing County.

When the lodes were exhausted, the boom days were over and many of these mining settlements were abandoned as quickly as they had grown up. Today, some are ghost towns, haunting reminders of the days when optimistic miners were pulling wealth from the rocks of Pershing County. Others have vanished completely, known only by local legend, a few mine tailings, or some broken masonry where there was once a vibrant town.

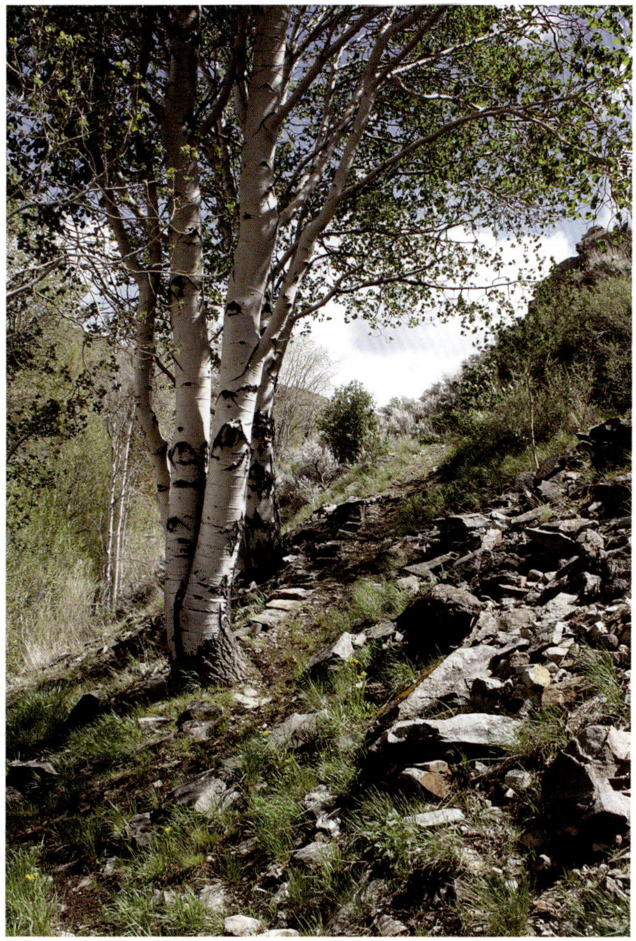

The Buena Vista Canyon, where Unionville is located, is one of the most scenic mining areas in the state.

One of these booms began in Buena Vista Canyon, undoubtedly one of the most beautiful of Nevada's mining canyons. Silver was discovered here shortly before the Civil War began, and its first settlers were miners who sympathized with the Confederate cause. They named their town Dixie. The name didn't last long. Very soon, northern sympathizers prevailed and began calling the area Unionville. By July 1861 the Unionville town site was platted. Miners continued to arrive. The years between 1863 and 1870 were the boom times for Unionville.

The area's most famous visitor was a young man named Samuel L. Clemens—not yet known by his pen-name, Mark Twain. He had been living in Carson City but left to strike it rich in the new silver-mining camp near the Humboldt River. Years later, in his book *Roughing It,* Mark Twain included an account that first appeared in Virginia City's *Daily Territorial Enterprise*: "I shall be candid with you. I shall express an honest opinion, based upon a thorough examination. Humboldt County [including today's Pershing County] is the richest mineral region upon God's footstool. Each mountain range is gorged

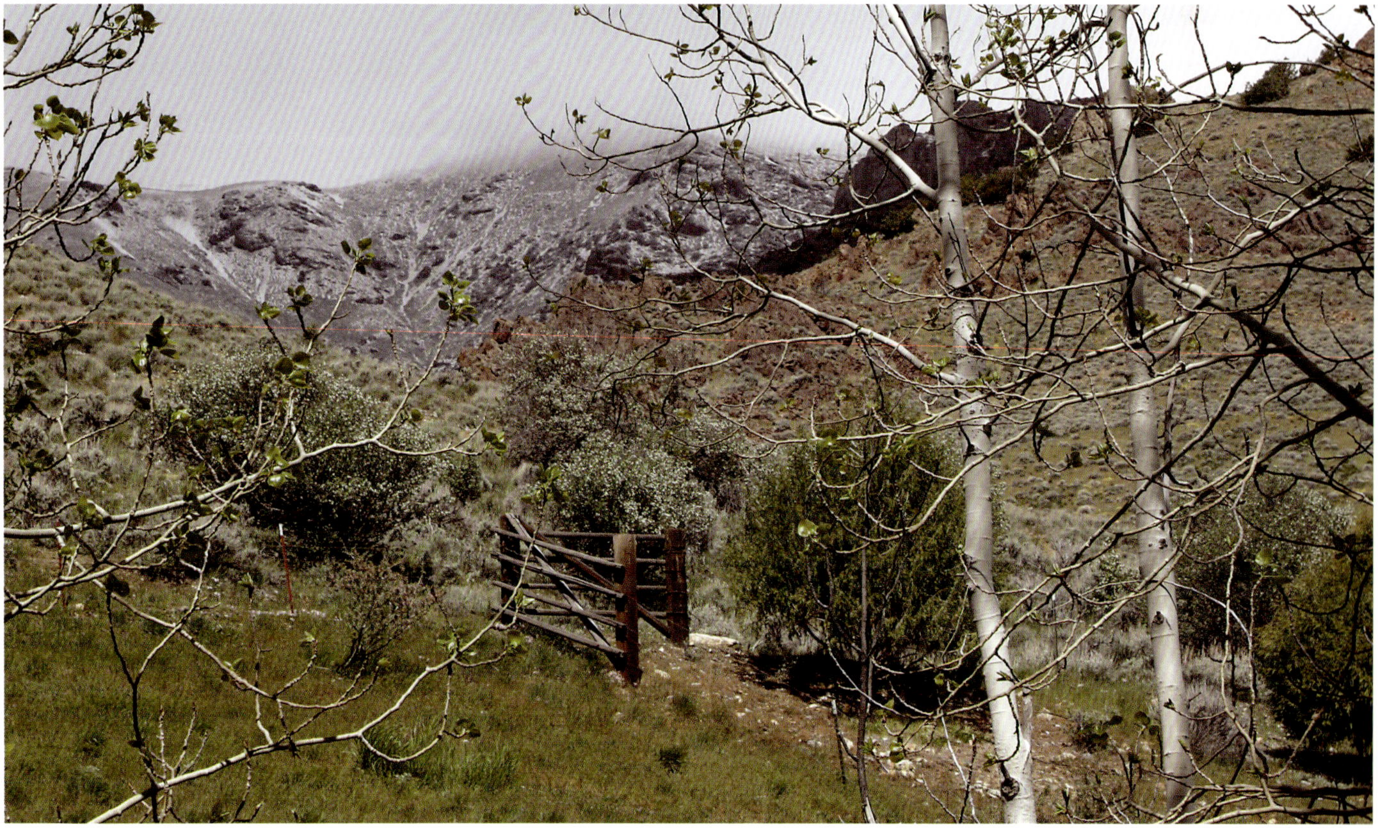

The ranges of Unionville.

with the precious ores. Humboldt is the true Golconda." Mark Twain's exaggerated prose convinced many miners that Buena Vista Canyon was "the place," and today, if visitors listen carefully to the winds in the canyon, they can hear the digging, the excitement, and the hope that echoed through Unionville over 150 years ago.

In the Humboldt Range, silver was the dominant ore, often found in inaccessible areas that made transportation expensive and challenging even after completion of the railroad. Rochester started out as a gold camp in the 1860s, but silver took over by 1900. According to historian Stanley Paher, "By 1913, 2200 men lived in Rochester and Lower Rochester: streets were laid out, buildings constructed between tents, two newspapers published, saloons, dance halls, a post office, and even the Rochester Philharmonic Orchestra civilized the inhabitants."

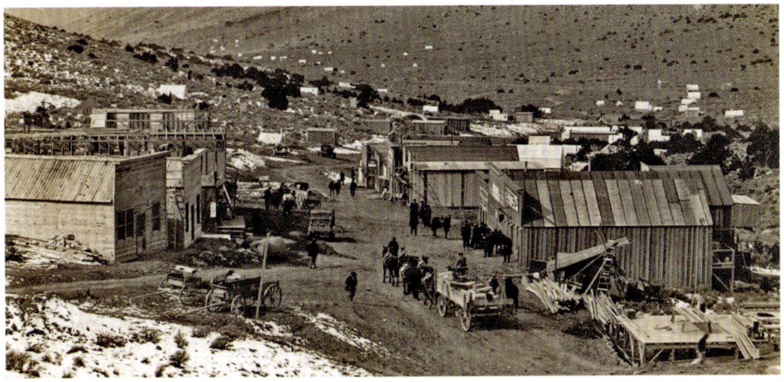

LEFT: *Rochester street scene, 1909. Courtesy Special Collections Department, University of Nevada, Reno Libraries.*

BELOW: *Standard Mine in the 1940s. Photo courtesy Paul Davidson.*

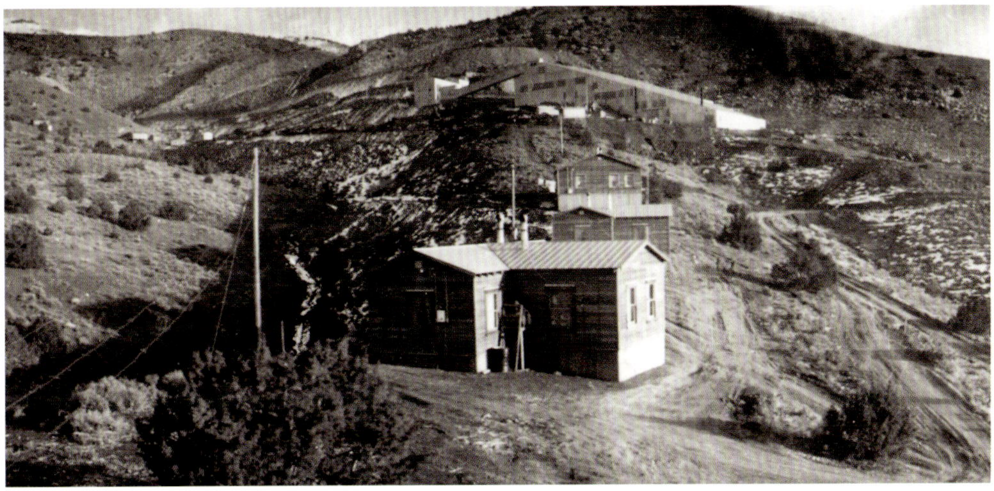

Dun Glen (also known for a short time as Chafey) dates to 1862, when silver was discovered nearby. In 1863, and again in 1865, U.S. Army troops were garrisoned at Camp Dun Glen to protect local settlers from Black Rock Tom and his band of renegades, who were terrorizing the area. Perhaps controlling the miners was also part of the garrison's orders. "In all events," a May 1867 advertisement for the Telegraph Saloon in Dun Glen, which both miners and soldiers would have frequented, tells readers, "you can take a chair and put your feet upon the card tables, and tell a pretty story about money you once had when stocks were up; and about how much better your ledge gets as you widen down where it pinches out. All that sort of talk gives tone to a well regulated saloon."

Seven Troughs is another mining camp that enjoyed a period of glory. When the mines around Tonopah and Goldfield petered out, miners from

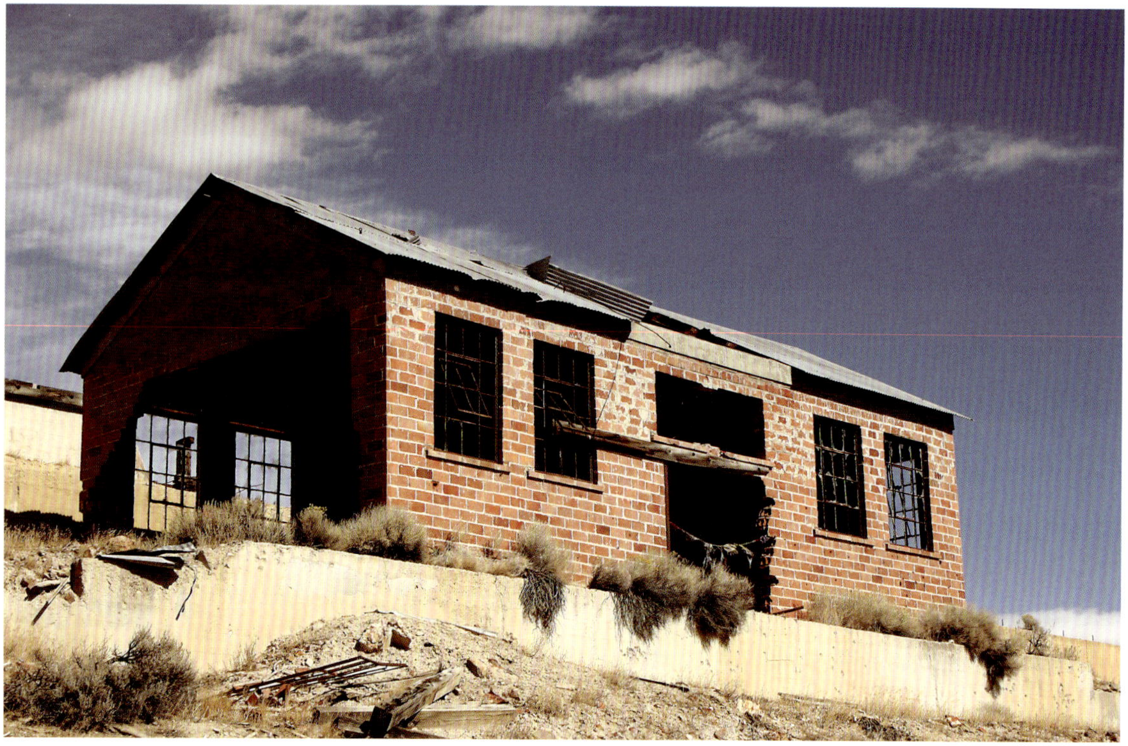

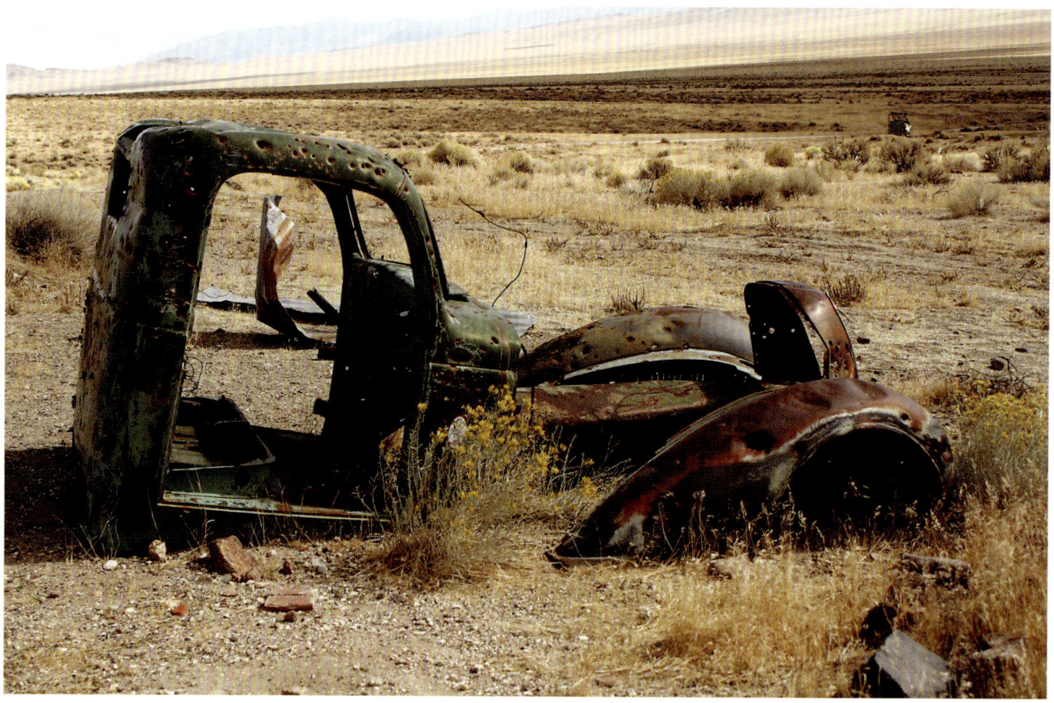

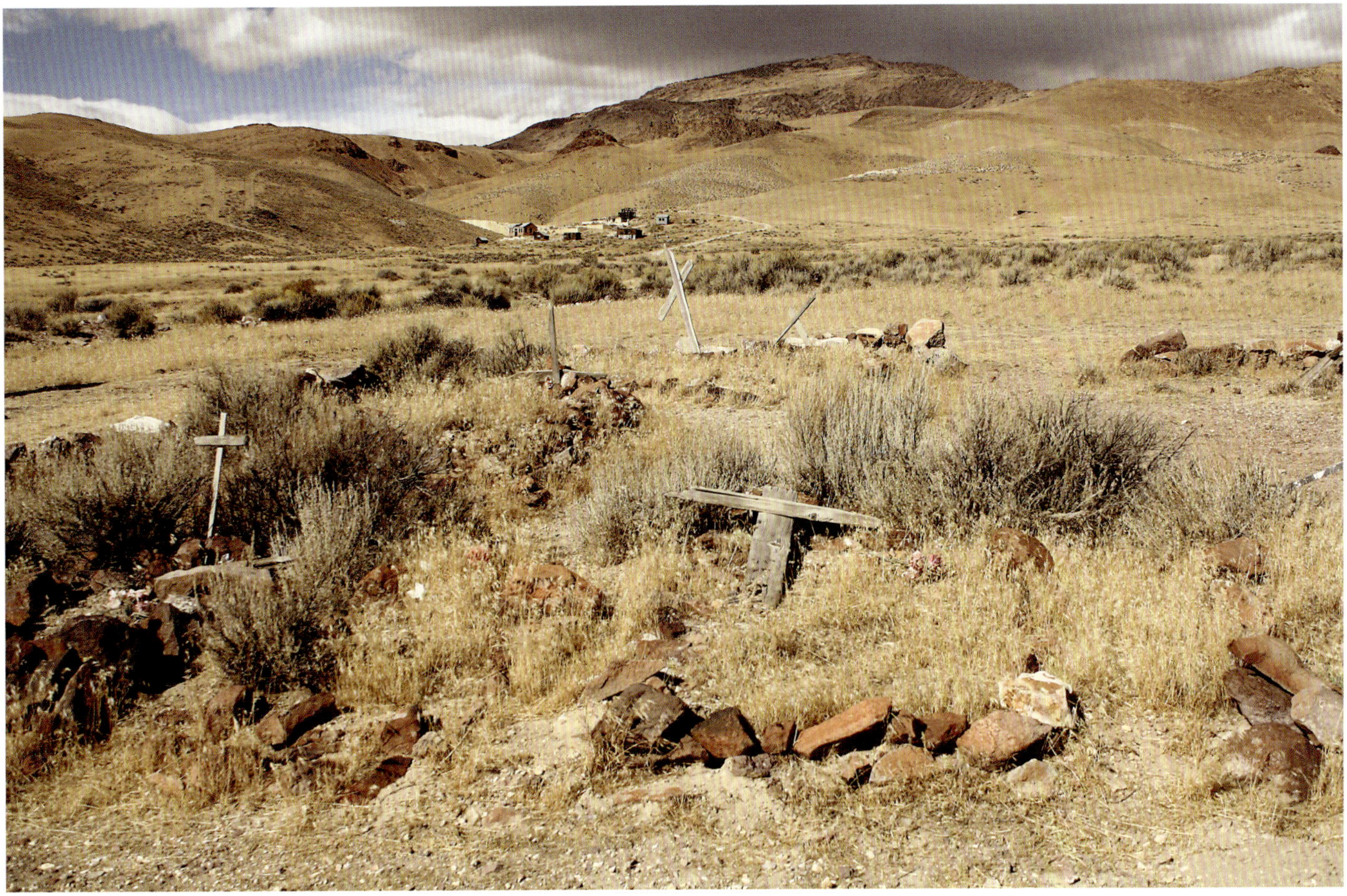

Seven Troughs cemetery.

FACING PAGE: *Abandoned at Seven Troughs.*

that area found success in Seven Troughs. The settlement soon grew to include families. Supplies were hauled in from Lovelock, and a school district was established there by 1908. Maude Frazier, who became one of Nevada's most prominent female politicians in the 1950s, began her teaching career in Lovelock but moved to Seven Troughs in 1908. By 1937 the gold veins had played out, and the camp declined. However, it was slower to fade than many of its counterparts, and its remaining residents eked out a livelihood until the end of World War I.

Scossa, forty-six miles northwest of Lovelock, was the scene of the last gold rush in Nevada. The mines became active in 1907, but the initial boom lasted only a few months. However, in 1930, brothers Charles and James Scossa staked out new claims in the area, and the *Saturday Evening Post* picked up news of their strike and wrote a feature article about it, prompting a new gold rush that lasted until the gold veins played out in 1937, when the camp declined and quietly passed into the limbo of ghost towns.

The history of mining in Pershing County can be broken into three phases. In the years before World War I, hardscrabble miners seeking precious metals scoured the hills and canyons, filing claims that were often worthless or produced just enough to pay their expenses. After the war, a wider spectrum of minerals was in demand, especially from industrialized counties that had to import the raw materials needed for their factories and manufacturing.

Today we are in an era of large-scale corporate mining. According to Dana Bennett, president of the Nevada Mining Association, "Mining today is a global industry. Some corporate offices are located outside the United States, many in Toronto, Canada, and many Nevada mines are part of larger companies that also have operations outside the United States. Certainly, a Nevada mine's production becomes part of the global supply chain." Modern exploratory drilling, sophisticated financial analysis, open-pit mining, and the ability to process relatively low-grade ores profitably have brought corporate mining to Pershing County, and these large-scale mining ventures have brought renewed energy to the county's economy.

Tungsten is one of the most important post-World War I metals. It is used as a hardening alloy in the manufacture of steel, and for much of the twentieth century it was a foundation of Pershing County mining. Scheelite ores (the source of tungsten) were discovered eight miles west of Mill City in 1914 by prospectors looking for gold and silver. This became the site of the Nevada Massachusetts Company, "the granddaddy of Nevada tungsten

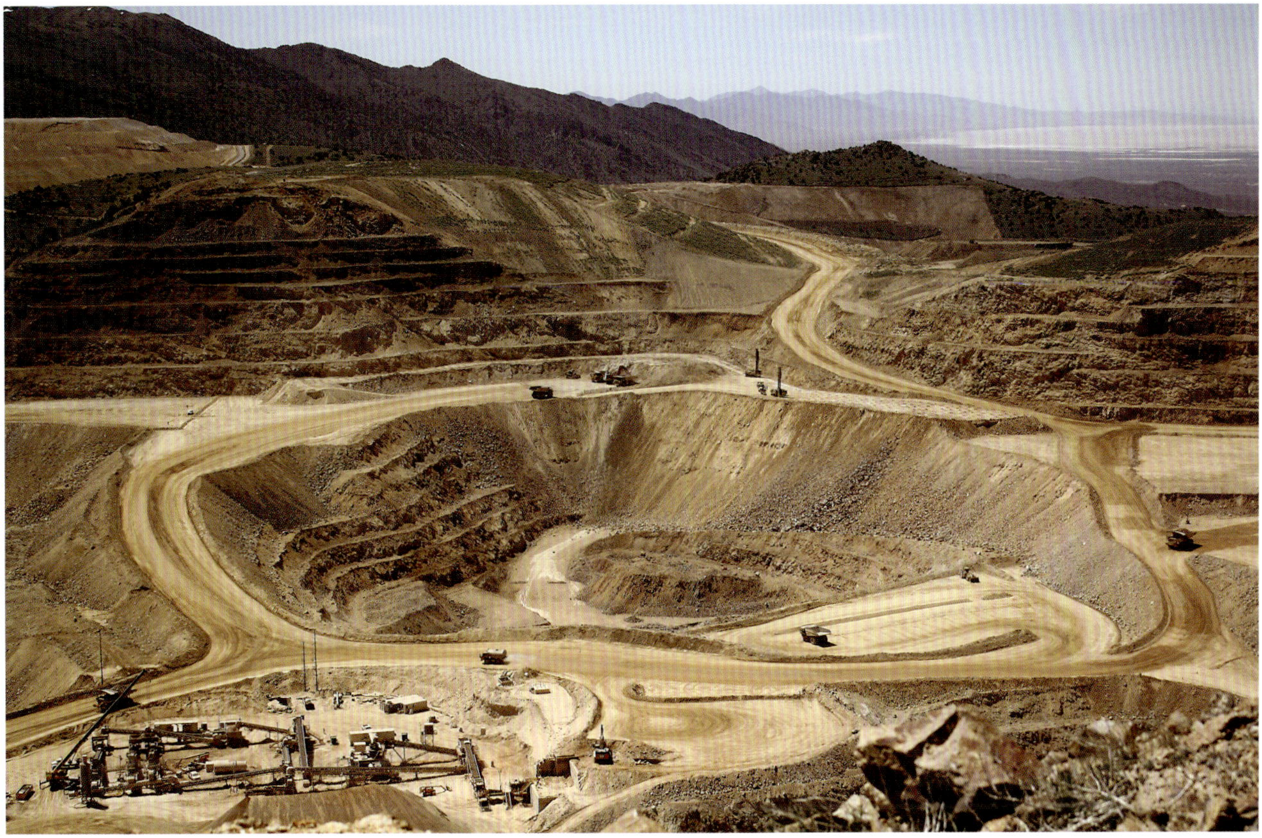

ABOVE: *The Coeur Rochester Mine is a vast open-pit, heap-leach operation northeast of Lovelock, extracting both gold and silver with the use of modern mining and extraction methods. It employs over 250 people and strives to operate in an environmentally responsible manner.*

RIGHT: *Coeur Rochester Mine.*

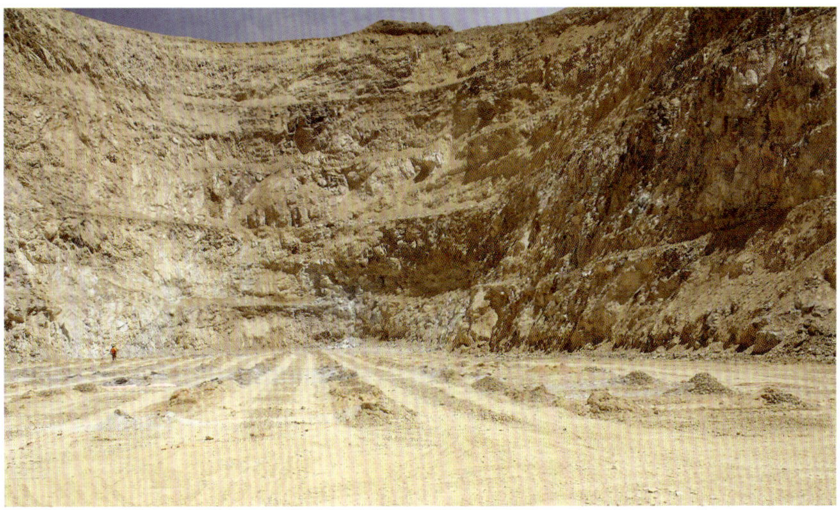

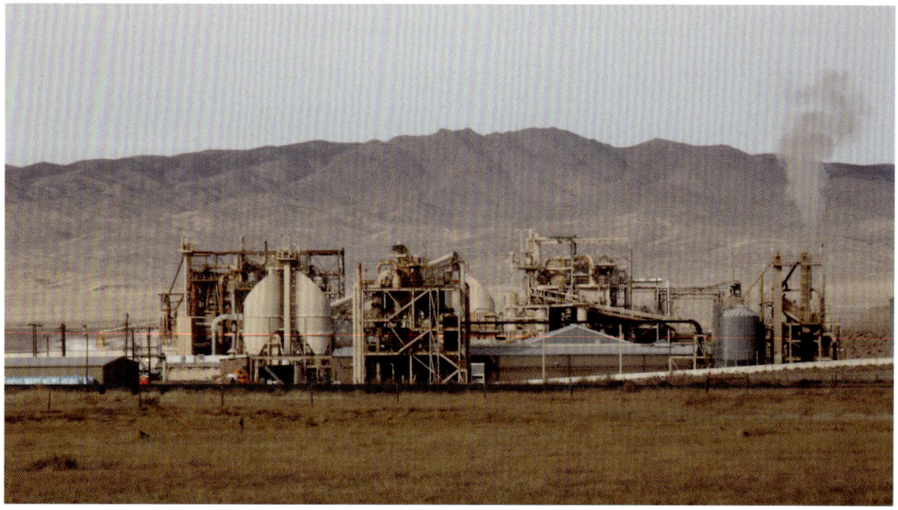

EaglePicher Minerals in the Trinity Range north of Lovelock. Pershing County is a major source of diatomite (diatomaceous earth), a versatile mineral with many uses in agriculture, explosives, water filtration, personal care, and even kitty litter.

mines." This company produced scheelite concentrates almost continually from World War I until 1958. The company town was called Tungsten and for a time was the second-largest town in Pershing County.

The Toulon Gravity Mill west of Lovelock was also a major tungsten producer, although not on the scale of Nevada Massachusetts. Pershing County tungsten production outpaced all other counties in Nevada from 1916 until 1982 by almost 2 million units.

Today, precious metals are once again an important focus of mining in Pershing County. The largest employer in the county is Coeur Rochester, Inc., which employs over 250 people. It is the only primary silver mine in Nevada, although gold is a secondary product of Coeur Rochester's huge surface mines.

There are several other major players in the Pershing County precious metals economy. Rye Patch Mining US Inc., which owns the Florida Canyon Gold Mine, is important, as are the Pershing Gold Corporation, the Newmont Mining Corporation, and several others. EP Minerals (formerly Eagle Pitcher Industries) is the second largest producer of diatomite in the world. But mining standards today are very different from the hasty and often careless practices of the past. Many of these corporate operations are located on public land, so by law they must consider the environmental impact of their operations and commit to the reclamation of the land once their mining activities are finished. In 2016, the Florida Canyon Mine received an award for its excellence in reclamation.

BURNING MAN

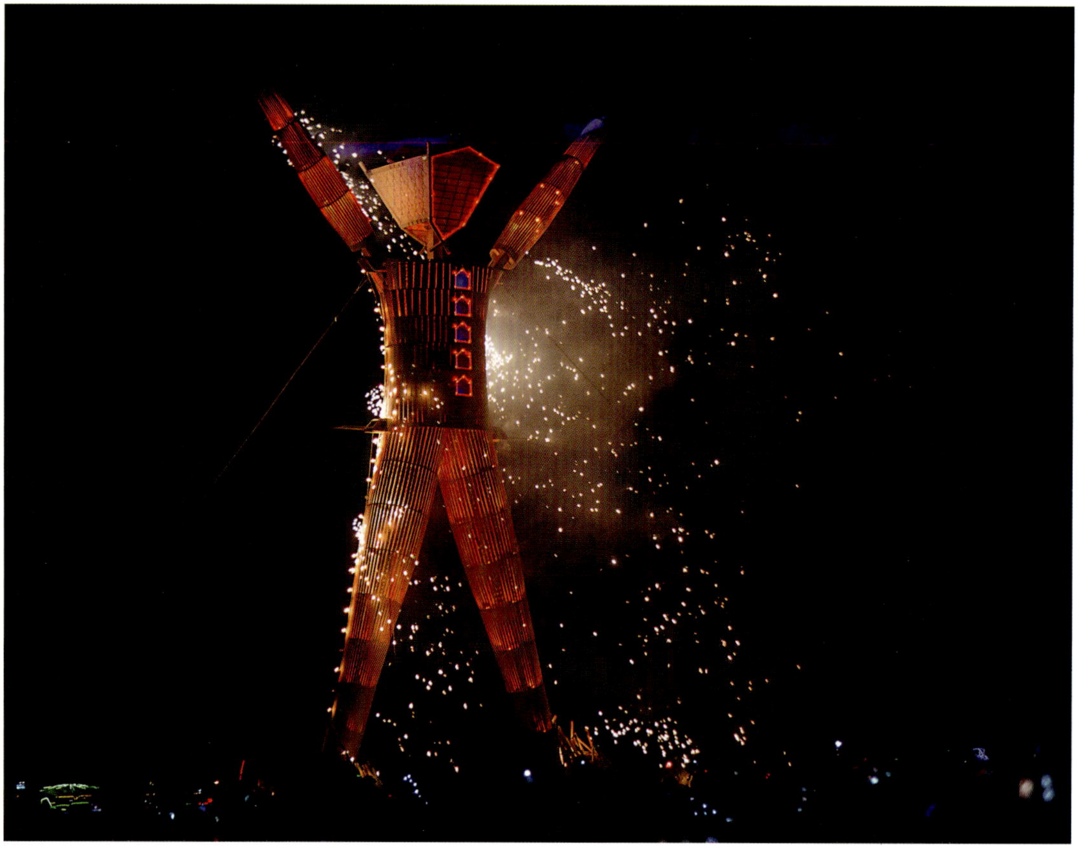

Burning Man, 2014. The Man. Photo by Spencer Jones.

For most of the year, Pershing County pursues its generally quiet and bucolic life, the scattered farms, ranches, and mines providing jobs and materials that enhance the lives of people far beyond the county's borders. But on the last Sunday of every August, all this changes. Suddenly, as if by magic, a city of 70,000 people appears in the middle of the county's least hospitable setting, the austere Black Rock Desert. Then, after a week of celebration it vanishes just as suddenly. No, this is not the mythical village of Brigadoon. It's Black Rock City, a community created by attendees of the world-famous Burning Man festival. And for these few days, it is also the sixth-largest urban community in the state of Nevada.

Although some people consider Burning Man an arts festival and others see it as a free-spirited, week-long bohemian party, it is actually part of a global cultural movement based on ten practical principles: radical inclusion, gifting, decommodification, radical self-expression, radical self-reliance, communal effort, civic responsibility, leaving no trace, participation, and immediacy. The attendees see themselves as a network of people inspired by the values embodied in the Ten Principles, united in the pursuit of a more creative and connected existence in the world.

Burning Man began in 1986 in San Francisco on Baker Beach, where founder Larry Harvey (d. 2018) and his friends met to explore various forms of artistic self-expression for the pleasure of all participants. The gathering ended with the ritual burning of a large wooden effigy of "The Man." In 1990, the event moved to Nevada's Black Rock Desert, where participants created Black Rock City, a temporary metropolis intended as an experiment in community and art. This community, limited to a population of 70,000 since 2015, encourages the active participation of all "Burners," as attendees call themselves. And their productions are prodigious: experimental and interactive sculptures; erection of "temples" and other structures; performances

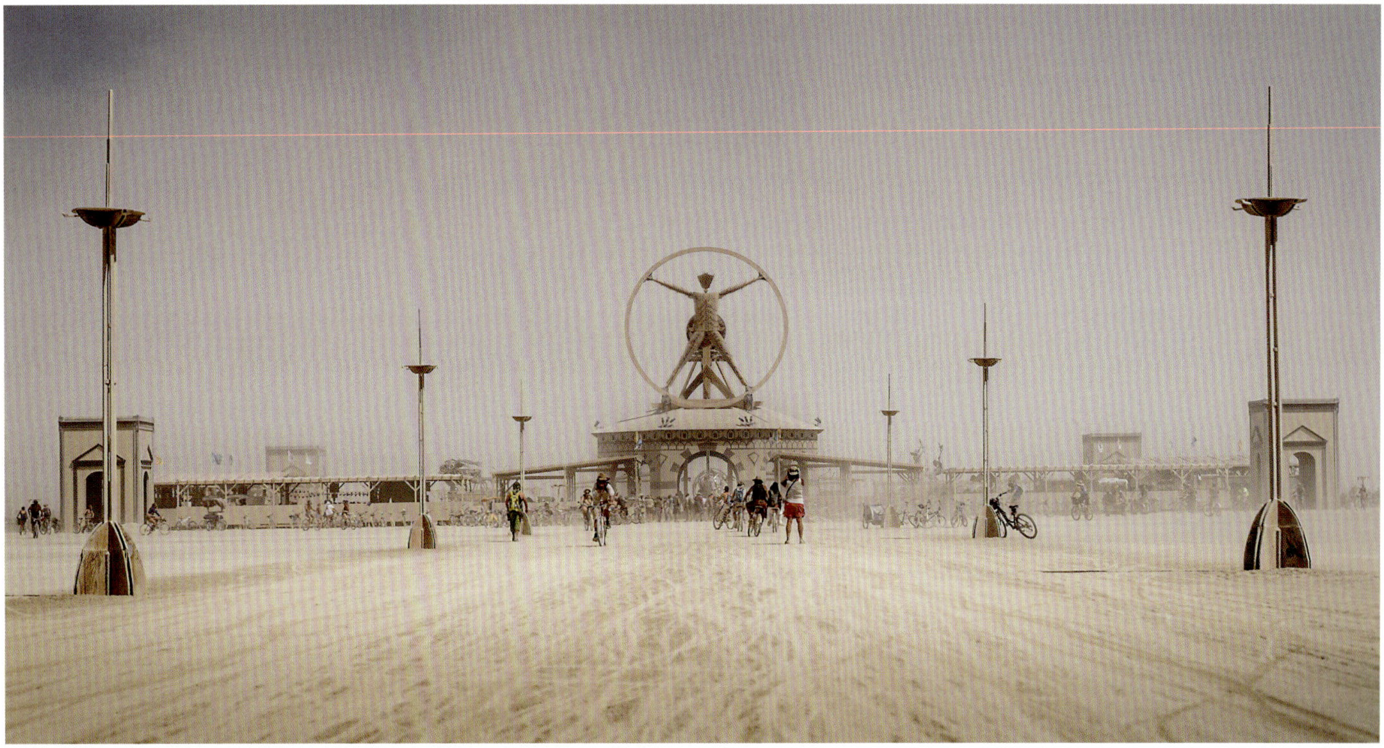

Burning Man street scene. Bicycles are a popular mode of transportation around the sprawling site. Photo by Spencer Jones.

of music and dance; and "art cars"—vehicles that have been modified to provide both an artistic contribution to the event as well as transportation around the sprawling site. On the final Saturday evening of the gathering, the ritual burning of The Man brings the community together in a moment of joy and wonder.

The creation of a community in the middle of the Black Rock Desert is possible because of the permission and cooperation of Pershing County and the federal Bureau of Land Management, and the aspirational principle of "leave no trace" is actively enforced. When Burners depart on Labor Day, they are required to bring out with them everything they brought in, and the site itself is expected to be left as pristine as it was before Black Rock City sprang from the hard playa and dust.

• • •

Annually, a small group of Pershing County seniors satisfy their curiosity about the Black Rock Desert's pop-up city on the playa, which is populated by people from all over the world. In late August 2017, on a Tuesday, the creators of this book joined twelve others who left Lovelock, turned right at Fernley, drove past Pyramid Lake, Nixon, Empire, and Gerlach, and finally arrived at the entrance to the famed playhouse on the playa. Little did we know how lucky we would be, because all veteran Burners traditionally sport tutus on Tuesday.

As guests of the Burning Man organization, the group from the Pershing County Senior Center in Lovelock visited the playa for a matter of hours to feel, see, and experience the drama in the desert in the county's northernmost region. We arrived in a cloud of dust, a famed Pershing County *haboob* or dust storm. However, we weren't there yet. Visibility for our driver was zero, and inside our van we masked our faces. Volunteers from the Burning Man organization huddled in tiny teepees at the entrance, and everything came to a halt. Twenty minutes later, the *haboob* lifted and moved on, and so did we, covered in the ritualistic playa dust.

We seniors visited Black Rock City as "Virgin Burners" from Lovelock and were overwhelmed by the panoply of color, activity, movement, and our desire to see everything at once. The hundreds of Porta-potties were reassuring, as was the location of the first-aid station, but, with that filed away, we began experiencing the extravaganza. The magnificence of unfolding scenes never before imagined took over. For this writer, the bicycles were

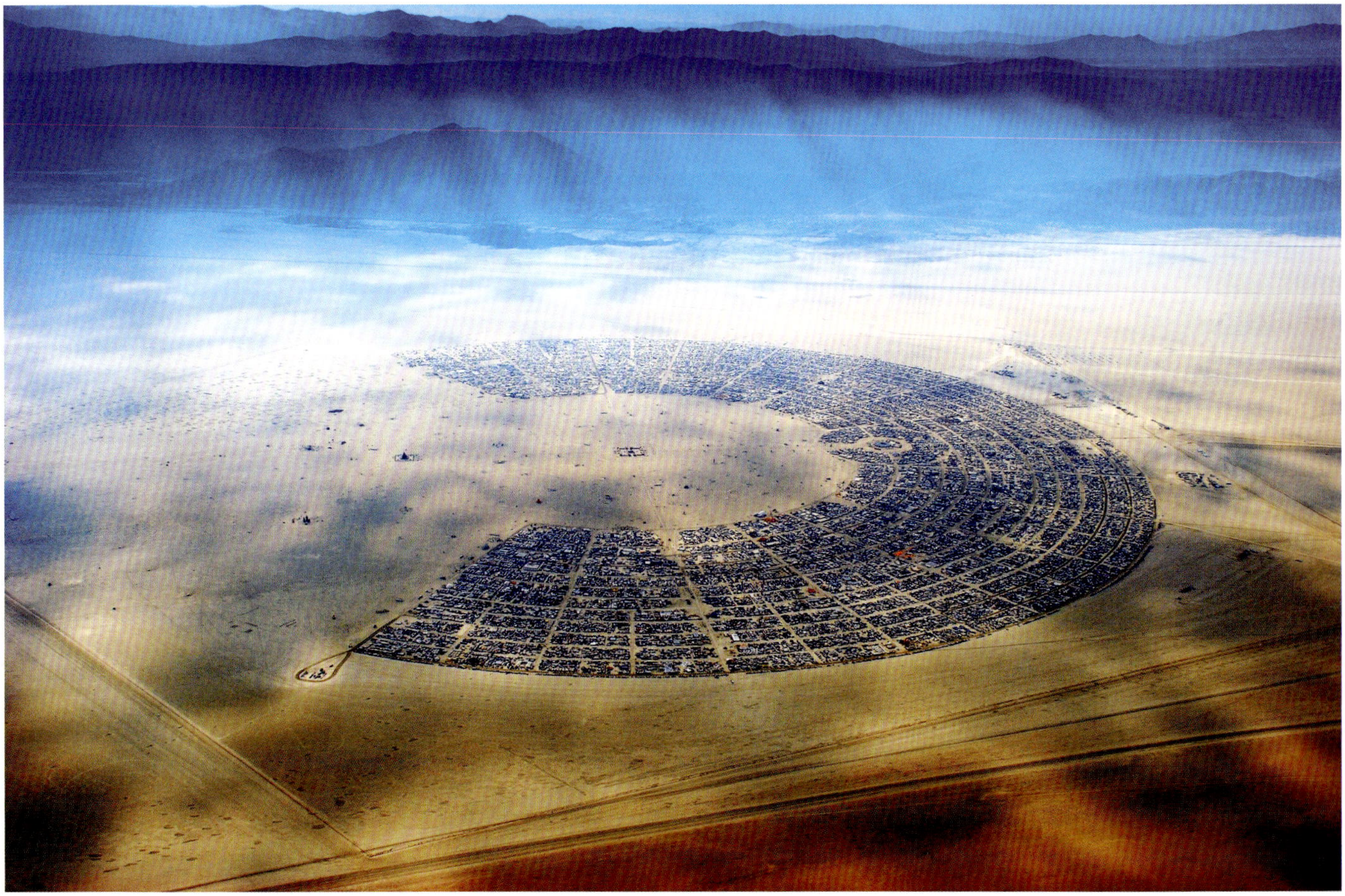

Aerial view of Burning Man City. Photo by Will Roger Peterson.

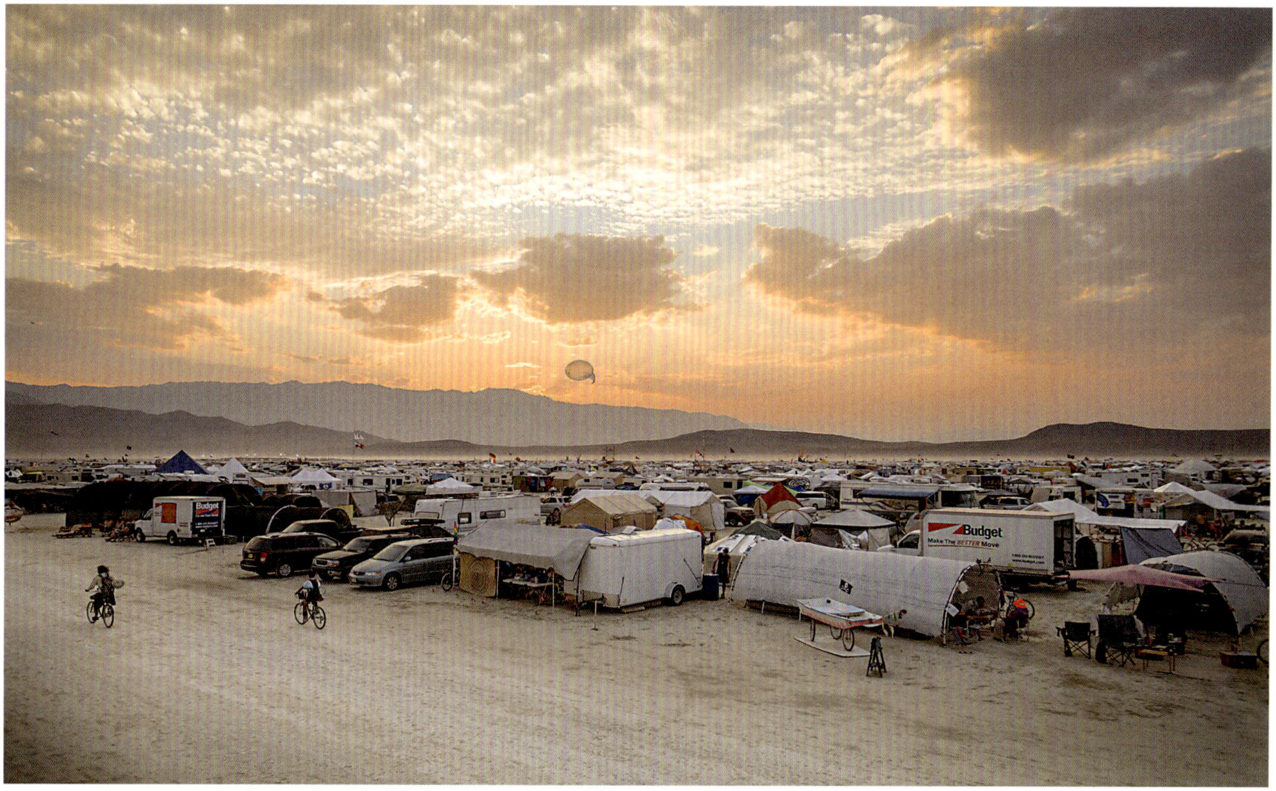

Burning Man City. Photo by Spencer Jones.

captivating, especially as the sun went down and they began to glow, sparkle, shimmer, and glide over the flat playa.

The Burning Man organization provides a double-decker art car for invited guests, and a narrator who explains that the "Community of Compassionate Care" began on the playa in 1990 after it left Baker Beach in San Francisco and has grown to the organized, people-friendly, safe gathering it is today. Literature and maps point out the busy airport that supports private planes from all over the world, the Center Camp where ice and coffee can be purchased (the only two items sold at Black Rock City), Kidsville (an area for children), and almost one hundred other locales satisfying every need and desire, from a cup of tea to wild and crazy dancing, plus all the titillating activities that have made Burning Man famous. Participants include

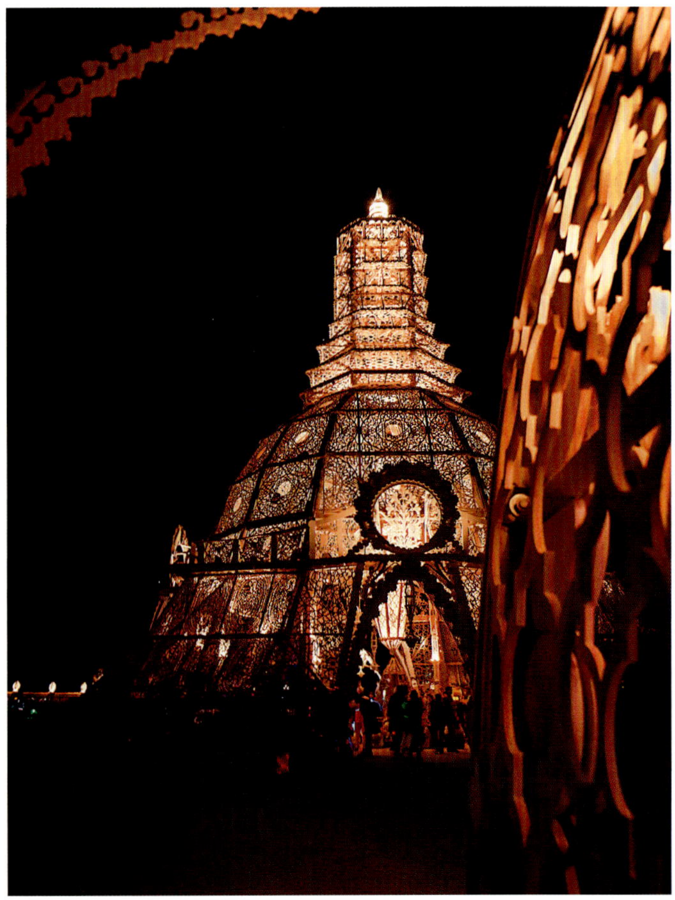

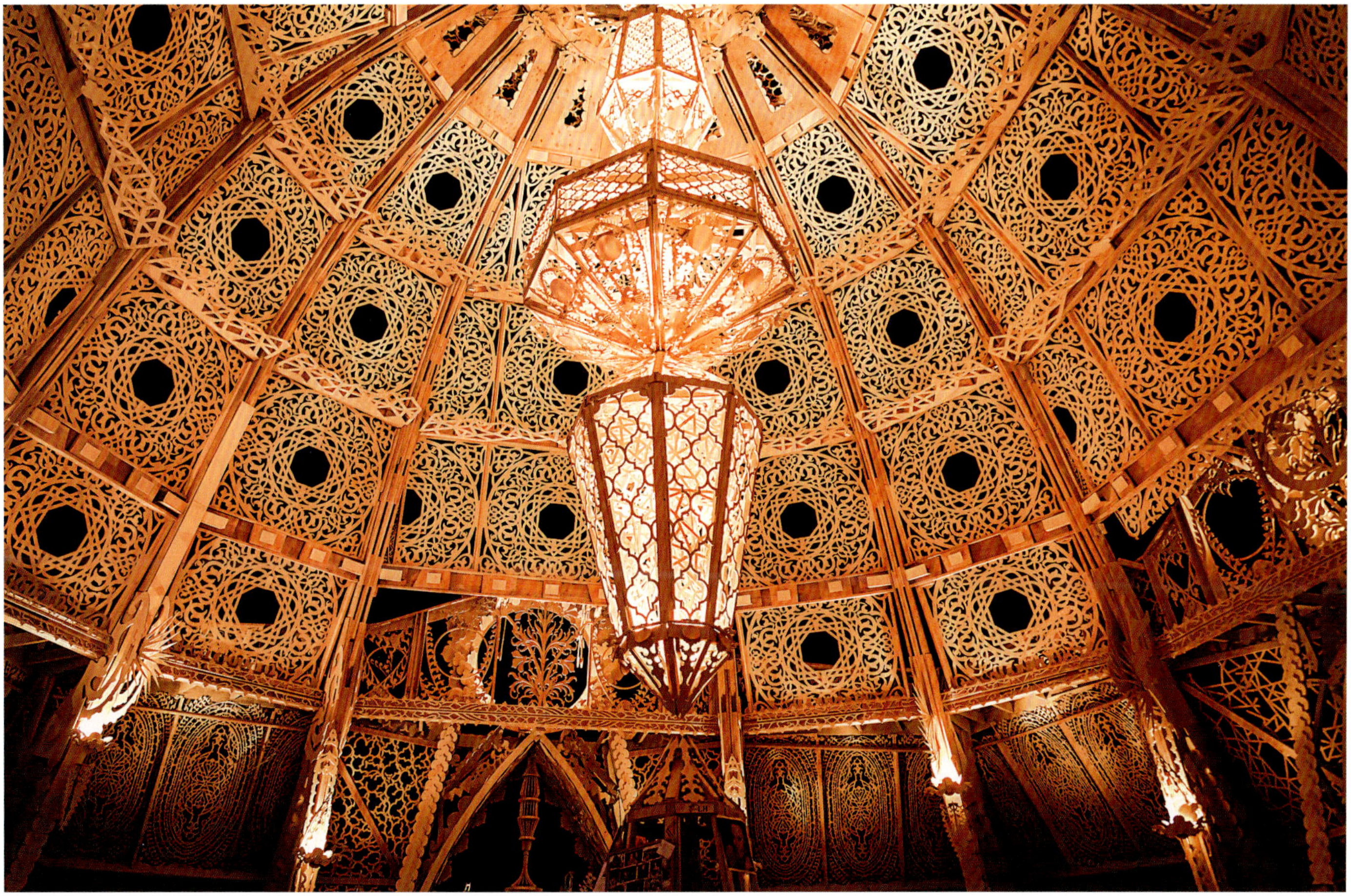

The Temple, 2014, interior. Photo by Spencer Jones.

FACING PAGE: *The Temple, 2014. Photo by Spencer Jones.*

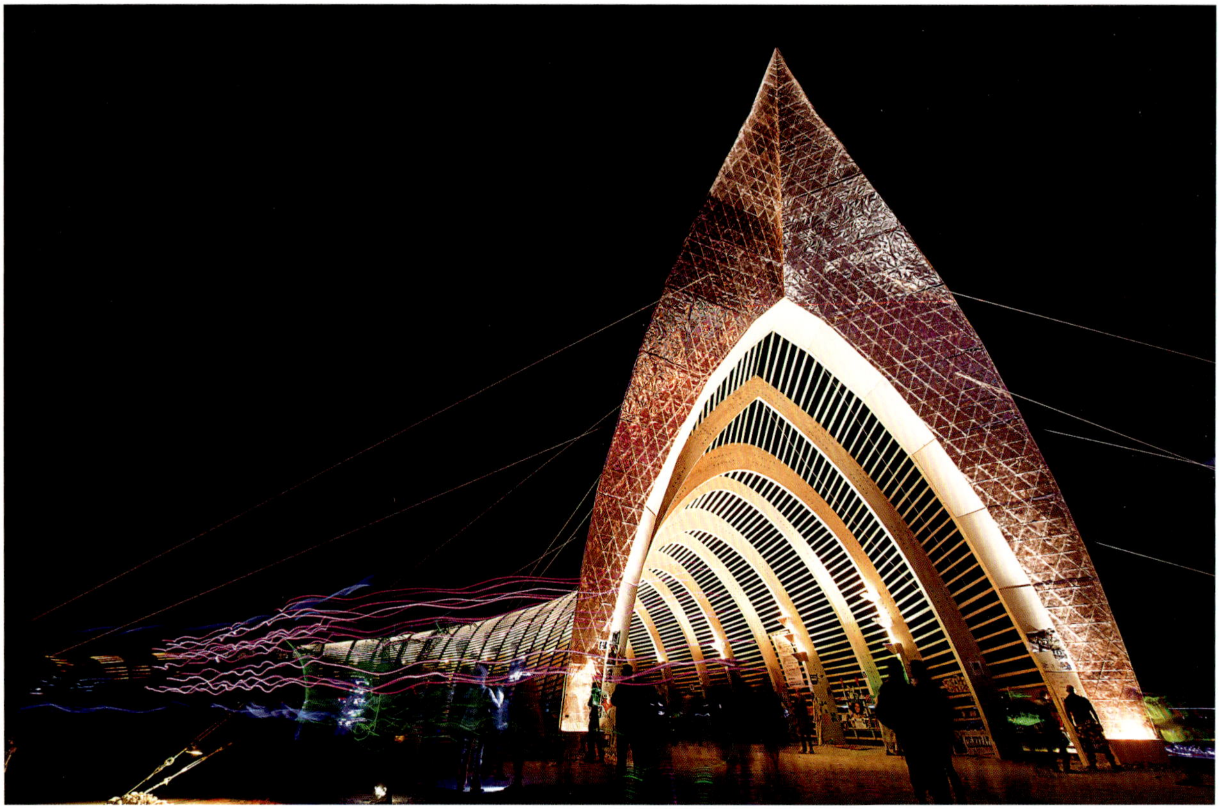

The Temple, 2015. Photo by Spencer Jones.

corporate CEOs, movie stars, rock stars, techies, folks who love "Radical Ritual," and the yearly seniors from Lovelock.

After the incredible dust at the entrance, our group had a night with a glowing half-moon, sharply focused stars, jet planes zooming above, and no dust! Our art car drove past The Man, which burns on the final Saturday night, The Temple, which burns on Sunday night, and all the other traditional and new installations, including a tree illuminated with seven thousand LED lights; statuary, including a massive bust of poet Maya Angelou; fifteen-foot-tall metal flowers spewing fire and groans; and art cars in every imaginable shape from dragons to frogs. The art cars, which debuted in 1991, must be registered with the DMV, the Department of Mutant Vehicles,

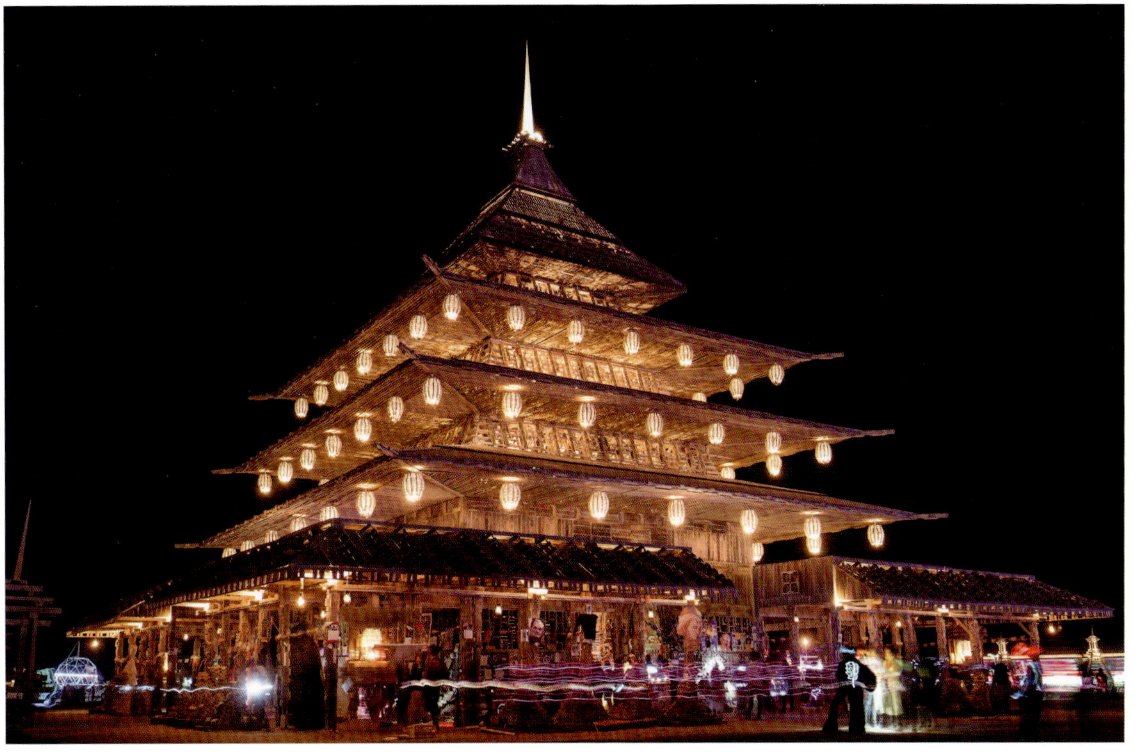

The Temple, 2016. Photo by Spencer Jones.

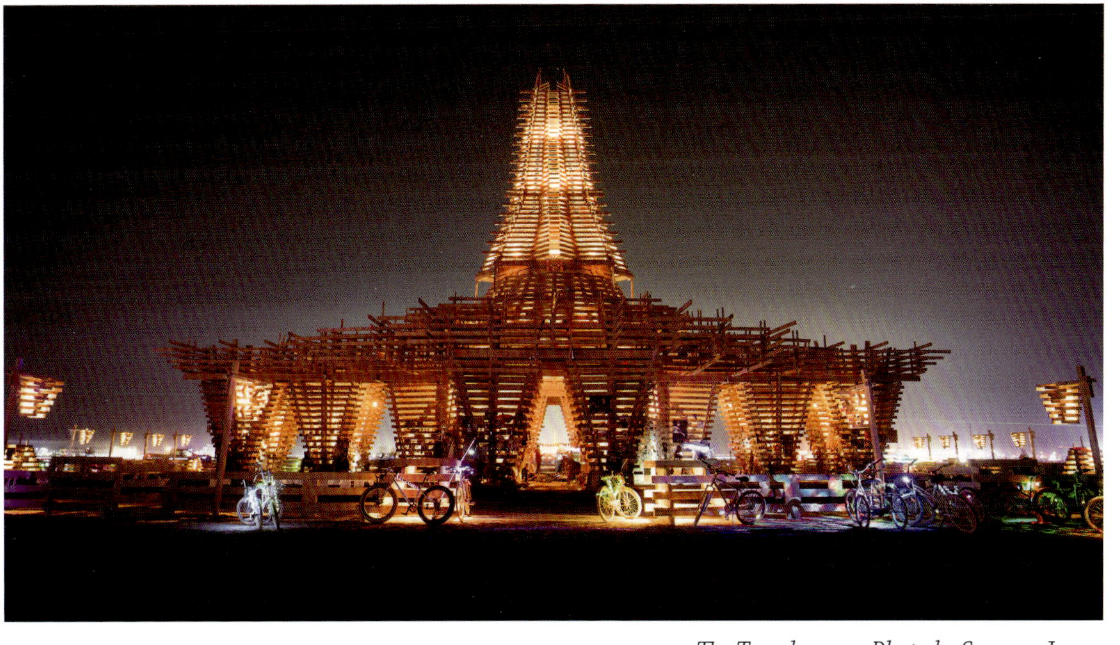

The Temple, 2017. Photo by Spencer Jones.

because all aspects of the community now have guidelines to maintain a safe environment for 70,000 people one week a year. This is no longer the free-for-all that began on the playa in 1990.

As official Burners, we became interested in MOOP—Matter Out Of Place—a perpetual endeavor to leave no trace on the playa: no feathers, no glitter, no paper, no cloth, no cans, no nothing! We were careful Burners. And we were educated Burners: we learned that the Burning Man organization catalyzed Black Rock Solar, which has funded solar installations in several Pershing County schools and at the county hospital and nursing home, and that it has sponsored a wide range of projects in other U.S. cities and rural areas intended to provide cultural enrichment and needed services to underserved populations. The organization also pays for the services of the county law-enforcement agencies and the Bureau of Land Management, which oversee the event.

Burning Man has had two locations in northern Nevada, and at one point even considered moving to Goldfield. The event started in Nevada in Pershing County in 1990, moved to Washoe County in 1997, and moved back to Pershing in 1998 and seems to have found its home there. Burning Man continues to "curate creativity and be a steward of the imagination." At his lecture at the Nevada Art Museum on July 13, 2017, Will Roger Peterson, Burning Man Founding Board Member and Board Chairman, said that about 65 percent of the people who attend return after their first visit.

• • •

And the spirit of Burning Man doesn't die when the Burners depart at the end of the gathering. Similar smaller events are held in many sites around the world to introduce the Ten Principles to new participants, and many of the art pieces that are displayed for the enjoyment of Burning Man attendees move on to become temporary or permanent works of public art around the U.S.

Putting the Principles of gifting and civic responsibility into action, for many years Burners have served as volunteer helpers when disasters have struck. One of the organization's programs, Burners Without Borders, provided assistance to victims of Hurricane Katrina in 2005. In 2017, when the Burning Man event concluded, a large contingent of Burners Without Borders headed for the Texas coast as volunteer workers to help victims of Hurricane Harvey. They brought with them massive amounts of supplies and cash, all donated by attendees. As Christopher Breedlove, BWB program

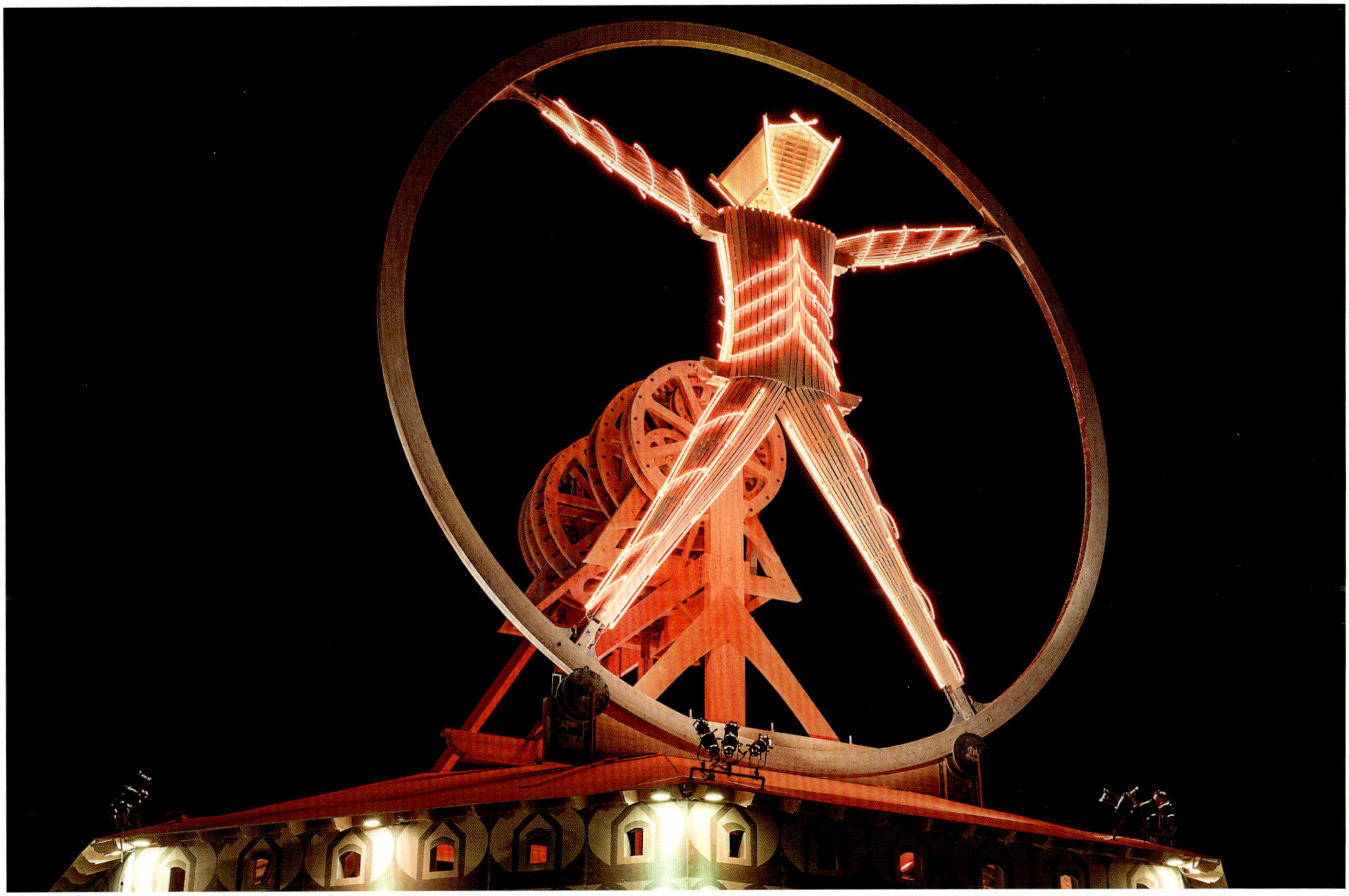

The Man, 2016. Photo by Spencer Jones.

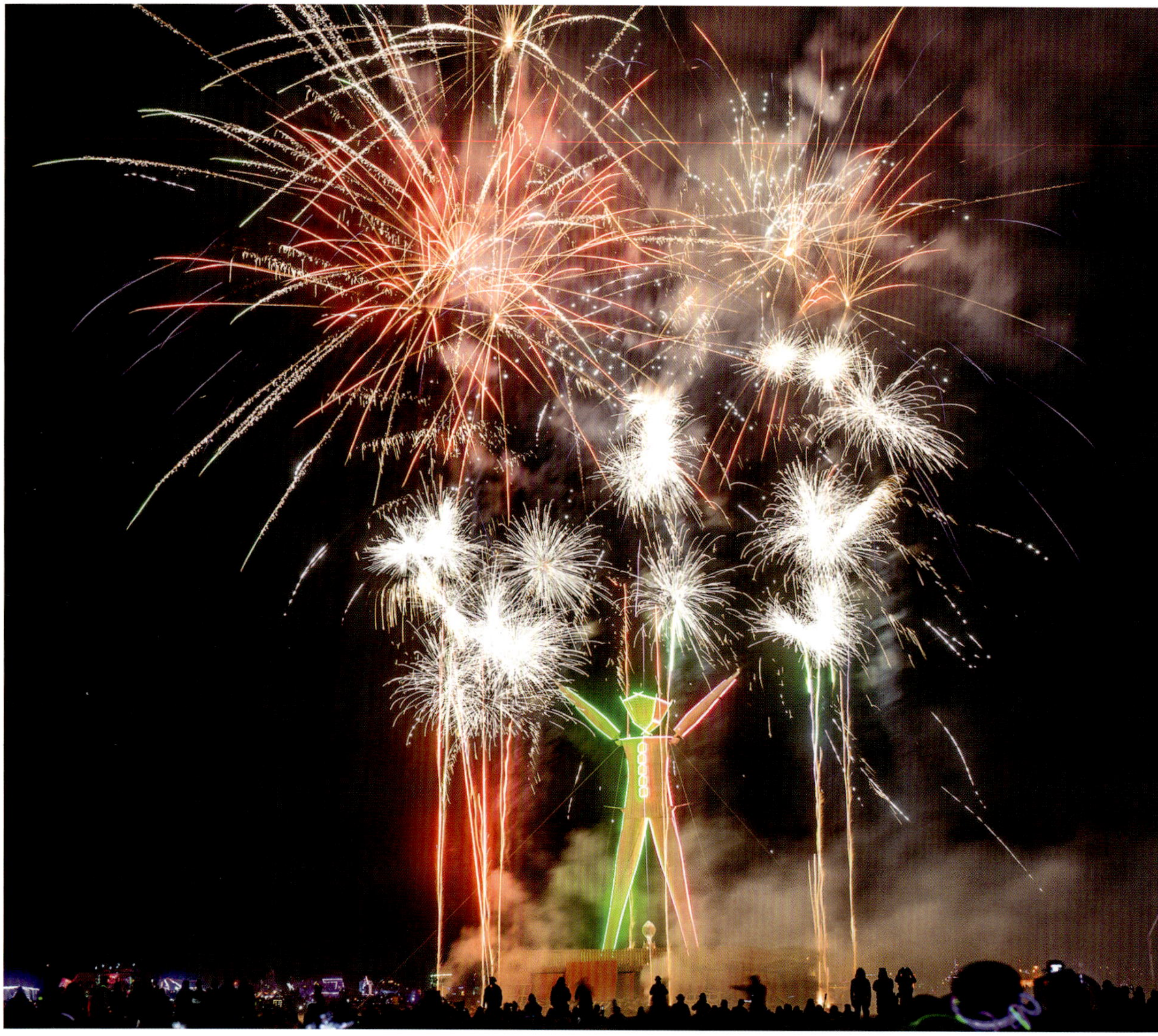

The Man, 2015. Photo by Spencer Jones.

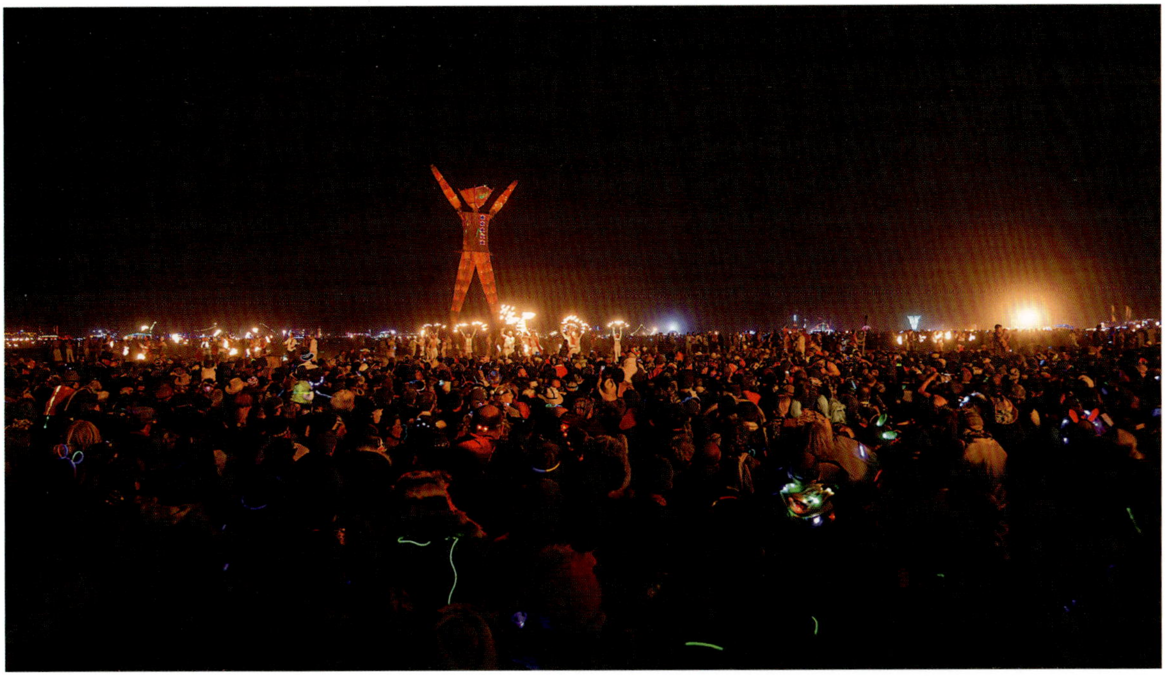

The Man, 2015. Photo by Spencer Jones.

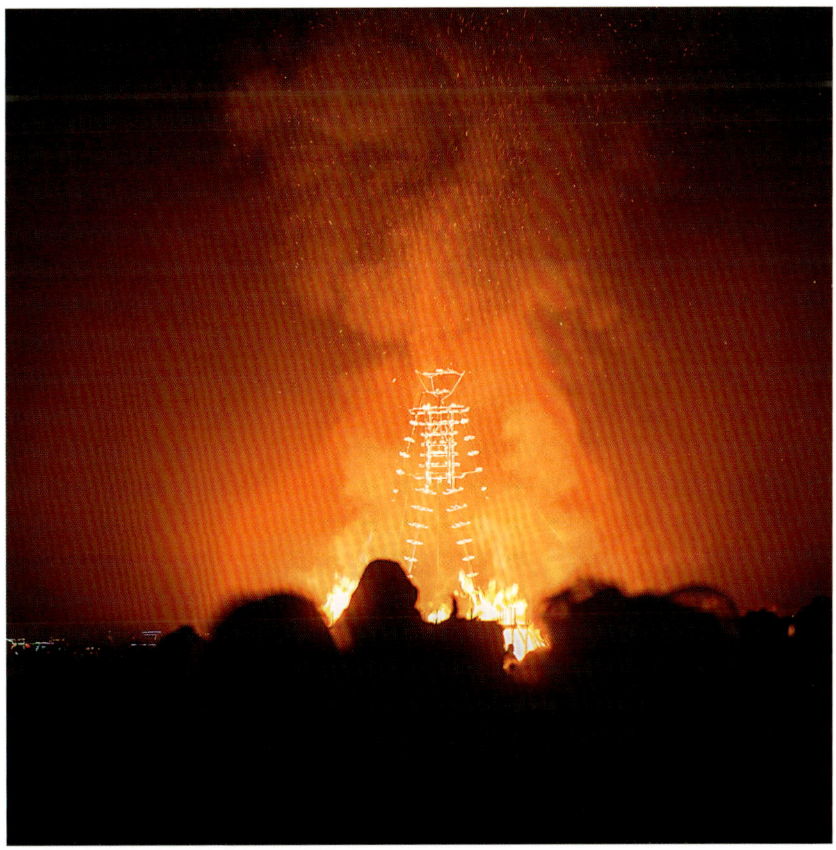

The Man burning, 2015. Photo by Spencer Jones.

manager, said, "Part of the vision is to take this camp and export it to Texas. We want to create a community center that isn't just doing direct relief but is also teaching children's art workshops and making a skill-sharing curriculum for people. We're cultural first-responders."

The deadly wildfires that assaulted Northern California in the autumn of 2017 also attracted assistance from Burners Without Borders. In late October, seven enormous shipping containers that had been modified to provide housing for attendees of the Burning Man event were sent to Santa Rosa, California—one of the communities most badly ravaged by the fires—to provide temporary shelter for up to seventy-five people left homeless by the conflagration. All the containers came with air-conditioning, kitchenettes, shelving, and bunk beds, and one included a full-service kitchen with refrigeration and a freezer. In addition, the Burners group provided supplies for fire victims who had lost everything, and their volunteers set up the shelters and offered victims a variety of needed services.

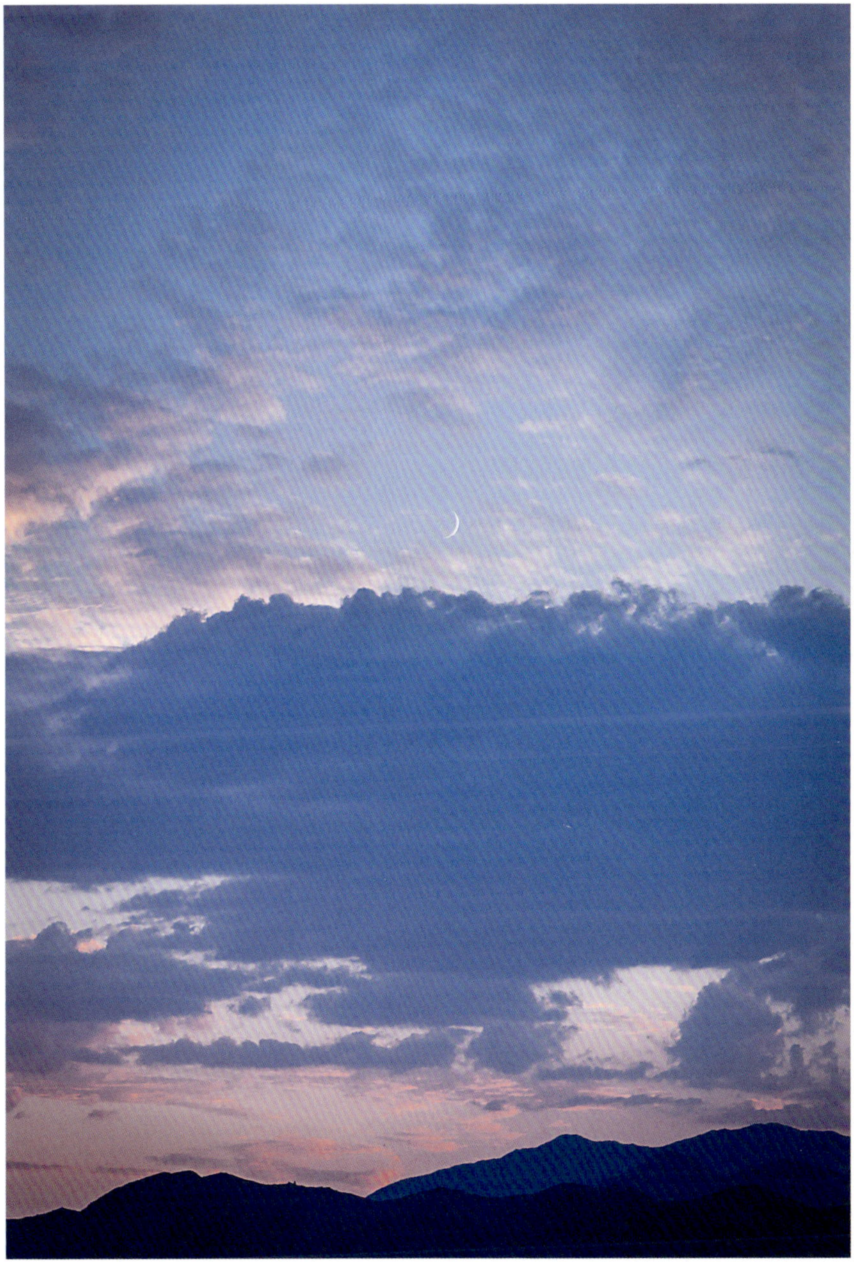

Sunset over the Black Rock Desert. Photo by Spencer Jones.

Appendix

BRANDS OF PERSHING COUNTY

The history of ranching in Pershing County is almost as old as the earliest Euro-American settlement there. As the number of herds—cattle, sheep, and often horses—roaming the open range grew, it became necessary for ranchers to devise an easy way to identify their own animals when they mingled with the herds of others. It was also necessary to find a permanent way to identify their animals in order to protect them from rustlers or to identify stolen animals.

Rustling was the scourge of the Old West, at least according to cowboy movies. A sharp-edged, distinct brand from a carefully designed iron could solve all that. In *On The Hoof in Nevada*, Velma Stevens Truett says, "There was the day when a long rope, a fast horse and a running iron put a man in the cattle business. There was also the day when a short rope with a noose at the end put him out of business."

Branding a cow or horse involves burning a mark on its skin—usually one of the rear flanks—in a way that inflicts no permanent harm but leaves a lasting scar in the shape of the iron used for branding. A brand that cannot be easily modified identifies each rancher's cattle, whether it was in the days before barbed wire or today on federally owned Bureau of Land Management (BLM) land.

Ranchers think in terms of AUMs—Animal Units per Month—when they pay the BLM a fee for each of their animals on the open range. The number of cows allowed to graze a certain area is determined by the BLM according to the condition and topography of the land—is it steep or flat? well-watered or arid? When cows from several different ranches are grazing an area together, the brand is a necessity. A rancher pays the AUM fee for each cow and her calf or calves, which covers unbranded calves called "oreanas" or mavericks—calves born after the herd is turned out. In the old days, each ranch had a "rep" to identify which calves were partnered-up with which cows; this practice has changed somewhat with the advent of more fencing.

Twelve miles north of Lovelock on the Humboldt River, the Duncan Ranch turns out its cows in the beginning of November, and Dan Duncan says, "You bring them in on the river [the Humboldt River] in July." That is when the Duncans get out the branding irons and brand the "slick-eared calves" born in the last season.

The student of branding irons—the long metal rod with the design of the brand on one end—learns that brands can be read top to bottom, inside out, left to right. Brands can reflect family names, as in Bing Crosby's brand, the +B in Elko County, or the Clark County brand of cowboy actor and former Nevada lieutenant governor Rex Bell for his Walking Box ranch, a box with little slanted lines below. Brands were not registered in Nevada before 1873, but since that time registration is required. However, a brand may be registered and never used, as in the case of one gentleman who bought a ranch, registered his brand, but never put livestock on the land.

The matter of identifying sheep is a little different. With sheep, identification can be by ear tags, tattoos, fleece brands, or ear notches. One of the major sheep ranches in Pershing County has a different brand for each band of sheep and uses a paint for the branding that can be scoured away after shearing. A short-handled brand of wood or sometimes metal is used for this kind of marking.

Cattle and horse brands are fascinating because of their design, history of ownership, and the ways an individual brand may change over time, often through simplification. The brands that follow are all from Pershing County, and they represent ranches from throughout the county.

Pershing County Brands—Cattle, Horse, Sheep

■ BRANDS BEFORE COUNTY APPROVAL IN 1919

Alves, A.J. – 1905, Lovelock

Anderson, J. – 1916, Lovelock

Anker, Chester – 1905, Lovelock

Anker, Peter – 1885, Lovelock

Anker, Phillip – 1916, Lovelock

Biddleman, F.C. – 1916, Lovelock

Blanchard and Hermelin – 1915, Lovelock

Carrel, J.B. – 1870, Unionville

Cooper & Scott – 1909, Mazuma

Cooper & Uniacke – 1915, Lovelock

Devita, R. – 1917, Lovelock

Farretta, M.D. – 1915, Lovelock

Fenton, Roger – 1915, Lovelock

Fratis, Mrs. Mary McCarthy – 1885, Lovelock

Fuss, H.W. – 1873, Lovelock

Gibson, W.B. – 1916, Lovelock

Gorr, L.J. – 1915, Lovelock

Hanson, Chris – 1904, Lovelock

Hendra, Lucy M. – 1901, Dun Glen

Hendra, Thomas – 1907 , Dun Glen

Holmstrom, J. Emil – 1917, Lovelock

Holmstrom, John – 1901, Lovelock

Holmstrom, Hugh – 1911, Lovelock

Jensen, Nels – 1917, Lovelock

Johnson, L.P. – 1900, Lovelock

Killebrew, Rachel L. – 1916, Lovelock

Lovelock, George – 1886, Lovelock

Mancebo, Frank R. – 1916, Lovelock

Marker Bros. – 1885, Lovelock

Marzen, Jos. (Lava Bed Ranch) – 1877, Lovelock

Marzen, Jos. (Stone House Ranch) – 1877, 1884, 1885, Lovelock

Marzen, Joseph – 1884, Lovelock

Meecham & Strowbridge – 1885 , Humboldt House

Monroe, Hugh & Miguel Baldees – 1883, Lovelock

Munk, Lester C. – 1915, Lovelock

Nelson, Omer – 1917, Imlay

Noctar, John – 1905, Oreana

Pearce, W.F. – 1874, Lovelock

Phillips, Josie – 1915, Imlay

Pitt, W.C. – 1887, Lovelock

Ruddell, Mrs. Jennie – 1884, Lovelock

Scilacci, Jos. A. – 1916, Lovelock

Serena, Peter – 1918, L. Rochester

Sommer, E.W. – 1917, Lovelock

Springer, Annie E. – 1916, Unionville

Springer, Mrs. L.E. tsfd. G.E. Springer – 1886, Unionville

Stoker, Mrs. C.E. – 1915, Lovelock

Strieff, S.E. – 1916, Lovelock

Strieff, Sam – 1875, Unionville

Taylor, H.W. – 1909, Lovelock

Taylor & Reed – 1915, Lovelock

Taylor, John G. – 1909, Lovelock

Taylor, John G. – 1909 (FJ)

Taylor, John G. – 1909 (J)

Taylor, John G. – 1910, Lovelock

Taylor, John G. – 1916, Lovelock

Thacker, E.J. – 1916, Imlay

Thies, J.H. – 1884, Lovelock (arch)

Thies, J.H. – 1884, Lovelock (circle)

Thornton, Sidney B. – 1892, Unionville

Van Reed, W.W. – 1915, Lovelock

Woodcock, Peter – 1885, Unionville

POST-COUNTY APPROVAL BRANDS – 1919+

Alfonso Talente Revocable Trust – 2015

Alves, John – 1946

Anderson, Clarence – 1943

Anderson, Mrs. Marie – 1939

Anderson, Mrs. Marie – 1940

Anderson, Robert Joseph – 2019

Anker, Leonard A. – 1935

Anker, Norman – 1940

Anker, Phillip – 1916, 1933, 1946

Arobio, C&L – 1929

Aufdermaur, John – 1920

Aufdermaur, John & Bobbie – 2019

Avery, Stuart & Janine, & Jason & Colleen Hill, & Tim & Nichole Owen, & Samantha Fontaine or Gene Heckman – 2015

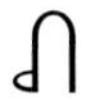 Bachman, Kit & Crystal – 2015

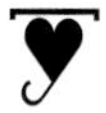 Baird, Glen – 1944

B+ Baird, Glen – 1945

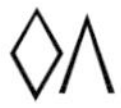 Bartorelli, Josephine S., Dolores S. Trigero and Marian S. Ferrigan – 2019

OI Big Meadow (Brinkerhoff) Ranching Company – 1945, 2019

BII Bixler, Keith, or Stephanie Mobley-Bixler – 2015

B-K Bradford, Hale H. – 1946

B5 Brink, H.T. – 1930

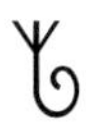 Brown, Geo. D. – 1949

B4 Burrows, Leonard – 2019

 C Punch Ranch Inc. – 2019

D+ Campbell, Bartt – 2019a

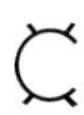 Campbell, Bartt – 2019b

N+ Campbell, Clayton; Roy Maier and Alice Maier – 1948

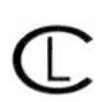 Cardinal, H. Leo – 1949

CL Carpenter, W.W. – 1935

JC Cavaney, Mrs. J.A. – 1919 - First brand recorded in Lovelock as the new county seat of the newly created Pershing County, Lower Rochester

D-S Cerini, Steve & Denice – 2019

EC Clinger, Carl F. – 2015

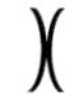 Cochran, D.T. tsfd. W.C. Pitt – 1919

 Costa, Susan M. or Joe – 1948

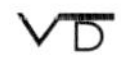 D'Allesandro, Vincent – 1943

 Dahl, Demar H. – 2019

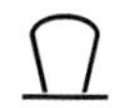 Davidson, H.F. (Hugh) – 1928

OY DeLong, John & Will & William T. – 2015

JG DeLong Ranches Inc. – 2015

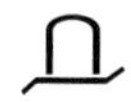 Dempsey, Jake & Lydia – 2015

E9 Depaoli, Robert R. or Debra – 2015

CR Devita, L. – 1920

JF Domenico, John & Guiseppe Ferretto – 1919

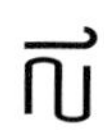 Dufrene, Nancy, and Robby Renfroe – 2015

AD Duncan, Jr., Abijah Elum – 1948

 Duncan, Berry – 1947

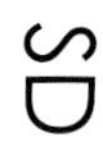 Duncan, Berry – 1948

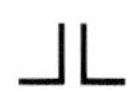 Duncan, Bige – 1947

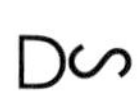 Duncan, Dan, or Joan or Abigah John – 2019

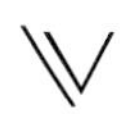 Duncan Family Trust – 2019

N-K Duncan, Jr., Gus – 1947

Duncan, L.B. & Dolack – 1949

Edmonds, Kelli, or Dan Duncan – 2019

Engle, Arthur W. – 1941

Ernst, C.A. – 1920

Esenarro, Dusti D. – 2019

Estill, James – 2019

M-F Estill, James – 2019 MF

Estill Ranches – 2019a

Estill Ranches – 2019b

SE Estill Ranches – 2019c

Evers, Vernon Z. – 1946

Fancher, Chas and Helen – 1949

M-G Gandraga, Martin – 1934

Garat, Peter tsfd. John G. Taylor – 1936

Giles, Donna Campbell – 2019

Gilliam, Kenneth – 1943

V7 Gottschalk, Joseph and Connie – 2019

Green, Harry R. & J.H. Jr. – 1946

Harrowa, Jack A. and Derita C. – 2019

Hart, Bill – 1942

Hay, Geo. M. & Thos. – 1934

Hay, Geo. M. – 1942

Hay Ranches, Inc. – 1946a

Hay Ranches, Inc. – 1946b

Heckman, Gene R., and Humboldt Ranches – 2019

Hetergard, Geo. N. – 1932

Hostman, Karl – 2019

Hull, J. Leonard & Virginia E. – 1947

Huntsman, Lyman and David – 2019

J & R Ranch – 1948

Jim DeLong Family Trust – 2019

John A. – 1925

J+ John DeLong Family Trust – 2019

John Espil Sheep Company – 2019

Kendricks, Charley A. & Carlinda – 2019

Kerscher, Jack – 1944

Kiel & Sons – 2015

Kjeldsen, J.J. – 1920

Knisley, Austin – 2019

Knisley, Ray & Barbara – 2015

Knisley, Wade – 2019

Leonard, Mrs. M.A., and Mrs. Spence, Jane Davidson – 1948

Lewallen, John L. – 1946

Leyra, Mrs. Irene – 1938

Liotard, Leon – 1922

Mahoney, Lawrence A. – 1939

Maier, Roy – 1949

Maigatter, Dixie, or Steve or Denice Cerini – 2015

Marker, Edwin – 1920

Marvel Family Trust – 2019

Mateas, V. – 1930

McDougal, Richard A. – 2019

Meissner, Nancy (Norcutt), Blaine & Kenneth A. Norcutt – 2019

Metche, Sam – 1938

Montrose, Mrs. Ella – 1919

Moura, Anthony, Lisa, Thomas – 2019

Moura, Thomas, Darlene, Anthony and Mark – 2019

Munk, N.C. – 1922

Munk, Wallace N. – 1949

Nevada Nile Ranch, Inc. – 2019

Nichols, Lee – 1949

Norcutt, Norman and Patricia – 2015

Nordman, Fred – 1934

Olagaray, John M. – 2019

Olson, Axel – 1946

Olson, Peter – 1942

Oro Vaca, Inc. – 2019

Overturf, Dorsey – 1945

Pennington, H.L. & Frances – 1945

Peters, Clyde – 1938

Portman, John T. and Blake – 2019

Portman, John T. and Paisley – 2019

Quilici, Mose – 1944

Reeves, Kelly E. & Nadine Dunham – 2015

Richards, Roger or Dixie – 2015

Richardson, Joe I. tsfd. A. Perry – 1927

Roberts, W. Lynn – 1949

Rodrigues, A.C. – 1937

Rodrigues, Gilbert – 1947

Rose, Edwin and Peggy J. – 2019

Ruddell, Ruth C. – 1929

Safford Land and Livestock – 2019

Scilacci, Jos. F. & Geo. – 1931

Scilacci, Randall Willis, & Scilacci, Christie Lynn – 2019

Shaden, Denver – 1942

Sheppard, O.L. – 1940

Smith, Ralph – 1946

Souza, Richard T. – 2019

Stevenson, Russell – 1920

Stevenson, W.H. – 1939

Stoker, Vernon C. – 1949

Sund, Gus – 1922

Talcott. David & June – 2019

Talcott, F.S. tsfd. Fern Louise Talcott – 1947

Talcott, Neil – 1940

Talcott, Reuben – 1942

Taylor, John G. – 1920

Taylor, John G. – 1926

Tenente, Joe F. tsfd. Arthur E. and Iris M. Rose – 1930

Thacker, Henry P. – 1943

Thacker, J.N. – 1940

Thornton, Victor A. – 1941

Villalobos, Art – 2019

W.C. Pitt Ranch Co. – 1920a

W.C. Pitt Ranch Co. – 1920b

W.C. Pitt Ranch Co. – 1920c

Wesner, Bingo G. & Karen T. – 2019

Whitaker, Timothy T. – 2015

Wilson, Frank C. – 1946

Young, Clarence L. – 1920

Brands researched by Pat Ferraro Klos. Brand images digitized by Danilo Thomas.

Notes

Preface

vii Allen C. Bragg, *Humboldt County 1905*. Bragg's account was originally a series of articles published in 1905 editions of the *Silver State,* a daily newspaper published in Winnemucca. Quote in second paragraph is from ch. 4, "Big Meadows," p. 85 (note chapter name pluralizes *meadows* although it is shown as plural and singular in various references in the book.) Quote in fourth paragraph is from ch. 2, p. 38. Quote in second paragraph is from ch. 4, p. 85. Quote in fourth paragraph is from ch. 2, p. 38.

A Little History

3 **the first white man to discover the Humboldt River**: Elliott, *History of Nevada,* pp. 33–38.

4 **in the vicinity of what became known as Lovelock"**: Hulse, *The Nevada Adventure,* p. 225.

the small settlement that became his namesake: Hart, "Location of Lovelock's Station," pp. 9–10.

6 **"the scat of the gods"**: Michael J. Ybarra, *Washington Gone Crazy.*

7 **at a trading post that was owned by George Lovelock**: Elliott, *History of Nevada,* p. 113.

8 **but that the time for "advancement" had come**: Earl, "The Development of Lovelock," pp. 14–22.

the bill creating Pershing County at 3:18 p.m. on March 18, 1919: Earl, "The Development of Lovelock," pp. 14–22.

8–9 **"Growing up to Man's Estate"**: Mrs. R. M. Hardy, "Nevada's Baby County, *Lovelock Review-Miner,* February 27, 1920.

The Land

20 **swaths of bright yellow blooms to the landscape**: Taylor, *Sagebrush Country*; Blackwell, *Great Basin Wildflowers.*

25 **"to the feral galaxy of spring"**: Shaun T. Griffin, "Rain Outside Lovelock, Late March."

tourmaline, turquoise, garnets, and numerous colorful quartzes: Castor and Ferdock, *Minerals of Nevada.*

28 **and amphibians that live both above and beneath the dry mud surface**: Wheeler, *Nevada's Black Rock Desert.*

The People

31 **based on the varied resources of their environment**: Wheat, *Survival Arts of the Primitive Paiutes*; Fulkerson, *Weavers of Tradition and Beauty.*

and coprolites (fossilized human waste): Loud and Harrington, "Lovelock Cave."

32 **(throwing stick) foreshaft from about 5088 B.C.**: Heizer, "Preliminary Report on the Leonard Rockshelter Site," pp. 89–98.

33 **"twisting and snapping its neck"**: Inter-Tribal Council of Nevada, *Numa: A Northern Paiute History,* p. 39.

33 **"Coyote built the dam to catch fish"**: Ibid., p. 39.

35 **the first book ever written by a Native American woman:** Sarah Winnemucca Hopkins, *Life Among the Piutes: Their Wrongs and Claims.*

private and museum collections around the world: Wheat, *Survival Arts of the Primitive Paiutes*; Fulkerson, *Weavers of Tradition and Beauty.*

36 **the government for three thousand dollars**: Inter-Tribal Council, *Numa,* pp. 41–42.

social, educational, and medical services to tribal members: www.lovelockpaiutetribe.com, https://en.wikipedia.org/ . . . /Lovelock_Paiute_Tribe_of_the_Lovelock_Indian_Colony.

An interesting book by Lalla Scott: Scott, *Karnee: A Paiute Narrative,* p. xv.

37 **inducted into the Wolf Pack's Hall of Fame in 1973"**: Murray, "Wolf Pack's Joe Bliss Last Link to Legendary Class."

39 **Thousands of Chinese workers**: McLeod, *Pigtails and Gold Dust,* p. 81.

according to the 1923 Sanborn map: From the middle of the nineteenth century, the Sanborn Map Company published detailed maps of American urban areas intended for assessing fire insurance liability. The University of Nevada, Reno, Library has a digitized collection of Sanborn maps for Nevada dating from 1867 to 1970.

The Chinese who remained in Lovelock: For further information about Chinese activities, see Liestman, "Horizontal Inter-ethnic Relations," p. 345.

41 **including 75,000 sheep and 10,000 cattle**: "John Taylor." Obituary, *Lovelock Review-Miner.*

42 **"They, too, have a right to know"**: Unpublished poem by Pat Ferraro Klos. Copyright © 1996 by Pat Ferraro Klos.

with several different business partners: Roger Mancebo Interview.

"the legacy of agriculture for both families": Tom Mouro Interview.

44 **stories about many of these families**: Pershing County Economic Development Authority, *Lovelock Historic Buildings Tour.*

played a role in determining settlement choices: Devoy Brinkerhoff Munk Interview.

the Union Mining District around Grantsville: Miranda, *A History of Hispanics in Southern Nevada,* p. 42.

11 percent of the population of Humboldt County was Hispanic: Miranda, *A History of Hispanics,* p. 60.

45 **bought a TV for all to enjoy**: Angie Sambrano Pommerening Interview.

many in the Winnemucca and Lovelock areas: Miranda, *A History of Hispanics,* p. 95.

including a house for their family: Alicia Arias Dyer Interview.

Some History Makers

49 **teach the English language to Numa children**: Inter-Tribal Council of Nevada, *Numa,* p. 41.

49 **secured her place in Nevada and Pershing County history**: Zanjani, *Sarah Winnemucca*; Zanjani, "Sarah Winnemucca," *Online Nevada Encyclopedia.*

50 **a boarding house called the Central House**: Pershing County Economic Development Authority, *Lovelock Historic Buildings Tour.*

51 **"we called her Miss Tumbleweed"**: Russell, *Charles H. Russell: Reminiscences of a Nevadan,* pp. 1–2.

52 **senator until 1974, when he retired**: Bible, *Recollections of a Nevada Native Son.*

53 **retired from teaching but still actively writing**: "Adrian Louis," in guides.library.unr.edu/nvwriters-hall-of-fame/louis-1999

54 **"frequently served one hundred people a night"**: Arias Dyer Interview.

opened **La Casita**: Alicia Arias Dyer Interview.

Lovelock and Imlay

57 **the library at the University of Virginia**: James and Harvey, *Nevada's Historic Buildings,* p. 128.

59 **"to bolster the economy during the depression"**: National Register of Historic Places-Nevada. US Post Office-Lovelock Main. NRHS# 90000134.

"about the hardest people in the world to please": National Register of Historic Places-Nevada. US Post Office-Lovelock Main, NRHS# 90000134.

60 **"ornate jigsaw cutout window moldings and cornerboards"**: National Register of Historic Places Inventory—Nomination Form.

62 **from local rancher James Blake**: Earl, "Welsh Miner Traveled Around the World Before Founding Lovelock."

63 **Lovelock also operated Lovelock's Hotel in 1866**: Hart, "Location of Lovelock's Station," pp. 9–10.

eventually owned all of the Lovelock family land: Hart, "Location of Lovelock's Station."

67 **the jewel-like stained-glass windows were undamaged**: *Lovelock Historic Buildings Tour.*

68 **this large, prominent Mormon farm family ever since**: Devoy Brinkerhoff Munk Interview.

and some detailed maps indicate a Perry Spring: Curtis McGowan Interview.

70 **Shoshone Mike and his band of Paiutes were apprehended**: Effie Mona Mack, *The Indian Massacre of 1911*, pp. 1–2, 110.

At the time of his death, he was living in Fallon: Monet Fabri Paputsidis Interviews.

"could pay $75 a month for the leased site": Sharon Stiff Calvert Interview.

74 **"the Pershing General hospital was established"**: Kirsten Gottschalk Hertz Interview.

75 **"which is about an average crop"**: *Lovelock Review-Miner,* August 21, 1925.

76 **"Truman said, 'must have gotten up before daylight'"**: Ybarra, *Washington Gone Crazy,* p. 399.

79 **"for their own self-guided tours"**: "Frank Van Zant (Chief Rolling Mountain Thunder), Thunder Mountain Monument," spacesarchives.org/explore/collection.environment/thunder-mountain-monument.

creations that comprise Thunder Mountain Monument: www.thundermountainmonument.com

Nevada Historic Site Restoration Project: "Frank Van Zant," spacesarchives.org.

Building an Economy

83 **covering an area of 11,970 acres**: "Rye Patch Reservoir," https://en.wikipedia.org/wiki/Rye_Patch_Reservoir; "Rye Patch Reservoir," https://www.usbr.gov/projects/index.php?id=268; "Rye Patch," parks.nv.gov/parks/rye-patch.

87 **"how we (all formers and ranchers) can work together"**: *Lovelock Review-Miner,* June 21, 2017.

Pershing Country Agricultural Extension Agent Steve Foster: Steve Foster Interview.

89 **"a large portion was being held by the receivers"**: Norman Biltz, *Memoirs of Norman H. Biltz,* p. 44.

this "oasis" of 2,200 acres for $66,000: Griffith Borgeson, *Errett Lobban Cord, His Empire, His Motor Cars,* pp. 261–62.

90 **3,500 of which have deeded water rights**: Louis Damonte Jr. Interview.

92 **"Humboldt is the true Golconda"**: Mark Twain, *Roughing It,* p. 212.

"Rochester Philharmonic Orchestra civilized the inhabitants": Paher, *Nevada Ghost Towns and Mining Camps,* p. 126.

93 **who were terrorizing the area**: U.S. Department of the Interior, Bureau of Land Management. Public Lands Guide, Winnemucca District Nevada (map).

"talk gives tone to a well regulated saloon": Paher, *Nevada Ghost Towns*, p. 139.

96 **into the limbo of ghost towns**: Paher, *Nevada Ghost Towns,* p. 121.

part of the global supply chain: Dana Bennett Interview.

one of the most important post–World War I minerals: Limbaugh, *Tungsten in Peace and War.*

98 **the second-largest town in Pershing County**: Gomes, "Mining Tungsten in Nevada in the 1950s," p. 20.

from 1916 until 1982 by almost 2 million units: Gomes, "Mining Tungsten," p. 21.

Burning Man

101 **a more creative and connected existence in the world**: https://burningman.org.

114 **"We're cultural first-responders"**: https://journal/burningman.org/2017/09/global-network/burners-without-borders.

a variety of needed services: "Burning Man Camp Sends Shelters to California Fire Victims," page 1A.

Appendix

117 **"a noose at the end put him out of business"**: Truett, *On The Hoof in Nevada,* p. 9.

118 **the "slick-eared calves" born in the last season**: Dan Duncan Interview.

List of Sources

Public Documents

State of Nevada, Department of Agriculture. *3rd Supplement to 2012 Nevada Livestock Brand Book*. Sparks: State of Nevada Department of Agriculture, Animal Industry Division, February 3, 2015.

State of Nevada, Department of Agriculture. *Nevada Livestock Brand Book*. Sparks: Animal Industry Division, 2016. agri.nv.gov/2016BrandBook_Web. Accessed November 13, 2017.

U.S. Department of the Interior, Bureau of Land Management. *Public Lands Guide, Winnemucca District Nevada* (map). May 1962.

Printed Sources

Blackwell, Laird R. *Great Basin Wildflowers: A Guide to Common Wildflowers of the High Deserts of Nevada, Utah, and Oregon*. Guilford, Conn.: Globe Pequot Press, 2006.

Borgeson, Griffith. *Errett Lobban Cord, His Empire, His Motor Cars: Auburn, Cord, Duesenberg*. Princeton: Automobile Quarterly Publications, 1984.

Bragg, Allen C. *Humboldt County 1905*. Winnemucca: North Central Nevada Historical Society, 1976.

"Burning Man Camp Sends Shelters to California Fire Victims." *Reno Gazette Journal*, 25 October 2017.

Castor, Stephen B., and Gregory C. Ferdock. *Minerals of Nevada*. Reno: University of Nevada Press, 2004.

Centennial Committee. *Lovelock Centennial 1868–1968*. Lovelock: Pershing County Chamber of Commerce, 1968.

Earl, Phillip I. "The Development of Lovelock and the Creation of Pershing County, Part II: 1917 Onward." *Humboldt Historian* (Winnemucca: Humboldt Museum, 1997): 14–22.

———. "Welsh Miner Traveled Around the World Before Founding Lovelock." *Reno Gazette-Journal*, April 1, 1984.

Elliott, Russell L. *History of Nevada*. Lincoln: University of Nebraska Press, 1973.

Fulkerson, Mary Lee. *Weavers of Tradition and Beauty: Basketmakers of the Great Basin*. Reno: University of Nevada Press, 1995.

Gomes, John M. "Mining Tungsten in Nevada in the 1950s." *Nevada in the West* 7, No. 1 (Spring 2016): 19–22.

Griffin, Shaun T. "Rain Outside Lovelock, Late March," from *Driving the Tender Desert Home*. Boise: Limberlost Press, 2014.

Hardy, Mrs. R. M. "Nevada's Baby County." *Lovelock Review-Miner*, February 27, 1920.

Hart, Phillip D. "Location of Lovelock's Station and Background of the Adobe Shed on the Ruddell Ranch Complex." Nevada Historical Society, clippings file, F 849/L 94/H 25. Pp. 9–10.

Heizer, Robert F. "Preliminary Report on the Leonard Rockshelter Site, Pershing County, Nevada." *American Antiquity* 17, No. 2 (October 1951): 89–98.

Hulse, James W. *The Nevada Adventure*. Reno: University of Nevada Press, 1965.

Inter-Tribal Council of Nevada. *Numa: A Northern Paiute History*. Salt Lake City: University of Utah, 1976.

James, Ronald M., and Elizabeth Safford Harvey. *Nevada's Historic Buildings*. Reno: University of Nevada Press, 2009.

"John Taylor." Obituary, *Lovelock Review-Miner*, May 29, 1941, pp. 1, 3.

Jones, Peggy. "A Touch of Hollywood Comes to Lovelock." *Lovelock Review-Miner*, October 12, 2016, p. 9.

Kane, Jenny. "30 Years of Burning Man." *Reno Sunday Gazette-Journal*, August 14, 2016.

Klos, Pat Ferraro. "Miss Urriola." Copyright © 1996 by Pat Ferraro Klos.

Liestman, Daniel. "Horizontal Inter-ethnic Relations: Chinese and American Indians in the Nineteenth-Century American West." *Western Historical Quarterly* XXX, No. 3: 345.

Limbaugh, Ronald H. *Tungsten in Peace and War, 1918–1946*. Reno: University of Nevada Press, 2010.

Loud, Llewellyn L., and M. R. Harrington. "Lovelock Cave." *University of California Publications in American Archaeology and Ethnology* 5, No. 1 (1929).

Lovelock Historic Buildings Tour. Lovelock: Pershing County Economic Development Authority, 2005.

"Pitt Mill to Start Soon." *Lovelock Review-Miner*, August 21, 1925.

Mack, Effie Mona. *The Indian Massacre of 1911*. Sparks: Western Printing and Publishing Company, 1968.

McLeod, Alexander. *Pigtails and Gold Dust*. Caldwell, Ida.: Caxton Printers, 1948.

Miranda, M. L. *A History of Hispanics in Southern Nevada*. Reno: University of Nevada Press, 1997.

Murray, Chris. "Wolf Pack's Joe Bliss Last Link to Legendary Class." *Reno Gazette Journal*, July 1, 2014.

Paher, Stanley W. *Nevada Ghost Towns and Mining Camps*. Las Vegas: Nevada Publications, 1984.

Sawyer, Byrd Wall. *Nevada Nomads: A Story of the Sheep Industry*. San Jose: Harlan-Young Press, 1971.

Scott, Lalla. *Karnee: A Paiute Narrative*. Reno: University of Nevada Press, 1966.

Taylor, Ronald J. *Sagebrush Country: A Wildflower Sanctuary*. Missoula: Mountain Press, 1992.

SE&A, Inc., Engineering and Planning. "Rye Patch Reservoir General Recreation Development." Sparks: April 1974. In Nevada Historical Society Library.

Truett, Velma Stevens. *On The Hoof in Nevada: An Ownership History of Nevada Cattle and Horse Brands 1854–1950*. Los Angeles: Gehrett-Truett-Hall, 1950.

Twain, Mark. *Roughing It*. 1872. Harmondsworth, England: Penguin Books, 1981.

Wheat, Margaret W. *Survival Arts of the Primitive Paiutes*. Reno: University of Nevada Press, 1967.

Wheeler, Sessions S. *Nevada's Black Rock Desert*. Caldwell, Ida.: Caxton Printers, 1978.

Winnemucca Hopkins, Sarah. *Life Among the Piutes: Their Wrongs and Claims*. Reno: University of Nevada Press, 1994.

Ybarra, Michael J. *Washington Gone Crazy: Senator Pat McCarran and the Great American Communist Hunt*. Hanover, N.H.: Steerforth Press, 2004.

Zanjani, Sally Springmeyer. *Sarah Winnemucca*. Lincoln: University of Nebraska Press. 2001.

Oral Histories

Bible, Alan. *Recollections of a Nevada Native Son: The Law, Politics, the Nevada Attorney General's Office, and the United States Senate*. Interview by Mary Ellen Glass. Reno: Oral History Project, University of Nevada Reno Library, 1982.

Biltz, Norman. *Memoirs of Norman H. Biltz: "Duke of Nevada."* Interview by Mary Ellen Glass. Reno: University of Nevada Oral History Archive, 1969.

Russell, Charles H. *Charles H. Russell: Reminiscences of a Nevada Congressman, Governor, and Legislator*. Interviewed by Mary Ellen Glass. Reno: University of Nevada Oral History Archive, 1967.

Websites

"Adrian Louis." guides.library.unr.edu/nvwriters-hall-of-fame/louis-1999. Accessed October 18, 2017.

"Burning Man." https://burningman.org. Accessed October 10, 2017.

"Burning Man." https://journal/burningman.org/2017/09/global-network/burners-without-borders. Accessed October 10, 2017.

"Frank Van Zant (Chief Rolling Mountain Thunder), Thunder Mountain Monument." spacesarchives.org/explore/collection.environment/thunder-mountain-monument. Accessed November 7, 2017.

"Lovelock Paiute Tribe." www.lovelockpaiutetribe.com. Accessed October 18, 2017.

"Lovelock Paiute Tribe." *Wikipedia*. https://en.wikipedia.org/wiki/Lovelock/Lovelock_Paiute_Tribe_of_the_Lovelock_Indian_Colony. Accessed October 18, 2017.

"National Register of Historic Places-Nevada. US Post Office-Lovelock Main. NRHS# 90000134. Registered February 28, 1990." shpo/nv/gov/state-and-national-registers. Accessed November 13, 2017.

"National Register of Historic Places Inventory—Marzen House Nomination Form, ID 81000384, entered August 27, 1981." https://npgallery.nps.gov/NRHP. Accessed December 15, 2017.

"Rye Patch Reservoir." *Wikipedia*. https://en.wikipedia.org/wiki/Rye_Patch_Reservoir. Accessed October 12, 2017.

"Rye Patch Reservoir." https://www.usbr.gov/projects/index.php?id-268. Accessed October 12, 2017.

"Rye Patch." parks.nv.gov/parks/rye-patch. Accessed October 12, 2017.

"Sarah Winnemucca." Sally Springmeyer Zanjani. *Online Nevada Encyclopedia,* 18 January 2011. www.onlinenevada.org/articles/sarah-winnemucca. Accessed November 9, 2017.

"Thunder Mountain Monument." www.thundermountainmonument.com. Accessed October 18, 2017.

"Thunder Mountain Monument." www.roadsideamerica.com. Accessed October 18, 2017.

Archival Collections

Hertz, Kirsten, Administrative Assistant Pershing General Hospital. Collected Papers, Pershing General Hospital Pink Ladies Auxiliary Collected Papers, Pershing General Hospital, Lovelock, Nevada.

Interviews

Interviews were conducted in person or by telephone. Asterisk indicates interviews conducted in person. Place indicates location of interviewee. Notes of interviews are in the author's possession.

Arias Dyer, Alicia. Lovelock, November 12 and 17, 2017.

*Bennett, Dana, President Nevada Mining Association. Reno, February 9, 2017.

Brinkerhoff, Kathie, Pershing County Librarian. Lovelock, May 31, 2017.

Calvert, Sharon Stiff. Minden, June 12, 2017.

Damonte, Louis Jr. June 29, 2017.

*DeLeeuw, Larry, Chinese Viewing Museum, Lovelock, March 1, 2017.

Duncan, Dan, September 16, 2017.

Espil, Carolyn Gottschalk. September 21, 2017.

Foster, Steve. Pershing County Agricultural Extension Agent. Lovelock, January 26, 2017.

Hertz, Kirsten Gottschalk. Assistant Administrator Pershing General Hospital. Lovelock, June 8, 2017.

*Maher, Robert N. Lovelock, October 14, 2016.

*Mancebo, Roger. Lovelock, October 13, 2016.

*McDougal, Robert. Lovelock, May 11, 2017.

McGowan, Curtis. Fallon, November 14 and 15, 2017.

*Moura, Tom and Darlene. Moura Ranch, Upper Valley, October 13, 2016.

Munk, Devoy Brinkerhoff. Lovelock, June 23, 2017.

Paputsidis, Monet Fabri. Emails, Reno, November 10 and 14, 2017.

*Peterson, Will Roger, and Crimson Rose. Reno, Nevada Museum of Art, July 13, 2017.

*Pommerening, Angie Sambrano. Lovelock, November 12, 2017.

*Reynolds, Jim. Reno, September 15, 2017.

A NOTE ABOUT THE TYPE

Designed by Carol Twombly for Adobe, Chaparral Pro combines the legibility of slab serif designs popularized in the 19th century with the grace of 16th-century roman book lettering. The result is a versatile, hybrid slab-serif design.